THE LIBERAL-REPUBLICAN QUANDARY IN ISRAEL, EUROPE, AND THE UNITED STATES

ISRAEL: SOCIETY, CULTURE, AND HISTORY

THE LIBERAL-REPUBLICAN

QUANDARY IN ISRAEL, EUROPE,

AND THE UNITED STATES

EARLY MODERN THOUGHT MEETS CURRENT AFFAIRS

Edited by Thomas Maissen
and Fania Oz-Salzberger

Boston 2012

Library of Congress Cataloging-in-Publication Data:
A bibliographic record for this title is available from the Library of Congress.

ISBN 978-1-936235-55-1 (cloth)
ISBN 978-1-61811-029-9 (electronic)
Book design by Adell Medovoy

Published by Academic Studies Press in 2012
28 Montfern Avenue
Brighton, MA 02135, USA
press@academicstudiespress.com
www.academicstudiespress.com

This book was published with the generous support of:

The German-Israel Foundation (GIF)
The Posen Forum for Jewish European and Israeli Political Thought, Faculty of Law, University of Haifa
The Chair in Early Modern History, Heidelberg University

Table of Contents

Introductory Remarks

Fania Oz-Salzberger and Thomas Maissen

This volume offers a threefold intellectual juncture. It counterpoises the political traditions of republicanism and liberalism, tracing tension-fields old and new. It solicits early modern political thought to meet with present-day political concerns. It also brings together Israeli political and legal culture with its European and American counterparts, pointing to their common origins and comparing their current topographies and concerns.

A major assumption in this book is that Israeli politics and law are derivatives of early modern European thought in ways that are both familiar and challenging to other descendants of the same tradition. The frequent stretching of the concept of Zionism to an analytical catch-all for all matters Israeli has obfuscated the country's basic political and legal structures that were aimed to steer clear of ideology. Alongside the heated rhetoric of nineteenth-century nationalism (some would say colonialism), Israel's founders deployed the cool scaffolding of a modern republic. Insofar as it imbibed major political legacies of modern Europe, many of Israel's current predicaments are more akin to those of other political societies than many scholars have previously surmised.

Modern Israel hails from a founding generation that was largely secular, an offspring of the Enlightenment (particularly the German Enlightenment), and steeped in European intellectual history. Many founders of Israel were educated in the high schools and universities of Eastern, Central and Western Europe. Most of them had strong European identities, often tragically destroyed before or during World War II. Whether socialist, liberal, or "revisionist"-nationalist, their European political compass was deeply relevant to the Jewish national awakening and state building. Zionism itself was a European movement first and foremost, deeply embedded in the broad education of its founders. Theodore Herzl and Ze'ev Jabotinsky were erudite liberals. David Ben Gurion proudly considered himself a self-taught democrat.

Consequently, the young state's main institutions were those of a liberal democracy; often flawed and gnawed by harsh circumstances, but a liberal democracy nonetheless. Its right-of-center ideologues were historically rooted in the age of nationalism, while its predominant left-of-center creed evolved from modified and mitigated Marxism, channeled into social democracy. The "center" itself, from Herzl onward, hailed from a bourgeois central-European liberalism strongly committed to the rule of law and deeply anchored in the Enlightenment. Most of Israel's governmental institutions, and almost all its juridical foundations, belong to the latter tradition.

Over the years, some thinkers and policy-makers have proposed to integrate "Jewish" elements into the largely secular framework of the state. For example, there have been attempts to make biblical laws relevant to the country's essentially modern legal system. Most of these attempts have worked well within the democratic framework, while others may seem nationalistic and even atavistic. One consequence is that Israel's public sphere today is often mired in the "Jewish or democratic?" debate, with Moses and John Stuart Mill playing tug-of-war over the country's political and moral identity. Israel's intellectual legacy, however, is far more complex and multifaceted than that.

Moses and Mill do not represent disparate and competing traditions. If one takes a closer look, some important Jewish legacies would disclose affinity to a broader European genome: the philosophy of Maimonides owes a great debt to Aristotle, and the modernizing project of Mendelssohn was part and parcel of the German Enlightenment. Converse impacts were at work, too: some crucial aspects of European political thought, specifically the ideas of liberty and justice associated with early modern natural law and maturing in the works of Hugo Grotius and John Locke, bear the fingerprints of those who looked at the ancient Hebraic republic for concepts of the good polity. Thus, "Jewish" ethics and politics drew sustenance from the same origins that fed European intellectual history, and vice versa.

Common legacies—the quests for liberty, civic equality and social justice—have enabled a strong and intimate dialogue between Israelis and Europeans in the immediate aftermath of the Holocaust and the founding of the State of Israel, from the 1950s to the 1970s. Israel was seen, not least through its own eyes, as a young European democracy rising from the ashes of the darkest European dictatorship. However, these intertwining traditions have lost some of their weight within Israeli society during the recent decades. Some Israelis find Europe and its political culture alien and menacing. Some critics, both in Israel and beyond, now tend to see Israel as a combination of religious fundamentalism and several despised aspects of the European legacy: chauvinism, expansionism and imperialism.

Yet the stamp of Europe, most specifically of Germany, on the Israeli constitutional structures covers far more ground than one may imagine. "Western" and "Jewish" elements are woven together: liberal discourse can underpin ultra-Orthodox sectarianism, and social democracy sometimes enlists biblical quotations to struggle against free market ideology. Significantly, the legal and moral justifications of civil equality for Israel's Arab minority, as well as the Palestinian bid for independence, are rooted in European political traditions. So was the historical Jewish demand for a sovereign state.

One purpose of a theoretical conversation involving Israel, Europe and the United States is to examine how much Israeli society still owes to its early modern legacies. European societies today may wish to do the same. Israel is a touchstone—at times extreme, but often revealing—for the current relationship between European legacies and European realities. On the other hand, early modern republicanism displays some Hebraic fingerprints, and the early liberalism of the Enlightenment engaged with Jews as a test case for civil rights and minority emancipation. On the other hand, Europe's present-day engagement with its new migrant minorities and with its recent religious differentials bears some similarities to Israel's complex relation with its own native Arab citizenry, as well as with the Palestinians residing in the Israeli-occupied territories. On certain points, notably the impressive influx of Israeli-Palestinians into the universities and the professions, Israel may be able to teach its European counterparts a useful lesson. On other points, notably the upholding of civil and human rights under occupation, Israel is requested to heed critical European voices.

Both Israelis and Europeans, however, may do well to become more attuned to the pre-nationalistic legacy of early European modernity, where ideas of liberty, civic commitment and political justice were played out in contexts relatively immune to the vicissitudes of ethnic strife. This is why early modern political thought, while not "Jewish" in any outright sense, is so interesting in our context. The tension field of republicanism and liberalism may well prove relevant to European and

Israeli current affairs in ways similar to its ongoing American relevance. Open issues of political deliberation today—cultural cohesion, migration, minority and collective rights, individual autonomy, sovereignty, universal jurisdiction, humanitarian concerns in peace and war—are all at stake. On a deeper level, citizenship, nationhood, freedom and maybe even rationality, are all part of the early modern resonance in current public affairs. Republican and liberal ways of thinking about the political and the social realm do not necessarily provide solutions for current problems; but they remain helpful analytical tools for understanding tensions in modern societies that are rooted in early modern options.

In this sense, republicanism and liberalism are not understood as two distinct and clear-cut ideologies, but as political languages and sets of ideas and values, conveying notable differences but also sharing significant similarities. It would be anachronistic to claim authors such as John Locke, Charles de Montesquieu, Thomas Jefferson or even Adam Smith for one camp in a hypothetical exclusivist struggle between republicanism and liberalism. The ongoing debates about these concepts—to which some of the authors of this volume have made important contributions in the last decades—have not produced general agreement on their definition. The spectrum of interpretations is also manifest in the articles gathered in this book. The liberal-republican quandary acquires new dimensions when dealing with different political cultures. As this collection of essays readily demonstrates, variegated national, cultural and scholarly backgrounds yield differing interpretations of the terms. In an ideal typical sense, it is nevertheless helpful to characterize the editors' own understanding of the two major concepts, from the perspective of early modern history of political thought.

Republicanism is understood as an essentially pre-modern way of thinking about power, liberty and participation, although it has had a lasting effect on modern political thought and political practice, too. In early modern societies, the individual rights of a citizen were not crucial for political order. Most men, not to speak of the women, were subjects, not citizens. If they had rights, those were collective rights of a social estate, a town, a monastery, or a university. It was not yet the sovereign state that generally guaranteed its citizens equal individual rights. Belonging to a circumscribed social or economic entity procured particular rights. Such rights were a privilege, and they demanded conformity—in religious faith, in political opinions, in manners and in values. Besides conformity, there were other prerequisites for citizenship that were barely questioned by anybody: a citizen had to be male, he had to be economically self-standing and contribute to the common weal by paying taxes and serving in the militia, he should sacrifice his own interests and even his blood for the sake of the common weal. Thus, the internal role of the citizen was closely linked to the external survival of the body politic in the dangerous world of sovereign states that developed in early modern Europe—a struggle for survival conceived in military terms by authors in the Machiavellian tradition, but increasingly seen as a commercial, and more generally economic, competition for prosperity and power.

Hence the republican insistence on individual virtue within a particular political community, discussed as the subject matter of moral philosophy recommending self-abandonment and disinterestedness. This set of beliefs derived sustenance not only from Aristotle, the Roman republicans and the Stoa, but also from Christian and (as we are increasingly aware) Hebraic sources.

In contrast to republican ideals, the natural law tradition leading to liberalism shifted its focus from the community to the individual, often understood in abstract and universal terms, and focused on individual rights. This opposition can be labeled, with Benjamin Constant, as *liberté des anciens* against *liberté des modernes* or, with Isaiah Berlin, as the positive liberty to exercise political participation versus the negative liberty from governmental coercion. For the republican, liberty is a virtuously achieved, but constantly endangered privilege and a duty with the aim to establish justice and concord in a predominantly agrarian world. For the liberal, it is the pre-politically founded and institutionally protected right to individual pursuit of happiness within the limits of law, guaranteeing property and eventually producing public wealth as an unintended side-effect of self-serving interest ("private vices") within an economy based on the division of labor. During the eighteenth century, these natural law based liberal beginnings flourished into a full-fledged philosophy. The Enlightenment developed ideas of universal rights and values, political representation instead of direct democracy, separation of powers and institutional checks and balances enabling and even legitimizing the co-existence of differing individual interests, culminating in the modern notion of political parties. This cluster of theoretical innovations formed a crucial juncture. The new, liberal republic of self-interested individuals began to part ways with the former republican ideal of a commonwealth of selfless citizens. At the same time, new ideas of the nation colored the collective sphere in cultural, linguistic and historical shades very different from the earlier republican citizenry, which seldom if ever depended on ethnic singularities as a major construct of identity.

The essays in this volume offer new ways of pondering these problems. The contributors—historians, philosophers, political scientists and legal scholars—were invited to reflect whether the political concepts and debates of the era preceding the nation state, and in particular the thought of the Enlightenment, might prove conducive to our understanding of the problems of our era, when nation states are undermined and their staying power is questioned. While common to all modern democracies, these newly sharpened questions are uniquely relevant to those European countries that are incorporating large minorities of recent migrants into their societies and cultures. At the same time, they are relevant for a European Union that, as a whole, has reduced all nations to minorities within a supra-national political and economic infrastructure. For such a meta-national body, not only do uniform laws and rules need to be established; but it also requires a shared identity that legitimizes redistributions and produces acts of solidarity, an identity that inevitably has its fundaments in history. The United States can serve as a model in some aspects; not because they have resolved these questions, but because they have to face them as well and do so within their own traditions. And other nations outside the European Union, such as Switzerland, are not immune to such challenges even if their citizens continue to believe in the exceptionalism of a chosen people. In general, such a self-perception may have survived better—for different reasons—in the relatively recent nation-states of Israel and the United States than among the European nations whose pasts, not only in the Nazi era, are laden with failure and atrocities.

Early modern political thought is fascinating in its own right. The major political issues of the early twenty-first century do not always yield easily to historical analysis. While this volume aims to juxtapose past and present, we do not propose to do this hastily. The coming chapters offer several novel attempts at a historical *cum* current affairs discussion of the shared and mutually tense republican and liberal legacies in Europe, Israel and the United States. Although the articles have been put in a roughly chronological order, they often refer to each other—in ways both affirmative and contradictory—in spite of the temporal gaps that might separate them. The chronological order should not be understood as a historical narrative of a single—republican and/or liberal—path towards, for example, liberty or modernity. The trajectory outlined here is just one of many ways to interpret challenges and responses in different states and within a converging world.

John G. A. Pocock begins with the European distinction between autonomous sacred and secular authorities, rooted in imperial Rome and leading to the early modern sovereign state that became the framework for both republican and liberal concepts of liberty, each similarly opposing the Church and the ecclesiastic claims for truth. Hence, historical narratives played a decisive role as alternatives for seeking out the fundaments of political thought. To a lesser extent than classical Rome, but recently of increasing interest to scholars, the Hebrew republic served early modern thinkers as a constitutional model for self-rule, distributive justice and civil legalism, a this-worldly institution existing in history, but ennobled by divine establishment (Fania Oz-Salzberger). A better-known matrix for analyzing the incorporation of citizens and the role of the political *demos* was the Athenian *polis*, discussed here by Christine Zabel. Moving on to the republican reassessments of the Enlightenment era, Urte Weeber presents the major republics of the eighteenth century, Venice, the Netherlands, and Switzerland, all of which stimulated debate on the best constitution, but, confronting the rise of commercial society, were increasingly disparaged as stagnated relics of the past. The future belonged to the new kind of republic that arose in the United States of America, where – alongside Rome – biblical republicanism and its Hebraic models again inspired the settlers erecting a "second Israel" (Eran Shalev).

While republican thinkers argued from historical precedence, liberal thought originated in a philosophy of nature. For Thomas Hobbes, this was a voluntary choice aimed at subordinating the rights of individuals, which he radically redefined, to the sovereign state that alone could guarantee them. Gordon Schochet explains also how Locke mitigated this interpretation of natural law and paved the way for inalienable rights to become the anchor of the American and French revolutions. From Hugo Grotius onwards, the natural law tradition was equally important to international law. Marco Geuna discusses critically how the concepts of just war and of human rights, which originated in early modern Europe, were reformulated and used to legitimize armed interventions in the asymmetric new wars of the last twenty years.

Further critical reflections on early modern legacies in present-day contexts are offered in the later chapters, which examine relevant tension-fields in three political cultures. Sam Fleischacker revisits Adam Smith to explain the danger awaiting states that leave poor relief to religious groups: support for the poor should be seen as a matter of justice among fellow citizens, not as charity invoking humility and veneration towards the morally superior donor. Raef Zreik explains the ambiguity of the civic discourse in Israel, which cannot be seen only as the triumphing liberal paradigm of equal rights. The political redefinition of citizenship and Israeli identity enabled an ethnocratic exclusion of the Palestinians in Israel who, while enjoying basic civil rights, are forbidden or unable to participate in seemingly abstract civic duties such as military service.

A different outcome of the ascending importance of legal procedure, this time in international relations, is the rise of extraterritorial and universal jurisdiction, considered by Amnon Reichman as acceptable if limited to exceptional cases of adjudication. On this turf, liberal and universalist juridical ideals may clash with traditional rule-of-law sovereignty. Israel has played varied roles, all of considerable importance, in this global development. It was also a party—however minor—to the claims put forward by Jewish organizations and in class actions against Swiss banks withholding assets of Holocaust victims. Thomas Maissen explains the litigation and the public debate surrounding these cases as a debate on collective memory, a confrontation between the Swiss glorification of their republican past and others' experiences, especially of the Holocaust, that have become the core element of supra-national human rights discourse. Such is also the argument in Diana Pinto's concluding essay, where she distinguishes between disparate lessons learnt from the War and the genocide. "Never again" has different meanings in Europe and in Israel, and this dissonance may shed light on numerous misunderstandings and tensions between these two partners.

The historical and geographical scopes of this volume of essays, as well as its range of contributing academic disciplines, make it a unique, and rather ambitious, attempt at expanding the horizons of our current-affairs debates. While eschewing any pretense to completeness or congruence, contributions to this volume are inter-conversing on many levels. Its editors and other authors all share a sense of intellectual urgency: if any of the major social, political and economic issues of our day are to be addressed responsibly, the broadening of comparative scopes across space and time is of utter necessity. We consider this book to be a proposed beginning, rather than a tidy conclusion, of such an opening of vistas from our non-distant past to our immediate future.

This book emerged from a research project led by the two editors and from an international conference held in January 2010, both funded by the German Israel Foundation (GIF) through a three-year grant, thoughtfully extended over a further year to complete the publication process. The conference received additional funding from the Posen Forum for Political Thought at the Haifa Faculty of Law and from the Department of History at the Hebrew University in Jerusalem, through the good auspices of Professor Avihu Zakai. The Faculty of Law at the University of Haifa hosted two meetings of the research team, as well as the concluding international conference. We are grateful to Tamara Krakovich, to Dorit Arbel, and to the conference team including Noemi Harari, Boaz Gur, and the inimitable Kalanit Kleemer. At the University of Heidelberg, the Department of History hosted several workshops of the research team, organized by Elisabeth Natour, Antoinette Saxer, Urte Weeber and Christine Zabel. Anne Brady, Philipp Flammer and Erika Lokotsch contributed their precious expertise to the editing of this volume. The editors most gratefully acknowledge their debt to all the aforementioned.

Thomas Maissen, Heidelberg
Fania Oz-Salzberger, Haifa

Republics, Revelations and Liberalisms: A Selective History of Early Modern Political Thought

JOHN G. A. POCOCK

In preparing this paper, I have had in mind that this book has two objectives. In pursuing the second—"can early modern concepts address current affairs?"—I shall offer an outline of the history of early modern political thought as I understand it, with attention to the problems early modern thinkers addressed, leaving open the question of how they may be translated into the problems we consider current. I shall return to the former objective—"Liberalism and Republicanism, past and present"—by asking in what ways early modern thought may be seen as anticipating that problem and perhaps addressing it for the first time in some earlier context. I believe in the uniqueness of distinctive historical contexts, but dismiss neither the possibility that historical processes may connect them, nor the possibility that the thought of one era may be translated into the language of another and made to address the latter's concerns.

What we call "early modern political thought" has, and has helped to shape, a history not only European, but which entailing a definition of Europe and its history renders it geographically and culturally distinctive. The extensive literature on the subject massively informs us that what we call Europe is not only Greco-Roman in its cultural foundations, but also geographically limited to those areas where the Latin language predominated over Greek among the learned, and the Roman Catholic Church with its Protestant and enlightened adversaries predominated over the Greek Orthodox. These limits were often exceeded but never abolished: during the medieval and early modern periods, the Latin Christian civilisation expanded, first into the European and the Scandinavian peninsulas, and then oceanically into the two American continents. In the latter expansion it began to encounter the question of rule over peoples not previously known in either its sacred or its profane histories; in the former, it entered a Europe defined in Orthodox Christian and Ottoman Muslim terms; and the dispersed

Jewish peoples found themselves marginal to the dominant concerns of all three. It is at this point that we encounter the third term I have used in my title: "revelation" was employed in all these cultures and affected their politics and political thought. It is a historical fact, however, that the "history of political thought" we speak of has been presented in terms overwhelmingly European and neo-Latin, so that the meanings given to the word "political" itself have been shaped by the encounters between Christian churches and Latin European forms of government: republican, imperial and monarchical; ancient, medieval and modern; early modern, modern and post-modern.

Let me begin with republics, as historically they appear earlier. They serve to remind us that the history we relate was Mediterranean before it became European—the latter word being used to introduce the interior spaces of the west Eurasian peninsula—and emerged from a heroic epic with the formation of city states surrounding that sea "like frogs round a pond" as Plato makes Socrates put it, constituting an ecumene held together as much by sea routes as by land.[1] It is worth asking whether any other civilisation has a history like this, beginning with the polis, or with liberty as both an ideal and a problematic. These cities—or so their historians tell us—were citadels of warriors engaged in agriculture and commerce. Out of the heroic virtue emerged the political: the rule by interacting groups of citizens who called their self-government "liberty." The word "republic" we employ to denote this form of polity, of course, appeared later; it is Latin rather than Greek in origin, and only by stages culminating in the European Renaissance and Wars of Religion came to be used as the opposite of several distinct kinds of monarchical rule. It is nevertheless lodged in both Greek and Roman consciousness and memory by political experience and by several forms of literature dominating both Mediterranean and European literacy and scholarship. We should repeat at this point the question whether this is peculiar to west Eurasian history. These cities were of course shaped by interactions with other civilisational structures, Egyptian and Persian, but there came a time when these are only interactions; *libertas* and *imperium*—to use the Latin words—constituted a subjective world to which a political consciousness addressed itself and developed concepts of the "political," which it denied to other civilisations and their forms of government.

---

1   Plato, *Phaedo*, 109b.

But the history of heroic political systems was tragic. Freedom produced power and what we call empire; the extension of *imperium* over the collective self to *imperium* over others. The two meanings of the word came into collision, and disasters ensued. In the intellectual history of Athens, these produced one great work of historiography, that of Thucydides, and have, for reasons too many to elaborate, played a dominant role in the history of political thought: that of the explosion of philosophy, which has sought to reorder political life at levels so far above the heroic as to transcend even the political. Here I seem to be repeating old-fashioned intellectual history, but I am doing so with the aim of reaching the specifics of early modern political thought. This was Latin rather than Attic in origin and was shaped by historiography as much as by philosophy, though the role of the latter appeared in the history of political thought far more prominently than that of the former. There appeared in Rome itself, and was developed by intensive study in Europe during what we call the Renaissance and the Enlightenment, a historical narrative relating how Roman liberty released energies (called *virtus*) that conquered an empire, how empire proved too great for virtue and corrupted it, and how the form of government we call the principate or rule by emperors replaced it. This narrative is too complex and morally ambiguous to be reduced to philosophy and theory, though it can inform both; and I argue that it was the chief legacy of republican Rome that influenced European political thought.

At the moment the Roman republic ended—the Romans, who continued to use the term *res publica*, called it *libertas* and used the same term for the rule of the *senatus populusque*—a "revelation" occurred.[2] I do not know how to exaggerate the significance of the circumstance that Jesus of Nazareth was born under Caesar Augustus and suffered under Pontius Pilate; that as Christians say, the Word was made Flesh and dwelt among us at perhaps the best documented and most contentious moment in all of Roman history. This is to say nothing of the coincident moment it occupied in Jewish history, which now became part of the vocabulary of the slowly-emerging political thought of Rome and Europe. The moment of Augustus was also the moment of Christ. Two developments now occurred. The Christian revelation, unlike (it would

---

2   I am using the word "occur" with an ambiguity that should keep both believers and unbelievers happy.

seem) its Abrahamic neighbours, offered a grace superseding law, from which churches and priests derived an authority unlike that of republics or emperors. In the same era, however, Roman empire gave birth to a universal civil law, in which the goods of social life were enjoyed under the protection of the sovereign, with the result that the *libertas* of the republic was replaced by the *legalitas* of the emperor: a new kind of liberty, which granted the freedom to hold property and engage in all manner of social pursuits under the protection of the law that the prince proclaimed and upheld. What would become the tension between "republican" and "liberal" concepts of liberty emerged when prince, law and church could be perceived as non-identical claimants to authority. This took a very long time, and the history of the decline and fall of the Roman Empire is needed to narrate it. A crucial moment in that much-debated process was the ransom and looting of the city of Rome by barbarian mercenaries in 410 A.D. This provoked two major narratives, both the work of Latin-speakers from the western provinces, written to argue that the disaster was not a consequence of the Christian abandonment of the gods of the city. One of these writers, the Spaniard Orosius, wrote what may be called a counter-history, designed to show that the conquering virtue of the pagan republic had caused disasters to both the Romans and those they conquered, far greater than the Goths were causing at Rome. The African Augustine wrote what it is better to call an anti-history, declaring that the redemption of souls from their sin did not occur in but rather outside any process of history, whether the work of humans or of God guided such a process (though no doubt He did). Both authors attacked the conquering virtue of the republic—Augustine calling *libertas* the *libido dominandi*—rather than the peaceable sociability of the empire, though both conceded that this might have been provided by God as a means to the spread of Christianity; Augustine merely insisted that the empire was not a preliminary to the return of Christ. A millennial language and its rejection are both integral to the formation of European political thought.

There is much to be said for treating the history of political thought in the Latin middle ages in terms of the conflict and co-existence of papacy and empire, with their theological and philosophical implications, capable of being related to Athenian political philosophy as rediscovered in both Christendom and Islam; the chief remaining theme being that of the encounter between Christianised barbaric kingship and the Roman-feudal law systems that took shape in the western kingdoms and the Germanic empire. This indeed is how the "history of political thought" was shaped as an academic discipline, beginning about a century ago, and helps account for the unsettled relationship between history and political theory or philosophy that still characterises it. In the last fifty years or so, however, a challenge has been posed to this view of the subject, which has changed it without overthrowing it. The recent *History of European Political Thought from 1450 to 1700*, edited by a team of scholars at the University of Hull, has offered to survey the literature of political thought in the principal European cultures, while continuing to arrange the topic of "political thought" under the three headings of "religion, philosophy and law."[3] The chapters of which it consists, however, displaying the thought shaped in many European contexts, reveal the presence of a fourth mode of thinking, to which the name "humanism" is given. In every case, furthermore, the political thought so described emphasizes the notion of the individual as an active participant in the deeds and decisions of a political society, and that society exists in order (among other purposes) to provide the individual with the opportunity for such an activity.

Historical consciousness and historical writing were not unknown in the political literature of papacy and empire, but it was possible to construct a narrative, which presented the conflict between them in the context of Roman history and its aftermath. Leonardo Bruni composed the first volume of his History of the Florentine People in the early years of the fifteenth century, and presented an account of Roman and European history strikingly like those we find in the works of the great enlightened historians three centuries later.[4] He retold the story of how republican liberty acquired an empire greater than it could bear, and wondered whether a league of free Tuscan cities might not have been preferable to the cannibal virtue of Rome. The rule of the emperors, however, destroyed the elites of free citizens and left Mediterranean culture without the warlike virtue needed to resist barbarian invasion. Italy found itself linked to a transalpine world of Goths, Franks and Saxons, in which the bishops of Rome took control of the ecclesiastical network

---

3   Howell A. Lloyd, Glenn Burgess, and Simon Hodson (eds.), *History of European Political Thought, 1450-1700. Religion, Law and Philosophy* (Yale: Yale University Press, 2008).

4   Leonardo Bruni, *History of the Florentine People*, 3 vol., ed. by James Hankins (Cambridge, MA: Harvard University Press, 2001-2007).

that had survived imperial authority. They were able to set up the Frankish kings as emperors in the west, but empire and papacy competed for universal authority until the temporary exhaustion of both in the fourteenth century left space for some cities in Italy to claim autonomy as republics. Their autonomy, however, was insecure, and their liberty and virtue were threatened by faction-fighting, both consequences of the struggle from which they had emerged. At this point, Bruni began to relate the history of Florence that had already begun to take shape.

Here we have the germ of both humanist and enlightened historiography, with both the values and the insecurity of republican citizenship—what I have ventured to call the "Machiavellian moment"—at its center.[5] Bruni is one of the central figures in the narrative of Hans Baron, who presented the Florentine rediscovery of liberty as the moment at which European political thought broke decisively with its papal and imperial-civilian pasts.[6] This thesis needs a great deal of historical revision, which however has been complicated by the strong desire of many scholars to keep "religion, philosophy and law"—as in the Hull volume I have mentioned—in their central role, relegating humanism and republicanism to the margins; and this is one source of the debate between "republicanism" and "liberalism." There are good arguments on both sides of this debate, and we are looking at a history of conflict and co-existence. Let us see how it might be told.

What Bruni's narrative seems to omit is the true victor in the struggle between the Popes and the Hohenstaufen: the kingdom of France, in his time disintegrated by the Anglo-Burgundian wars. His enlightened successor historians, three centuries later, had to consider its recovery, together with that of the kingdom of England from its own civil wars, which furnished—rightly or wrongly—the dominant themes of our standard histories of early modern political thought, where the germs of a concept of "liberalism" are usually located. These conventional histories have focussed, though never exclusively, on themes neither papal nor imperial: namely the rise of the state and civil society in the king-

---

5   John G. A. Pocock, *The Machiavellian Moment: Florentine Political Thought and the Atlantic Republican Tradition* (Princeton: Princeton University Press, 1975).

6   Hans Baron, *The Crisis of the Early Italian Renaissance: Civic Humanism and Republican Liberty in an Age of Classicism and Tyranny* (Princeton: Princeton University Press, 1955). For a reappraisal of Baron's work see the *AHR*-Forum: "Hans Baron's Renaissance Humanism," *American Historical Review* 101 (1996), 107-144.

doms of France and England. They have dealt with the conflicts between monarchical sovereignty and systems of civil and customary law, the latter entailing an ideology of property at a time when land-tenure and its history were being transformed by mercantile capital; and between sovereignty and ecclesiastical authority, ranging from papal to sectarian under the revolutionary impact of the Protestant Reformation. Hence we re-encounter the theme of my title, "republics and revelations," and the history of Florence reminds us that Machiavelli's account of the republic, neo-pagan if not yet secular in the Enlightened sense, coincides in time with that given by Savonarola, in which, since all citizens are equal in authority, Christ must be king if there is to be any king at all.

If republics could be situated in apocalyptic and messianic narratives of sacred history arising from revelation, the same is true of monarchies and empires. Histories of political thought, centered on that of the west European kingdoms in the early modern period, have focussed on the rise of the sovereign state and its interactions with the liberties of estates, parliaments and the individual. This was the origin for everything we mean by the terms "liberalism"—anachronistic though it is when used of this period—and it is vital to keep in mind that the companion term "liberty" was being used in more senses than one. In ancient, i.e. Greco-Roman, usage it meant the autonomy of the city and the individual's participation in exercising that sovereignty. In post-feudal Europe it came to mean the individual's freedom to enjoy what was called his "property"—a word of great philosophical complexity—under the protection of a law to which he enjoyed access. The term "right" in due course appeared at this point; it is a term of law, and it was perceived on all sides that a system of law implied the presence of a sovereign who might or might not be identical with it. Political thought in the early modern period was therefore preoccupied with a dialectic between right and sovereignty, and this is the point at which the history of political thought becomes hardest to distinguish from the political theory that has emerged from it and has offered to control the ways in which it is to be written.

The giant figures of the history of political theory—Jean Bodin in France, Thomas Hobbes and John Locke in England—made their appearance during this period, and each of them had as much to do with the relations between state and Christian religion as between sovereignty, liberty and law. Bodin's philosophical Judaism, Hobbes' ferocious anti-

Hellenism, and Locke's cautious Socinianism connected all three with the impulse to diminish the Trinitarian account of Christ's nature, on which the Church's claim to an other-worldly authority chiefly rested. One can never overestimate the importance—which is not to say the success—of the campaign to reduce the independence of divine grace from civil authority in the early history of the modern state, and there was a powerful theological component in the history of "liberalism" itself.

There is a double vision here: the relation of law to grace is one story, that of law to will another. If we set alongside the history of political theory the history of historiography as a species of political thought, what is now to be noted is that English and French controversy in the early modern age entailed the historiography of historically specific political nations, each defined by a particular set of relationships between law and sovereignty, church and state, and by the ramifying controversies over these relationships that went on in the narrative of a particular collective experience. This species of historiography is now defined as "nation-state history," a term intended to dismiss it as obsolete and potentially harmful; but it is a major presence in the history of European historiography, and it is worth enquiring what political intentions underlie the present impulse to do away with it. If we now need other kinds of historiography—as we do—it does not follow that we have ceased to need this one, for reasons that may include the political.

Reverting to the political thought of the early modern period, we note that much of it went on within the contexts of this kind of history, and that to study it within these contexts—as has been a main theme in the scholarship of the last half century—leads to the discovery of several kinds of political thought that enlarge our definition of the term. In England it was debated whether the central institutions of law and sovereignty were Anglo-Saxon or Norman in origin—the ancient constitution against the feudal law; the French debate went back further still and discussed how far the central institutions were Roman or Frankish—the *thèse royale* against the *thèse nobiliaire*. It is worth enquiring how far other emergent national societies brought comparable debates to as high a level of organisation. Underlying but not controlling them, we find concepts drawn from philosophy (how is custom related to the law decreed by the sovereign will and how are both to be seen as exercises of reason?) and concepts arriving at philosophy by way of jurisprudence (how far is the individual's reason exercised through his property, and what happens if he has none or if it is in reality the property of another?). Here the word "property" takes on a diversity of meanings, some of them entailing the construction of new historical narratives. In England particularly, where "property" had above all the meaning of "tenure," James Harrington traced a history of tenures back to the point where it made contact with the Mediterranean notions of the republic as a community of armed freeholders, and with the Roman notion of the republic's decay as the disappearance of such a class's *libertas*. This was a point at which the political historiography of the western kingdoms became connected with both antiquity and republicanism. Before pursing its encounter with modernity and liberalism, however, there are some preliminaries to be noted.

In giving priority (not primacy) to Harrington in the English seventeenth century, I have reached a point where my reading of the relevant history differs from (without disagreeing with) that of Quentin Skinner. He has given priority to the much greater philosophical figure of Hobbes, and has reduced (at least I would call it reducing) the republican notion of liberty to the neo-roman (the term is his) contention that if your will, or the property through which you exercise it, is in the power of another, you are not your own master but another's servant or slave.[7] Against this Thomas Hobbes sets up the terrifying thesis that all you can do with your will is consent that it be exercised in your name by another, at which point he and you become not master and slave but a single artificial person, or even god. I am drastically simplifying an interpretation and a historical narrative with which I have no intention of disagreeing. But in offering to relate another narrative, with Harrington at its center, I shall be asking what and where were the historical consequences of Hobbes (probably in the history of philosophy), while offering to relate the historical consequences of Harrington, which lie in the fields of historiography and political economy, as well as in the relations between republics, revelations and civil society.

In addition to Harrington and Hobbes, a third major figure emerges, that of Hugo Grotius, and The Laws of War and Peace, a classic in the literature that deals with the relations between the states we begin to

---

7   Quentin Skinner, *Liberty Before Liberalism* (Cambridge: Cambridge University Press, 1998). Idem, *Hobbes and Republican Liberty* (Cambridge: Cambridge University Press, 2008).

call nations.[8] From 1560 to 1660, Latin Europe was devastated by wars between principalities and civil wars—sometimes hard to tell from each other—that were impelled by religious divisions and could be called wars of religion, and were rendered uncontrollable by the ability of princes to raise large armies and set them fighting, but not to pay them long or regularly enough to prevent them from devastating territories by living off the land and ceasing to be manageable instruments of state. Grotius, a Dutchman whose thinking was impelled as much by maritime and mercantile lawlessness at sea as by religious and mercenary warfare by land, helped develop the concept of an ecumene in which the relations between states were those of either peace or war and could be thought of as governed by systems of law originating in nature. The ability of a state to control its relations with other states was as important as its ability to exercise authority over its own subjects and components, and both became aspects of the concept of sovereignty. Though we think of international law as limiting the sovereignty of a state to act as it chooses, the works of Grotius heightened the notion of sovereignty to a point where sovereigns could escape religious and civil war and enter a world of sovereigns interacting with each other. This is the world we seem to be losing.

It is no surprise, then, to find Grotius' theology tending—as did that of Harrington and most radically Hobbes—towards a vision in which God enacted himself in the form of natural and civil law, and a grace which may transform or transcend law, but never negates or supersedes it. Grotius was certainly an Arminian and possibly a Socinian, who saw Christ as a being divine in mission but not in substance, who had come more to preach a doctrine conducive to salvation than to affect it by the sheer power of what he was. This is a point at which Protestantism began to mutate into Enlightenment, and the great debates of the third and fifth Christian centuries were revived in early modernity.

I propose to consider "Enlightenment" as a name, not a thing; a name for a number of processes that can be grouped together, but differ sufficiently, and occur in a sufficient diversity of contexts, to make it undesirable to speak of "The Enlightenment" as a unified process calling for unified explanation. It will also appear that I consider these phenomena, during the hundred years preceding 1789, as occurring in early

---

8   Hugo Grotius, *De Jure Belli ac Pacis* (Paris, 1625).

modern history and to be narrated as part of it; this for the reason that enlightened historiography, which I have made my subject, retained as dominant many of the characteristics of Renaissance humanism. Subject to these waivers, it is possible to say that developments of great importance began occurring in the later seventeenth century and that it is useful to apply the concept or word of Enlightenment—as contemporaries were beginning to do—in speaking of them. I suggest that there is to be found a general determination to have done with the religious civil wars (conducted by mercenary armies) that had afflicted peninsular and insular Europe since the mid-sixteenth century, and to do this by means of a plurality of sovereign states rather than by any single hegemony. At the levels of religion and philosophy, this entailed a determination to reduce the capacity of belief in divine grace to act contrary to the laws of civil society, though it is of the first importance to realise that what was entailed was less the commands of the sovereign (Leviathan) than the shared culture of a society increasingly seen as commercial. This is the story I propose to tell under the heading "Enlightenment"; that other stories could be told under the same heading is not at issue.

We tell this story as beginning from "the Anglo-Dutch moment" of 1688.[9] The overthrow of King James II was possible, without plunging England into a civil war like that of 1642, because it was conducted by two professional armies, those of James and William of Orange. The individual was spared the necessity of choosing a side, drawing his own sword, and facing the terrible problems of conscience and sovereignty that had made the English conflict one of the great moments in the history of political thought. The English were delivered from the political thought of Hobbes and Locke by an army, maintained by Dutch merchant capital, that neither lived off the land like those of the Thirty Years War nor attempted revolution to avoid doing so like the New Model Army in 1647. But the consequences were such that England found itself a new sort of state, obliged to maintain an army (to say nothing here of the navy that transformed its role in world history) capable of acting in both European state politics and the competition for global empire. This was achieved by instituting a system of public investment that maintained a professional army as an arm and extension of the state. Thus it came to be realised that the power of the state rested on an investing public's

---

9   Jonathan I. Israel, *The Anglo-Dutch Moment* (Cambridge: Cambridge University Press, 1991).

confidence in the future stability of its regime and the prosperity of its commerce, and this led to a rapidly increasing concern with civil society as the precondition of the state.

With surprising speed—in England during the decade following the revolution of 1688, and no doubt the same process is traceable in other national cultures—political society came to be defined in terms of commerce, and the individual citizen as transactor more even than proprietor. The philosophical consequences were many and various. Europe, for example, was redefined as a republic or commonwealth of sovereign states, maintained as a system of relationships by three major forces: the capacity to engage in war and peace, culminating in the power to sustain treaties; commerce, in the usual sense of trade, which made the states interdependent upon each other; and culture, known by the name of manners or *mœurs*, a system of social usages and social roles dependent on commerce but also on cultural heritage, which Europeans had in common and which polished and refined their dealings with one another. This was the profile of the *ancien régime*, which Burke denounced the French Revolution as aiming to destroy; but it was modern in the sense that it was neither ancient nor medieval, one reason I have for calling it early modern.

As property became transactional, so too did philosophy and religion. The progress of society was re-described as the establishment of sedentary cultures, constituting a social space through which the exchange of goods, values and ideas could go on; but philosophy in the wake of Locke began to enquire what could be known of a thing or idea beyond its changing meanings as it passed from one user to another. There were those who aimed to remove philosophy from the schools and situate it in the clubs and the drawing-rooms (an important step in the history of gender), but this was to convert it from knowledge to conversation, and the words "commerce," "conversation" and "intercourse" took on a diversity of meanings, from the mercantile to the sexual. The conversion of knowledge into opinion was of vast importance in the programme of ending religious war by establishing regimes of toleration, some of which were less concerned with the rights of the individual against authority than with the rights of the sovereign against the church: the sovereign's authority might be the more absolute when he was no longer obliged to persecute at religion's command. But the impact of toleration upon religion, that is to say upon revealed religion, was profound. Christ became a being concerning whom one held opinions, but with whom one had no experiential encounter; and if one's opinion of him could never become knowledge of his nature, it followed that he had no nature that could be known. Dissolution of transcendent experience, and of doctrine concerning it, was a necessary consequence of the creation of a tolerant society and its state. One of the earliest appearances of the word "liberal" to denote anything more than generosity is its use to devote a form of Christianity which placed tolerance above definable belief.

Ten years after the English Revolution of 1688, when it was being debated whether to maintain the standing army founded on public credit that had been created to maintain the new regime, a Scottish historical philosopher, Andrew Fletcher, wrote to enquire what was being lost in attaining the immense goods of commercial society. He looked back— necessarily with nostalgia—to a Mediterranean or Gothic past in which the hoplite or freeman had appeared in arms, which were his because he owned his own land, at the *ekklesia* or folkmoot in which he and his equals governed themselves. He did not deny that such a life had often been poor and brutal, but he feared the loss of republican virtue which must follow if standing army and public credit were necessary means of attaining commerce and enlightenment. To this Daniel Defoe—a brilliant observer of contemporary historical change, which in itself was something historically new—replied that one might not only be richer and more enlightened, but actually more free, if one were prepared to pay another to fight for oneself, and elect another to govern as one's representative. How this might apply to one's relationship with God was a further question which neither Fletcher nor Defoe considered in 1698. What they were doing was putting forward two opposed conceptions of liberty: the freedom to be oneself in participating in self-government, and the freedom to pursue one's self in taking part in the innumerable social pursuits that opened up once commerce and the exchange of goods and values with others had revealed that there were other things to be done in society than taking political decisions, perhaps under the terrible conditions of religious civil war.

The former idea was of course ancient; the latter would very soon be called modern, and commerce would take its place beside Christianity as one of the forces which had displaced antiquity. One can read the eighteenth century as a series of debates between the ancient and modern ideas of liberty and even of the republic: particularly in Britain, where kingless government was not a possibility. This was a series of brilliant debates, dominated by the English in the first half of the century, and the Scottish in the second. In what was to become the United States, debates over the Constitution and the founding ended in the triumph of the modern republic, but the idea of ancient virtue survived as a means of criticising its corruption. In France, there was the devastating re-enactment of the history of a neo-Roman conquering republic followed by a neo-Caesarean empire, after which liberalism was born as a philosophy, a practice, and a term of art, while Europe struggled to reconstitute the enlightened states-order of the ancient regime. We enter modern history, the world of the nineteenth and twentieth centuries, with the emergence of new problems in political and historical thought.

I have presented the early modern period as a culture obsessed with the presence of antiquity—two antiquities, indeed, one pagan and the other Christian—and able to envisage the ancient world as an era of heroic simplicities, in which the individual's engagement in politics was immediate and unmediated and the commitment of the self to action heroic and unspecialised. The commercial revolution, as we may call the earlier phases of Enlightenment, substituted a world in which the self was offered freedom to be many things, but might depute the management of self to many others, and was left wondering where in all this freedom of choice the choosing self was still to be found. Was not the self the sum of its roles, the value of property the sum of its debits and credits, and reality the sum of its images? These are questions we are once again asking ourselves. After the two centuries from 1789 to 1989, in which revolution and empire, state and war, seemed to exhaust the human capacity for self-assertion, we may now be facing a Second Enlightenment, directed not against the church but against the self: its freedom to know itself and to associate in communities whose autonomy consists in the freedom to debate histories of their own. If these are our problems, early modern thought will certainly not supply us with the answers, but may assist us in seeing how the questions came to be asked.

Political Hebraism, Past and Present

FANIA OZ-SALZBERGER

"Political Hebraism" is defined as the early modern, and mainly seventeenth century, set of attempts to read the Hebrew Bible, and to some degree the Talmud, Hellenistic Jewish authors such as Philo and Josephus, and later Maimonides, as genuinely historical sources which offer political forms and legal doctrines that might be usefully deployed in modern political and legal theory and practice.[1] In this essay I will offer a discussion of the surge of research into political Hebraism in recent years, assessing its genealogy, and offer a new analysis of its particular importance for understanding two partially overlapping traditions in early modern political thought: the modern reworking of classical republicanism, and the political deployment of natural jurisprudence. Finally, I will consider the potential importance of political Hebraism for enriching Israeli political discourse and debate in current-affairs perspective, and suggest that there is value in demonstrating that Israel's "democratic" component, hailing from both liberal and republican European traditions of discourse, includes a Hebraic legacy channeled through the works of major European thinkers.

Thus, I will argue, Israel's "Jewish" and "democratic" constitutional facets, often combined or counterpoised in recent public discourse, are by no means mutually alien. By adding a Hebraic component to the list of origins of early modern political thought, I am not contesting John Pocock's assertion that it was "Latin rather than Attic in origin," and I am indeed relying on his second point, that it was "shaped by historiography as much as by philosophy."[2] Indeed, it is only when the Hebrew Bible was grasped historically, as an ancient source akin to Thucydides or Titus Livius, that political Hebraism emerged. The Hebraic impact was never

---

1   The term was coined, or at least reached mainstream attention, in the early 2000s. Cf. Arthur Eyffinger and Gordon Schochet, "From the Editors," *Hebraic Political Studies (HPS)* 1,1 (Fall 2005): 3-6; for an account of the speedy recent growth of this field see Carlin Romano, "Who Took the 'Judeo' Out Of 'Judeo-Christian'?" in *Chronicle of Higher Education* (January 23, 2007).

2   See Pocock's contribution in this volume.

as powerful as the Greek, let alone the Roman; but it has some claim to being a minor third antiquity, alongside Pocock's two major antiquities, the pagan and the Christian. Importantly, it is not a mere component of Christian antiquity.

1.

If there is indeed a distinct political Hebraist chain of impact in seventeenth century thought, why did it go almost wholly unacknowledged for so long? Let us begin by exploring three main scholarly lineages of political Hebraism: the study of late medieval and early modern European Hebraism; research into the Jewish political tradition; and the history of political thought, primarily in early modern Western Europe. For a while, each of these lineages developed separately, with very little overlap. Since the 1980s there has been a set of studies on Renaissance Hebraism and cabbalism, Reformation biblicism and post-Reformation Christian Hebraism,[3] buffered by research of Jewish-Christian personal encounters and cultural go-betweens in Italy, the Netherlands and elsewhere.[4] Of prime importance was the scholarly attention drawn to the immense rise in late Renaissance and post-Reformation interest in ancient Hebrew texts and the rising numbers of Hebraist scholars, particularly philologists. The seventeenth century emerges as the era most attuned to the Hebrew language in European history. More European scholars could read Hebrew at that time than can now.

Much of the earlier research did not dwell specifically on *political* Hebraism. To be sure, the political impact of Bible reading has not gone unnoticed, especially in revolutionary societies. Two pivotal studies dealt with the biblical underpinnings of the Dutch war of independence and the English civil war and interregnum: Michael Walzer[5] and Christopher

---

3   Aaron Katchen, *Christian Hebraism and the Dutch Rabbis: Seventeenth Century Apologetics and the Study of Maimonides' Mishneh Torah* (Cambridge, MA: Harvard University Center for Jewish Studies, 1984), Frank Manuel, *The Broken Staff: Judaism through Christian eyes* (Cambridge, MA: Harvard University Press, 1992), Allison P. Coudert and Jeffrey S. Shoulson eds., *Hebraica Veritas? Christian Hebraists and the Study of Judaism in Early Modern Europe* (Philadelphia: University of Pennsylvania Press, 2004).

4   David B. Ruderman and Giuseppe Veltri eds., *Cultural Intermediaries: Jewish Intellectuals in Early Modern Italy* (Philadelphia: University of Pennsylvania Press, 2004).

5   Michael Walzer, *The Revolution of the Saints: A Study in the Origins of Radical Politics* (Cambridge, MA: Harvard University Press, 1965).

Hill[6] respectively highlighted the revolutionary import of Calvinist and Puritan perusals of the Old Testament. The radicals' Bible was the most striking, but over time, new studies began to look at the biblical deployment of other currents of early modern political theory and rhetoric— from the monarchist to the republican.

The difference between these earlier studies and the current interest in "political Hebraism" is important. Neither the young Walzer nor Hill assumed that the Hebrew Bible offered its readers anything but an arsenal of quotations, picked and endlessly rehearsed for their rhetorical moving-power, ignited by the messianic fire of Protestant extremism. There was no question of what the Bible, or the Talmud, appeared to be saying. No tests were suggested for the viability of readers' interpretations. The Bible was a quotation-toolbox for radicals, just as it could, and did, serve monarchists.[7] It was not approached as a self-standing source of political reflection in its own right.

This is precisely where new work on the Jewish political tradition— not necessarily emphasizing its Christian reception—that has blossomed since the 1990s[8] becomes relevant to the recent study of political Hebraism. New research, especially the project undertaken by Michael Walzer and his co-editors, suggests that despite the absence of ancient Hebrew and medieval or early modern Jewish political textbooks akin to Aristotle's *Politics* or Machiavelli's *Discourses*, systematic political thinking can nevertheless be found in the Hebrew and Jewish sources, accommodating one or several major strands of political philosophy.[9]

The idea that the Hebrew Bible, especially, harbors not only a set of quotable phrases, but rather a political theory—and perhaps even displays a tension-field between several political theories—is in some

---

6   Christopher Hill, *The English Bible and the Seventeenth Century Revolution* (London: Allen Lane, 1993). Earlier works on similar themes include Peter Toon, ed., *Puritans, the Millennium and the Future of Israel: Puritan Eschatology 1600 to 1660* (Cambridge and London: James Clark, 1970) and Richard H. Popkin, "Jewish Messianism and Christian Millenarianism," in *Culture and Politics from Puritanism to the Enlightenment*, ed. Perez Zagorin (Berkeley: University of California Press, 1980), 67-90.

7   Robert Filmer and Jacques-Benigne Bossuet are two cases in point. Cf. Emile Perreau-Saussine, "Why Draw a Politics from Scripture? Bossuet and the Divine Right of Kings," *HPS* 1, 2 (2006): 224-237.

8   Daniel J. Elazar, *Covenant Tradition in Politics*, 3 vols. (New Brunswick and London: Transaction Publishers, 1995-8); David Novak, *The Jewish Social Contract* (Princeton: Princeton University Press, 2005); and especially the multi-volume *Jewish Political Tradition*, ed. Michael Walzer et al. (New Haven: Yale University Press, 2004).

9   Walzer et al., ibid.

ways as old as Josephus, who defined the ancient Israelite state as a full-fledged theocratic republic. In other ways, it is a new and controversial assertion.[10] Looking at the Hebrew Bible, and in some cases at the Talmud and other Hebraic texts, through the eyes of political-minded Hebraists of early modern Europe may well shed some light on the viability of these ancient texts as sources for political thought, somewhat independently of their status as holy scriptures. In other words, both early modern (Christian) Hebraism and the history of Jewish political thought are scholarly fields that might benefit immensely from mutual interaction.

For about two decades, both Hebraist scholarship and research into the Jewish political tradition proceeded mostly unlinked to—and usually unheeded by—the prominent and immensely fruitful work on early modern European, and specifically English, political thought, that emerged from the pioneering work of J.G.A. Pocock and Quentin Skinner, alongside John Dunn, Richard Tuck, and their numerous colleagues. Neither Pocock, in *The Machiavellian Moment*[11] nor Skinner has granted much attention to the Hebraic sources of the political thinking of their seventeenth-century protagonists. Skinner, in a recent work, put great onus on the "neo-Roman" grain of early modern republicanism. His monograph, *Liberty before Liberalism*,[12] cuts the Bible altogether out of seventeenth-century republicanism. In several important studies of the 1980s and 1990s, the Bible itself (whether you call it thus, or the Hebrew Bible, or the Old Testament or the Holy Scriptures) fails to appear in the bibliography and index although it is mentioned and quoted in numerous locations in the text.[13] The Bible was either transparent or politically uninteresting.

Recent studies are setting out to rectify the chasm between history of political thought, especially in seventeenth-century England and the

---

10   Cf. Yoram Hazony, "Does the Bible Have a Political Teaching?" *HPS* 1, 2 (2006): 137-161.

11   J. G. A. Pocock, *The Machiavellian Moment: Florentine Political Thought and the Atlantic Republican Tradition* (Princeton: Princeton University Press, 1975).

12   Skinner, *Liberty Before Liberalism* (Cambridge: Cambridge University Press, 1998).

13   Thus, Peter Laslett's impressively thorough edition of Locke's *Two Treatises of Government*, published in the Cambridge Texts in the History of Political Thought (Cambridge: Cambridge University Press, 1960) with numerous later editions and amended reprints), has no "Bible," "Hebrew Bible," or "Old Testament," nor indeed "New Testament," in its bibliography or index. Individual biblical tomes are similarly absent; the book of Genesis, the focal point of the present essay, is thus non-existent as a source of Locke's thought. By contrast, all authors known to Locke, from Aristotle to Tyrell, are duly listed and indexed.

United Provinces, and the study of early modern Christian Hebraism. They focus on the political import of the Hebrew Bible, Talmud, rabbinical and other Jewish sources on prominent political thinkers in early modern Europe.[14] The story they tell runs as follows: political Hebraism flourished in European thought for about a century and a half, roughly from Bodin and Grotius to Locke, with Machiavelli as a significant predecessor. The greatest tide of political and legal-minded Hebraism emerged in mid-seventeenth century England, when jurist John Selden built his excellent scholarly reputation upon it, and republican theorists John Milton and James Harrington endowed it with hands-on political significance. Its ebb began in the early eighteenth century, when the Enlightenment threw out the political baby along with the theological bathwater. By the nineteenth century no major political thinker read the Old Testament politically.[15]

There are both "weak" and "strong" arguments at work here. The "weak" argument is a continuation, in greater detail and sharper focus, of the scholarship of previous decades that suggests that Hebraic sources could buttress almost every political stance in early modern European discourse. The "strong" argument is that several intellectual traditions, in particular modern natural law from its incipient phase in Grotius, could draw sustenance from biblical sources in the most privileged way. Moreover, a range of republican political stances—associated with the Dutch revolt, the English civil war, and the Glorious Revolution—relied on the Hebrew Bible, and at times on the Talmud, in ways more consistent, methodical, and persuasive—intellectually more interesting, one might say—than the use of Hebraic texts by other contemporaneous political creeds.

The Hebrew Bible, according to the "strong" argument, is particularly useful in the junctures where natural law feeds republican claims.[16] A

---

14   I have offered a preliminary view of this intersection and some of the research problems involved in Fania Oz-Salzberger, "The Jewish Roots of Western Freedom," *Azure* 13 (2002): 88; for significant recent work see Adam Sutcliffe, *Judaism and Enlightenment* (Cambridge: Cambridge University Press 2003); Steven Grosby, "The Biblical 'Nation' as a Problem for Philosophy," *HPS* 1, 1(2005): 7-23; and Eric Nelson, *The Hebrew Republic: Jewish Sources and the Transformation of European Political Thought* (Cambridge, MA: Harvard University Press, 2010).

15   Oz-Salzberger, "The Jewish Roots"; eadem, "The Political Thought of John Locke and the Significance of Political Hebraism," *HPS* 1, 5 (2006): 568-592.

16   Most helpful on this juncture is Richard Tuck, *Natural Rights Theories: Their Origin and Development* (Cambridge: Cambridge University Press, 1979), ch. 7.

substantial argument, emanating from Grotius, derives good human laws harmoniously from the laws of God, the light of Nature, and human reason. The principle of law-governed society can accommodate legitimate kings, as long as they are not *legibus solutus* and do not transcend the law and transform themselves into tyrants; but it is more conducive to republics. The Israelite polity, at least in its early phase from Moses to Samuel, could be seen by its early modern students (leaning on Philo and Josephus) as a law-governed republic. Indeed, it could, and often was, seen as the best republic in history. To wit, its laws were directly God-given and at the same time sanctioned by human reason, and deployed by virtuous magistrates, mostly or wholly without a king. But despite the divine origin of its constitutional text, it was still a republic *in history*. As such, it was comparable to other republics ancient and modern, and it offered a "usable past" to modern republicans.

This view becomes more convincing as new scholarship exposes both the scope and the depths of early modern, especially seventeenth-century, engagement with the Hebrew sources. Grotius, Petrus Cunaeus, and John Selden studied the juridical infrastructure of ancient Israel and it informed the works of James Harrington, John Milton, Algernon Sidney and John Locke. While many of the latter group deployed the Bible against monarchist rivals who used biblical props for their own theory, nevertheless their engagement can be seen as far more sophisticated than the biblicism of their rivals, from Bodin to Bossuet.

Thus, Milton's *Defence of the People of England* displays a different, better-grounded biblicism than that of his nemesis, Claudius Salmasius. Similarly, Locke's use of the Bible in the *Treatises of Government* arguably goes deeper into the biblical subject matter than Robert Filmer's *Patriarcha*. Milton and Locke's advantage does not necessarily stem from their superior acquaintance with the biblical text, but rather from their adherence and contribution to one of the most effective intellectual stances of the age, Grotian natural law. According to this line of argument, Hebraic sources, if taken seriously by their own political lights, *lend more support* to both republican and natural law based arguments.

I find the "strong" argument appealing, especially in view of a further distinction. Evidently, the Bible served many early modern readers as a historical textbook akin to the Greek and Roman canons. The history of the people of Israel was prominently cited in seventeenth-century texts alongside the two classical models, at times teaching similar lessons, and elsewhere punctuating dissimilarity. As the editors of a recent edition of Sidney's *Court Maxims* put it, "Next to Roman History, biblical history from the Old Testament made him understand the nature and dangers of monarchy, as it provided ample insight into godly inspired rule . . ."[17] Seventeenth-century political use of the Bible was coupled by a sharply increased awareness of the ancient Israelite nation in early modern treatments of classical antiquity.[18]

This novel emphasis on ancient Israel, or the *Re(s)publica Hebraeorum*, supplies a justification for using the term "Hebrew Bible" rather than "Old Testament" (or, for the matter, Hill's "English Bible"). Whereas "Old Testament" is most easily contextualized in a Christian theological prism, "Hebrew Bible" is closely associated with attention to the history and historicity of ancient Israel. As such, for example, it predominates Locke's *Two Treatises*, almost to the full exclusion of the New Testament. The present essay therefore normally uses the term "Hebrew Bible," *not* to indicate that most of the relevant authors read the book in its original language (though Selden and Cunaeus certainly did), but that they consciously related it to the historical and political contexts of the ancient Hebrews.

2.

Niccolò Machiavelli pioneered a non-theological political use of the Hebrew Bible.[19] Between the twelfth and the sixteenth centuries, several thinkers stand out as political-minded readers of Hebrew scriptures in theological contexts.[20] Political readings of Hebrew texts flourished when late Renaissance Hebraism, coupled with post-Reformation interest in the vernacular Old Testament, became a staple of scholarship in both

---

17 Hans W. Blom and Eco Haitsma Mulier, introduction to their edition of Algernon Sidney, *Court Maxims* (Cambridge: Cambridge University Press, 1996), xxii.

18 Adam Sutcliffe, *Judaism and Enlightenment* (Cambridge, 2003), ch. 2. Gordon Schochet, Fania Oz-Salzberger and Meirav Jones, eds., *Political Hebraism: Judaic Sources in Early Modern Political Thought* (Jerusalem: Shalem Press, 2008).

19 Christopher Lynch, "Machiavelli on reading the bible judiciously," in *Political Hebraism*, ed. Schochet et al., 29-58.

20 See David Novak, "Maimonides and Aquinas on Natural Law," in *St. Thomas Aquinas And The Natural Law Tradition: Contemporary Perspectives*, ed. John Goyette et al. (Washington, D.C.: The Catholic University of America Press, 2004), 43-65; Wilhelm Schmidt-Biggemann, "Political Theology in Renaissance Christian Kabbala: Petrus Galatinus and Guillaume Postel," in *Political Hebraism*, ed. Schochet et al., 1-28.

Protestant and Catholic milieus. Rome, Basel and Heidelberg boasted Hebraist scholars and collections of *Hebraica*. Basel also spearheaded a torrent of printed editions of the Hebrew bible, Talmud and rabbinical texts, both in Hebrew and in translations, as well as new commentary and lexicography.[21] From Jean Bodin onwards, political theory began to take up the *Re(s)publica Hebraeorum* as a regular model for political inquiry. The term, gleaned from Josephus' *Jewish Antiquities*, became a genre in humanist literature: tracts bearing this title were published as early as 1546, and would continue to appear until 1710. But it was primarily Bodin's *Methodus ad Facilem Historiarum Cognitionem* (1566) that granted ancient Israel a status similar to that of other polities of antiquity on the desk of late Renaissance scholarship.[22]

In Amsterdam, Hugo Grotius was an enthusiastic promoter of this line of learning. In 1614, he prompted the United Provinces to allow Jews to settle everywhere, in anticipation of their most welcome contribution as teachers of Hebrew to Christians.[23] Grotius himself made political use of the Hebrew Bible on several occasions, notably in his pamphlet *De Mare Libero* (1609) and in the posthumously published *De Republica Emendanda* (circa 1600), where he put ancient Israel as a model for the young Dutch Republic.[24] Grotius was personally acquainted with, and exercised significant intellectual influence on, several younger authors of great importance to political Hebraism, notably Petrus Cunaeus (Piet van der Cun) and John Milton.

Grotius' formulation of natural law proved fundamental for the republican appropriation of the ancient Israelite polity. Turning away from the Calvinist orthodoxy that prohibited human questioning of the divine will, Grotius pronounced human reason, guided by the light of Nature as well as God's commands, capable of grasping what is right.[25] Hence, justice was not a sword in the hand of the sovereign alone. When Milton revolutionized this doctrine by putting the "sword of justice" in the hands of individuals, he referred to Grotius' *De Jure Belli ac Pacis*

---

21 Sutcliffe, *Judaism and Enlightenment*, 27ff.
22 Ibid., 43. Anna Maria Lazzarino del Grosso, "The Respublica Hebraeorum as a Scientific Political Model in Jean Bodin's 'Methodus'," *HPS* 1, 5 (2006): 549-567.
23 Jonathan Israel, *European Jewry in the Age of Mercantilism 1550-1750* (Oxford: Clarendon Press, 1985), 64.
24 Arthur Eyffinger, "'How Wondrously Moses Goes Along with the House of Orange!' Hugo Grotius' 'De Republica Emendanda' in the Context of the Dutch Revolt," *HPS* 1, 1 (2005): 71-109.
25 Ibid.

(1625) when stating that "men, free in the state of nature, entrusted their right of self defense to kings or magistrates to be thir [sic] Deputies and Commissioners, to execute, by vertue [sic] of thir intrusted power, that justice which else every man by the bond of nature and of Cov'nant must have executed for himself."[26]

Petrus Cunaeus was Grotius' younger colleague, and his theoretical and political rival. Like Grotius' *De Republica Emendanda*, Cunaeus' *Re(s) publica Hebraeorum* discussed ancient Israel, its grandeur and especially its doom, with the modern Dutch Republic firmly in mind. He wrote this grand-scale opus in the wake of Grotius' unpublished tract, and in consultation with Grotius. The impact of Cunaeus' book was significant: it went through at least seven editions before 1700 and had a demonstrable effect on Dutch constitutional decisions. Richard Tuck pronounced it "one of the most remarkable pieces of political theory to come out of the early seventeenth-century United Provinces."[27]

Addressed to the Dutch Estates General, Cunaeus' book analyzed the fall of the federal republic of the Israelites in terms of religious strife and extremism, and prefaced his opus with a direct plea to the "illustrious members of states" to avoid discord and factions and to pursue peace and harmony.[28] Cunaeus then aired and developed Grotius' (unpublished) account of the federal structure of the Israelite tribal republic in direct reference to the requisite federal balance of the Dutch Provinces. He thus established ancient Israel into the origin of a subsequent genealogy of European theories of federation. The Hebrew republic for Cunaeus was a unique embodiment of the rule of law, and its intricate system of social justice. Using biblical historical narrative from Exodus to Kings, as well as Josephus' *Jewish Antiquities* and *Contra Apion*, and Maimonides' *Mishneh Tora*, Cunaeus translated the Bible's political imagery into familiar Greco-Roman terms. Despite its uniquely divine

---

26 John Milton, "The Tenure of Kings and Magistrates," in *Political Writings*, ed. Martin Dzelzainis (Cambridge: Cambridge University Press, 1991), 9. Cf. the editor's Introduction, xvi-xvii.
27 Richard Tuck, *Philosophy and Government 1572-1651* (Cambridge: Cambridge University Press, 1993), 167.
28 Petrus Cunaeus, *The Hebrew Republic*, translated and annotated by Peter Wyetzner with an introduction by Arthur Eyffinger (Jerusalem: Shalem Press, 2006). The following quotations, however, are from Clement Barksdale's English translation of 1653, read and used by several English republicans: Petrus Cunaeus, *The Commonwealth of the Hebrews* (edited with an introduction by Lea Campos Boralevi, Florence, 1996). Subsequent page-number references for Cunaeus reflect the facing Latin/English pagination.

origins, Israel's codex of laws was, he claimed, within easy reach. "[T] hat people had Rules of Government, excelling the precepts of all wise men that ever were; Which Rules, we have shewed, may in good part be collected out of the holy Bible."[29]

The Hebrew legal code included highly advanced and humanely construed Agrarian Law.[30] If anything could postpone (in the Hebrew case) or prevent (in the Dutch case) the fall of the republic in the wake of religious strife, it is a system of social justice and stability, anchored in the certainties of land ownership rather than the vicissitudes of commerce. After a first chapter dealing with the origins of law, five chapters—a substantial part of the First Book of Cunaeus' opus—are dedicated to aspects of the Israelite agrarian law: distribution and ownership, reasons underlying the agrarian laws, the rustic lifestyle of the ancient Hebrews, their shepherd culture distinguished from Egyptian farming, and the laws of jubilee and sabbatical, which Cunaeus pointedly admired.[31]

Here was a system of social balance based on landed smallholdings broadly dispersed among tribes and families. Distributive retuning and balancing acts included tithes, leaving part of one's field for the poor, and the sabbatical and jubilee practices of forgiving debts, redistributing land, and freeing slaves. Enacted in the biblical Hebrews' nomadic period and listed in Leviticus, Numbers, and Deuteronomy, these social laws of justice continued to act as a permanent corrective after the Land of Israel was settled in the generation of Joshua, ensuring that "the avarice of a few should not invade the possessions distributed with so fair equality."[32]

The pioneering element in Cunaeus' presentation of the Israelite Agrarian Law, as Eric Nelson points out, is his very choice of the term "Agrarian Law," which he goes on to contrast with the notorious Roman _lex agraria_. This is where some of my colleagues and I would take issue

---

29   Ibid., 6/7.
30   See Tuck's discussion, 167-168, and more recently Nelson, _Hebrew Republic_.
31   Jonathan R. Ziskind, "Petrus Cunaeus on Theocracy, Jubilee and the Latifundia," _The Jewish Quarterly Review_, New Ser., 68, 4 (1978): 235-254
32   Cunaeus, _Commonwealth_, 60/61. Cunaeus quotes at length, in this context, from Leviticus 25, emphasizing the mechanism of invigorating and renewing the division of land and of agrarian justice by means of the sabbatical and jubilee years, as well as the prevention of poverty and harmful urbanization by means of the laws governing treatment of the stranger and the widow, the first fruits, and tithes—in contrast to the centralization of land ownership, degeneration, and ethical corruption in ancient Rome.

with John Pocock's broad claim that it was the Roman universal civil law that underpinned early modern notions of state *legalitas*.[33] Cunaeus was the first to suggest that Hebrew social legislation was far superior to the Roman. It kept most people well provided and civic-minded, preventing gross enrichment and generally promising peace and concord. Its main instrument, which the Romans lacked, was the extreme legal tool of land repossession "at the solemn feast of Jubily."[34]

Cunaeus' understanding of biblical social justice in terms of distributive justice (alongside or beyond commutative justice) offers a possible corrective to Sam Fleischacker's recent claim that "'distributive justice' in the way we today use that phrase" did not exist prior to the late eighteenth century.[35] Fleischacker defines modern distributive justice as a state-sanctioned guarantee of a universal access to material means of subsistence by means of property distribution. To be sure, Mosaic law was not meted out by a "state" in the modern sense, but stipulated a periodic redistribution of landed property among numerous (though not all) members of society: the jubilee. Other Mosaic laws created a set of procedures to maintain all needy persons (resident foreigners included) on a subsistence level (*shemitah, leket, shichecha, pe'a*). All these were legal duties anchored in a written constitution, they were non-voluntary, and had nothing to do with charity.[36] Thus, the Hebrew Bible stipulates (re)distribution of both land and foodstuff. The latter, too, is property. Unlike Fleischacker, I believe that these arrangements—whether or not they were practiced by ancient Israelites is beside the point—convey a full-blown theory of distributive justice. Several important early modern readers, from Cunaeus onward, understood them as such.

If agrarian law is the essence of ancient Hebrew republicanism, its

33 Pocock, *Machiavellian Moment*, ch. iv and passim. Cf. Pocock, "The Ideal of Citizenship Since Classical Times," *Queens Quarterly* 99 (1992): 33-35.
34 Cunaeus, *Commonwealth*, 53/54. See Nelson's well-argued further discussion in *Hebrew Republic*.
35 Samuel Fleischacker, *A Short History of Distributive Justice* (Cambridge, MA: Harvard University Press, 2004), 4.
36 Fleischacker, *Distributive Justice*, 40-41, confuses calls for compassion, included both in the Mosaic code and in the Prophets, with the strictly legal instructions pertaining to redistribution of land and food. He is right to mention that Deuteronomy states that "the poor shall never cease out of the land" (Deut. 15:11), but wrongly assumes that this verse proves that Mosaic justice was non-distributive. For one thing, he ignores a contradictory statement, only seven verses earlier, where a debt-dropping law is enacted only temporarily, "save when there shall be no poor among you; for the Lord shall greatly bless thee in the land which the Lord thy God giveth thee for an inheritance to possess it" (Deut. 15:4). The prophets, too, often deemed poverty as temporary.

constitutional arrangements are its solid framework. The Sanhedrin, that Cunaeus and others took to exist since the nation's inception at Mount Sinai,[37] was the Israelite senate. A rather better one than the Roman, to be sure, that seamlessly incorporated judges and priests and deftly bridged between God-given laws and human adjudication. In the terms of Grotius (and possibly of Aquinas) here was a system of positive law neatly rooted in natural law. Guided by God's own hand, it was a near-perfect match of the natural and the positive; yet it went on to live and die as a normal historical construct. Precisely because ancient Israel existed in history, the Dutch republic could hope to emulate it. The initial model—created by God but not permanently reliant on transcendental resuscitation—was about adherence to "the light of nature" and human reason, particularly in matters of social justice.

3.

By the time Cunaeus' book on the Hebrew Republic had been translated into English, in 1653, England had overshadowed the United Provinces in its bid to become a Second Israel. John Selden was a foremost figure in English political Hebraism of the seventeenth century. Selden was an English jurist—a practicing lawyer at the London bar and a prominent historian and philosopher of law—who devoted his entire life to the study of the ancient Hebrew legislation. His greatest opus was the monumental *Law of Nature and the Nations According to the Hebrews*, published in 1640.[38] Other works included a three-volume work on the Hebrew Sanhedrin and juridical system, *De Synedriis & Praefecturis Juridicis Veterum Ebraeorum* (1650-3).[39]

Though no republican, Selden was member of the Long Parliament and a staunch believer in the supremacy of the legislature over kingly

---

37 "Sanhedrin" was the Great Council of Jewish elders during the era of the Second Temple. The term itself, Jewish-Aramaic and derived from the Greek *synedrion*, is obviously anachronistic when pertaining to the era preceding the First Temple, but the seventeenth-century Hebraists followed the lead of Josephus in using it for the assemblies mentioned in the Torah.

38 John Selden, *De jure naturali & gentium juxta disciplinam Ebraeorum* (The Law of Nature and the Nations According to the Hebrews) (London: 1640).

39 On Selden see, most recently and most eminently, Jason Rosenblatt, *Renaissance England's Chief Rabbi: John Selden* (Oxford and New York: Oxford University Press, 2006); important also is Tuck, *Natural Rights*, ch. 4; and on the Hebraist contexts, Sutcliffe, *Judaism and Enlightenment*, 46-49, and Jonathan R. Ziskind's "Introduction" in *Selden on Jewish Marriage Law: Uxor Hebraica* (Leiden: E. J. Brill, 1991).

prerogative and church-centered theocracy. His legal theory was based on the prominence of law as mediator between ruler and subjects, and as superior to both secular and clerical magistrates. It was through this conviction that Selden's work affected the deep-end uses of biblical essence in republican discourse: his ambition was to demonstrate that the laws of the Jews, given in the Pentateuch and interpreted in the Talmud and in Maimonides' *Mishneh Tora*, constitute the historical core of the natural law common to all mankind. "I cannot fancy to my Selfe what the law of nature means," he extrapolated in his *Table Talk*, "but the law of God."[40]

Like Cunaeus, but on a far broader scale, Selden used the modern natural law theory expounded by Grotius to introduce ancient Hebrew law as an ultimate exemplar of the human reworking of natural law. Selden divided his *Law of Nature* into seven parts, corresponding to the seven Noahide Laws of the Hebrews. Selden was not the first, but the most important commentator to see these seven precepts as the Hebrew *jus gentium*, law of nations, and thus natural law at its purest and most universal basis. According to Selden, the early Israelites created, with divine guidance, the first juridical state in history—today we might call it a veritable *Rechtsstaat*—that became the paradigm for the rule of law thereafter. The law given by God at Sinai was natural law *per se*, hence the Israelite laws deriving from it belong not in the realm of canon law but in that of civil law in the most proper sense. Selden's hidden agenda was Erastian and pertained to England of his time: all rule, including that of king and church, ought to be mediated through laws.[41]

Selden's thorough acquaintance with a wide range of Hebrew and Jewish source materials makes his use of Torah, Midrash and later texts, notably Maimonides' Mishneh Torah, a powerful testimony to our case. Selden may have imposed seventeenth-century English sensibilities on his source material, but his use of the texts was systematic and subtle: it attests to his awareness of the presence of a Jewish legal and political philosophy, a philosophy original and coherent enough to buttress his own world view. Furthermore, Selden's extensive use of Maimonides' interpretation of the Pentateuch amounts to a reception not merely of Jewish exegesis, but more precisely of a self-aware Jewish intellectual

---

40   John Selden, *Table Talk* (London: Quaritch, 1927), 69.
41   Cf. Sutcliffe, *Judaism and Enlightenment*, 47.

tradition with an emphasis similar to Selden's own. Maimonides, in other words, was not just a "primary source"; he informed Selden as a fellow-philosopher, and gave him a glimpse into a prominent and strand of Jewish political and legal philosophy. This philosophy is, in essence, civil legalism. The Jewish tradition appealed to Selden precisely because it offered him an alternative both to monarchical absolutism and to God-ordained Church domination either based on a Calvinist commitment to God's unmediated and unfathomable will, or on a more traditional adherence to superiority of canon law.

4.

The English republicans, Harrington, Milton, and Algernon Sidney, brought the political deployment of the Hebrew Bible, and in some cases the Talmud, to new levels of radical outspokenness. James Harrington's *Oceana* (1651), John Milton's *The Tenure of Kings and Magistrates* (1649) and *A Defence of the People of England* (1651), and Algernon Sidney's *Court Maxims* (written in 1664-5 but unpublished until 1996) are three of the most remarkable English republican works that draw heavily on biblical and post-biblical texts. For these authors, the Hebrew and Jewish sources presented a republican theory of government on top of a historical narrative conducive to republicanism.

Eric Nelson's work deftly depicts the Hebraist works of these "Talmudical Commonwealthsmen" as an escalating road to republican radicalism: the more deeply they delved into the Talmud, the more radical their monarchomach and commonwealth politics could become.[42] English revolutionary Biblicism developed along the two strands already noted in Cunaeus—social justice and the right of the people to a just government. Both strands had numerous variations. For the revolutionary generation, Moses had come into his own alongside Solon, Lycurgus and the Romans. The Hebrew Bible was a privileged source of Truth, of *Hebraica Veritas*. The Bible, Milton wrote in an early polemical pamphlet, is the perfect "rule and instrument of knowledge."[43]To be sure, not all theorists and pamphleteers of the English revolution were equally seri-

---

42   Nelson, *Hebrew Republic*.
43   John Milton, "Animadversions upon the Remonstrants' Defence, Against Smectymnuus" (1641), in John Milton and Charles Symmons, *The Prose Works of John Milton: With a Life of the Author* (London: J. Johnson, 1806), 64.

ous about it—but Milton and Sidney surely were.

The claim is more opaque with regard to James Harrington, a polit-ical-minded reader of the Hebrew Bible to be sure, but a Machiavellian rather than political Hebraist. Harrington harks back to Roman *libertas* more than to Deuteronomy or the book of Judges, no matter that he furnishes his work with biblical quotes and allusions.

It was John Milton, along with Algernon Sidney, who, in the wake of Grotius and Selden and parallel to Cunaeus, took the ancient Hebrew republic as a theoretical offering, as well as a historical model for what England ought to become. Milton's justification of regicide in *The Tenure of Kings and Magistrates*, followed by a vindication of the Revolution and the Commonwealth to a European audience in *A Defence of the People of England*,[44] combined references to Roman authors and to the Hebrew Bible. The Bible allowed Milton to radicalize the theory of resistance to unlawful rule developed by previous writers who sought justification of tyrannicide. According to such predecessors as Theodore Beza and the anonymous author of *Vindiciae Contra Tyrannous*, individual citi-zens, who were not magistrates, were not allowed to resist legitimate monarchs turned tyrants, although they could be suffered to oppose usurpers. The Bible, however, related many instances in which indi-vidual persons resisted Israel's kingly enemies and conquerors. Milton cited the slaying of King Eglon by the Ehud (Judges 3:12-26), asserting that Eglon was sovereign over Israel and that Ehud was a private person and no magistrate, in order to justify and legitimize the revolutionary army's responsibility for the execution of Charles I.[45]

The biblical free-lance tyrannicides, Milton said, were acting purely upon natural justice; direct divine guidance, when they got it, was mere-ly an affirmation of an act already made legitimate through natural law. Jehu's slaying of King Jehoram (2 Kings 9:1-2) is another case in point. The deep end is this: for Milton, natural law serves as both a necessary and a sufficient condition for justifying tyrannicide. Like Selden, and quite likely following Selden, Milton relied on Jewish legalism to reject the extreme Calvinist concept of God's incomprehensible will. The Book of Judges and the Books of Kings afforded Milton sustenance for his

---

44 John Milton, *Political Writings*, ed. Martin Dzelzainis (Cambridge: Cambridge University Press, 1991).

45 Milton, "Tenure," in *Political Writings*, 17-19; see the illuminating discussion in Dzelzainis' "Introduction," xii-xiv.

idea of the right of the people (rather than their magistrates, includ-ing the English Parliament) to dispose of a monarch turned tyrant. A reasonable man, even without magisterial status or a divine command, can oust the oppressor when guided "by the very principles of nature in him."[46]

Thus, the Hebrew commonwealth was the rule of God, under whom there are only men, and men were capable of self-rule or of electing their own magistrates. "The man who sets over him an earthly master, who is above all laws, is near to erecting a strange god for himself." This claim is made on the authority of Samuel, Hosea, Gideon, and Isaiah; also on that of Josephus, the Jewish-Hellenic historian who conceptual-ized the Hebrew polity in Greek terminology: "Hence Josephus calls the Commonwealth of the Hebrews, in which God alone held sovereignty, a theocracy."[47] Josephus' theocracy is—as far as Milton is concerned—Milton's republic.

Algernon Sidney worked along a similar route as Cuneaus and Mil-ton, but his emphasis was parliamentarian rather than individualistic. The Bible, Sidney asserted, presents us with a Hebrew republic, or, more accurately, a mix of democracy and aristocracy, where kings are either non-existent or elected by the better-placed citizens. Analyzing the bib-lical Law of the King, he concluded that monarchy was no necessity for the Hebrew commonwealth, and that wherever it clashed with the laws, it was law that trumped king, or ought to have trumped him.

Elsewhere, I have taken issue with Jeremy Waldron, who rightly emphasized Locke's Christian sources, but wrongly assumed that his use of the Hebrew Bible was fully ensconced within that intellectual Christianity.[48] I pointed out that in the *Second Treatises of Government*, having finished with Filmer and moved on to his own trailblazing politi-cal philosophy, Locke sticks with the Old Testament and mentions the New Testament with barely a footnote. Instead, the *Second Treatise* is swarming with Aaron, Abel, Abimelech, Abraham, Adam, Adonitzedek, Ahaz, Cain, Esau, Eve, Isaac, Ishmael, Jephthah, Moses, and this is only up to the letter M. For Locke, the Bible was the record of a people in

---

46   Milton, "Tenure," 17.
47   Milton, "Defence," in *Political Writings*, 102. Cf. Josephus, *Contra Apion*, ii: 165.
48   Jeremy Waldron, *God, Locke, and Equality: Christian Foundations in Locke's Political Thought* (Cambridge: Cambridge University Press, 2002); Fania Oz-Salzberger, "The Political Thought of John Locke and the Significance of Political Hebraism," *HPS* 1, 5 (2006): 568-592.

history—the Israelites—divinely endowed, and humanly struggling, with a model system of law and governance. The Hebrew Bible informed his ideas of the state of nature and early society. In dealing with several aspects of dominium, with both governmental power and property ownership, Locke used a sustained theoretical reading of the Hebrew Bible, and paid attention both to the right-of-the-people biblicism of Harrington and Milton and to the agrarian law biblicism of Harrington (and possibly Cunaeus).[49]

What, then, were the specific and unique drops that the Hebrew Bible might have added to the rich and bubbling waters of early modern political thought? To begin with, it offered an ancient model of a law-ruled polity exercising civil legalism; a polity whose divine original sanction is precisely what allowed its citizens to fend for themselves, either by self rule or by the elimination of tyrants; an interesting model of tribal federalism; a non-Roman republicanism based on the idea of mutual responsibility and a higher moral calling, firmly encapsulated in social laws. Last but not least, it offered its readers a historical stage swarming with strong-willed, voluntarily acting, intervening and highly opinionated individuals. As John Locke noticed, the Bible, as well as the Talmud, spreads out a plethora of distinct personal voices, sometimes a cacophony and seldom a harmony: individuals arguing and disagreeing among themselves, and sometimes with God himself. Here was a human platform for political theory, steeped in differentiated opinion and open debate, where disagreement could be taken on board and political interlocution legitimized.[50]

Of course, everyone used the Bible to their ends: monarchists and cardinals, budding imperialists and all-out levelers. It was particularly conducive to two overlapping groups: the natural law theorists and the republicans. Such authors, unlike the bible-minded supporters of monarchy and the divine rights of kings, were keen on finding a theory of government wedged between Deuteronomy and I Samuel.

The reason, I suggest, for this biblical allure was twofold. First, of course, here was the Godliest of human political creations, a divinely or-

---

49   Oz-Salzberger, ibid., 571ff.

50   Of the numerous biblical characters inhabiting Locke's two *Treatises of Government*, Jephthah stands out as arguably the most interesting. For a recent controversy on Jephthah's role in Locke's Second Treatise, cf. Oz-Salzberger, "Jewish Roots," with Andrew Rehfeld, "Jephthah, the Hebrew Bible, and John Locke's 'Second Treatise of Government'," *HPS* 3, 1 (2008): 60-93.

dained polity of the highest order, which could either match or surpass the Greek and the Roman models in its bright light of authentic truth. Dutch revolutionary Calvinism and the English republican politics of saintliness could not hope for a better prop for their earthly aspirations.

But this is just part of the story. The second, and more interesting, aspect of the usefulness of Bible and Talmud to natural lawyers and republicans is what I have proposed to call their civil legalism. From Mount Sinai onwards, the Hebrew polity is adamantly constitutional. Its dramas are legal—not least, of course, because humans keep eluding or challenging the statutes. Biblical man and woman's relations with God, king, elder and community are invariably law-mediated. Exodus, Leviticus, Numbers and Deuteronomy add up to a legal codex, and Talmud is a broad compendium of legal exegesis upon it. The narrative-historical parts of the Pentateuch, and their continuation in Joshua through II Kings, supplied a series of human engagements with the laws in a civil environment of everyday strife, in a political environment of contingent historical challenges, and in an intellectual environment of debate and exegetical creativity. For the post-Grotian natural lawyers, including Cunaeus and Selden, this was an exemplary model of positive law, derived from God-given/natural law but nevertheless freestanding, man-made and historically evolving. For the republicans, from Cunaeus to Sidney (in some significant ways up to Locke), the legalist components of ancient Israel were coupled by its lively human magistracy, which included assemblies, elders, "Sanhedrin," and judges. Israelite kingship was preceded by a kingless polity, darkened by premonitions and fraught with failures and qualms. But here was the earliest, best, and most sustained proof that every polity must be self-governing, subject to good civil laws, that no ruler may rise above them.

5.

For present-day Israeli society, and its unique political and legal debates, the importance of political Hebraism is more than historical. It suggests that Israel's two constitutional appellants, the "Jewish" and the "democratic" state, do not form a dichotomy, nor do they represent a superficial amalgam of disparate traditions.[51] Insofar as Israel's liberal

---

51   Israel's *Declaration of Independence* of May 14, 1948 defined the new country as "a Jewish State in

democratic legacy hails from a post-Lockean understanding of modern democracy in terms of the rule of law and civil equality, this lineage carries several capsules of ideas derived from Hebrew antiquity itself.

Not only do the Hebrew Bible and later Jewish texts belong to the genome of modern rule of law; they also affected, as we have seen, modern ideas of social justice and modern understanding of the importance of free debate. This set of ideas combines the biblical influence on early liberal thought, from Locke to the American founding fathers, with the strand of early modern republicanism, from Cunaeus through Milton (and arguably Locke), that sets high value on civic engagement through virtuous public discourse.

Each of these elements is crucial for current Israeli discussions of the compatibility of full liberal democracy with the state's "Jewish" character—whether the adjective is taken in national, religious, or cultural context. Recent voices from the political right, calling for the supremacy of "Jewish" over "democratic," thus ignore the uniquely Hebraic component of modern democracy's appeal for legal equality to all. As former Supreme Court President Aharon Barak has recently written, Israel ought to perfect the civil equality of Arabs and Jews. Such equality befits the mutually complementing constitutional appellants of the State. Barak, a secular Jew, quotes Leviticus 24:22: "Ye shall have one manner of law, as well for the stranger, as for one of your own country."[52] By delving deeper into the intellectual history of Western democracy, Israelis might therefore achieve a better perspective of their Jewish as well as their democratic legacies, intertwined in the past as well as the present.[53]

---

the Land of Israel." Without mentioning "democracy," it nevertheless committed the newfound state to "ensure complete equality of social and political rights to all its inhabitants irrespective of religion, race or sex; it will guarantee freedom of religion, conscience, language, education and culture; it will safeguard the Holy Places of all religions; and it will be faithful to the principles of the Charter of the United Nations." See *The Declaration of the Establishment of the State of Israel*, May 14, 1948, http://www.mfa.gov.il/MFA/Peace%20Process/Guide%20to%20the%20Peace%20 Process/Declaration%20of%20Establishment%20of%20State%20of%20Israel. The conjoining of "Jewish" and "democratic" first appeared in the *Basic Law: The Knesset*, in its amended form of 1985, and reinforced in the two Basic Laws pertaining to civil rights of 1992. See Knesset website, http://www.knesset.gov.il/description/eng/eng_mimshal_yesod1.htm.

52   Aharon Barak, "The State of Israel as a Jewish and Democratic State," *Iyuney Mishpat* 24 (2000): 9-14 [Hebrew].

53   Cf. Fania Oz-Salzberger, "But Is It Good for Democracy? Israeli's Dilemma," *World Affairs* (May/June 2010): 62-69.

The Polis in Seventeenth-Century Political Discourse:
Athens Mirrored by Francis Rous, Marchamont Nedham, George Guillet de Saint-George and Jonathan Swift

Francis Rous the Younger (1615-1643), son of an English Puritan, politician and Member of Parliament, was one of the first authors in early modern England who dedicated a whole work to the ancient Greek city-state of Athens. In 1637, he published his study entitled *Archaelogiae Atticae Libri Tres*.[1] The work saw great success, and was reissued several times. The 1649 third edition was augmented with four additional books by Zachary Bogan.[2] Now consisting of seven books, this work described in almost four hundred pages the customs, rites, and political and judicial regime of ancient Athens.

Rous considered the study of ancient Athens important for seventeenth-century education, blatantly rejecting the tendency to read philosophical and theoretical texts without knowledge of ancient Attic customs and rites as well as of the political history of Athens. In his dedication to the reader, Rous confirmed his scholarly interest:

> It is not a thirst of empty glory that makes me runne
> bazard of your censure, but a consideration of the
> weaknesse of School-masters, who undertake to read
> the Greeke Orators to raw Scholers, themselves being

---

1   Francis Rous, *Archaeologiae Atticae Libri Tres: Three bookes of the Attick antiquities Containing the description of the citties glory, government, division of the people, and townes within the Athenian territories, their religion, superstition, sacrifices, account of their yeare, as also a full relation of their iudicatories. By Francis Rous scholler of Merton Colledge in Oxon* (Oxford: Printed by Leonard Lichfield, for Edward Forrest, M.DC.XXXVII, 1637).

2   Francis Rous, *Archaeologiae Atticae Libri Septem. Seven Books of the Attick Antiquities. Containing the description of the Citties glory, Government, division of the People, and Townes within the Athenian Territories, their Religion, Superstition, Sacrifices, account of the Yeare, a full relation of their Judicatories. With an Addition of their Customs in Marriages, Burialls, Feastings, Divinations, & c. Third Edition Much enlarged* (Oxford: Printed by Leonard Lichfield, for John Addams and Ed. Forrest Junior, 1649). In the following notes I will cite the seven books containing longer versions.

not ripe in the Attick custumes.[3]

Throughout his work, Rous praised Athens for its achievement in philosophy, reason and art, especially in the development of the theatre, as well as for its political eloquence and military triumphs. In his epistle, Rous stated:

> That City once the nurse of reason, which flourisht in eloquence, & brave atchievments more than all Greece, could not, unlesse in her miserable ruines, have without her disgrace been spoken of by me. [...], as Devotion paid to Antiquity, by you well esteemed of, though among most of these our daies accounted durt; whose labour it is to seek new fashions, and like nought but what may be accounted novelty. Resembling the brute [...] never caring for what is past. But you weigh well the excellency of talking with those Champions of Learning, hundreds of years since gathered to their former dust By whose pensills wee see drawne the lively Images of deceased Monarchs, the formes of government, and very lives of States.[4]

In this short abstract, we can observe three major features of Rous' reception of ancient Athens, which are pivotal to the reception of the *polis* in seventeenth-century political discourse:

1. An awareness of a period of florescence and glory in Athens
2. An awareness of the end of this "Golden Age" and of Athens' downfall
3. A great interest in the study of the forms of government based on the historical example of Athens

This article's aim is to examine the function of the Attic city-state as a historical example in seventeenth-century political discourse, and furthermore to focus on what seventeenth-century political thinkers

---

3   Rous, "To The Reader," in *Archaeologiae Atticae Libri Septem.*
4   Rous, "The Epistle," in *Archaeologiae Atticae Libri Septem.*

writing about the Attic *polis* tell us about citizenship. Consequently, although we identify the Attic city-state rather as a direct-democracy, I do not aim to analyse early-modern attitude towards (direct-)democracy—considering that *polis* denotes first of all a community of citizens and does not necessarily determine a specific political regime like democracy, aristocracy or monarchy. However, in the context of political and religious dissensions in sixteenth and seventeenth century England and France, this discourse on the Attic *polis* may have generated new prospects and opportunities for the creation of a body political with participating citizens.

In order to analyse the *polis'* function in seventeenth-century political discourse, this article will present and analyse four works significant for the reception of the Attic polis. These works have several points in common. First, all were read with attention and were received in the following decades, and consequently shaped the discourse on the Attic *polis*. Second, they all show an issue pivotal to this reception: the connection between politics and culture.

Furthermore, it seems that political writers became increasingly interested in the ancient Attic *polis* beginning in the 1640s. Reading Latin, Greek, and especially Attic political philosophers in order to think about a free state and its suitable constitution which allowed for liberty and stability, English political thinkers seem to have been particularly intrigued not only by Rome or Sparta, but by Athens, too.[5] These writers

---

5   In his *Leviathan* Thomas Hobbes stressed the influence of the Attic city-state blaming Greek and Latin philosophers to be accountable for political turmoil in his days. According to Hobbes their theoretical assumptions were wrong, because these writers had not conceived of their political categories on natural, but on criteria they had observed in their own environment. Thus, especially Greek philosophers such as Aristotle, had had the Attic polis in mind, when they had written their political works: "But it is an easy thing, for men to be deceived, by the specious name of Libertie; and for want of Judgement to distinguish, mistake that for their Private Inheritance, and Birth right, which is the right of the Publique only. And when the same error is confirmed by the authority of men in reputation for their writings in this subject, it is no wonder if it produce sedition, and change of Government. In these westerne parts of the world, we are made to receive our opinions concerning the Institution, and Rights of Common-wealths, from Aristotle, Cicero, and other men, Greeks and Romanes, that living under Popular States, derived those Rights, not from the Principles of Nature, but transcribed them into their books, out of the Practise of their own Common-wealths, which were Popular; as the Grammarians describe the Rules of Language, out of the Practise of the time; And because the Athenians were taught, (to keep them from desire of changing their Government,) that they were Free-men, and all that lived under Monarchy were slaves; therefore Aristotle puts it down in his Politiques, (lib.6.cap.2) In democracy, Liberty is to be supposed: for 'tis commonly held, that no man is Free in any other Government. And as Aristotle; so Cicero, and other Writers have grounded their Civill doctrine, on the opinions

began to realize that there had been a cultural florescence in the Attic *polis*, and, hence, they tried to explain this period of florescence as well as the collapse of the Attic greatness.

First, the article will present the already mentioned *Archaeologicae Atticae* by Francis Rous. Second, *The Excellencie of a Free State: Or, The Right Constitution of a Commonwealth*, published in 1651 and written by the journalist and pamphleteer Marchamont Nedham. In this work, Nedham compared Roman and Attic "Liberties and Freedom of the People," and reflected on the governmental and constitutional lives of both of the ancient Republics.[6] Third, the article contains an analysis of the work by the French comedian and first historiographer of the "Royal Academy of Art and Sculpture" George Guillet de Saint-George entitled *Athènes ancienne et nouvelle*, which was first published in 1675 under the name of the author's brother, La Guilletière.[7] The work contains a description of Athens by Guillet's imaginary brother who had just escaped from Turkish captivity in Athens. La Guilletière was the pen name used by Guillet de Saint-George. The latter has received all necessary information for his account from French priests in Athens.[8]

Finally, I will examine *A Discourse of the Contests and Dissensions*

---

of the Romans, who were taught to hate Monarchy, at first, by them that having deposed their Soveraign, shared amongst them the Soveraignty of Rome; and afterwards by their Successors. And by reading of these Greek, and Latine Authors, men from their childhood have gotten a habit (under a false shew of Liberty,) of favouring tumults, and of licentious controlling the actions of their Soveraigns; and again of controlling those controllers, with the effusion of so much blood; as I think I may truly say, there was never any thing so deerly bought, as these Western parts have bought the learning of the Greek and Latine tongues." See Thomas Hobbes, *Leviathan*, ed. Richard Tuck (Cambridge: Cambridge University Press, 2007).

6   Marchamont Nedham, *The Excellencie of a Free-State: Or, The Right Constitution of a Common-wealth. Wherein All Objections are answered, and the best way to secure the Peoples Liberties, discovered: With Some Errors of Government, And Rules of Police* (London: Printed for Thomas Brewster, at the three Bibles near the West-end of Pauls, 1656).

7   George Guillet de Saint-George, *Athènes ancienne et nouvelle. Et l'estat present de l'empire des Turcs, contenant la vie du sultan Mahomet IV. Le ministere de Coprogli Achmet Pacha, grand vizir. Ce qui s'est passé dans le camp des Turcs au siege de Candie. Et plusieurs autres particularitez des affaires de la Porte...* (Paris, chez Estienne Michallet, ruë Saint Jacques, à l'Image Saint Paul, proche la fontaine S. Severin. M. DC. LXXV. Avec privilege du Roy, 1675). The English edition was published in 1676: George Guillet de Saint-George, *An account of a late voyage to Athens containing the estate both ancient and modern of that famous city, and of the present empire of the Turks, the life of the now Sultan Mahomet the IV, with the Ministry of the Grand Vizier Coprogli Achmet Pacha : also the most remarkable passages in the Turkish camp at the siege of Candia and divers other particularities of the affairs of the port / by Monsieur de La Guillatiere, a French gentleman; now Englished* (London: Printed by J. M. for H. Herringman, 1676).

8   David Constantine, *Early Greek Travellers and the Hellenic Ideal* (Cambridge: Cambridge University Press, 1984), 18-19.

Between the Nobles and the Commons in Athens and Rome with the Consequences they had upon both those States by the Irish writer Jonathan Swift, published in 1701.[9] As the title indicates, Swift, like Nedham, compared Attic and Roman political history, but focused much more on the dangers of civic dissensions.

In analysing seventeenth-century political discourse, historical and political researchers most often stress the reception and proliferation of Roman political ideas and models for political conceptions, rather than those of the Greek city-states.[10] Indeed, Roman political models played a dominant part in this discourse. In my analysis, I do not want to deny the importance of Roman heritage—in fact, in most cases, Athens appears in conjunction with other ancient republics like Rome or Sparta—but I will rather show that it is not the only political language of this period.

In his article "Republican Visions," Eric Nelson describes a Roman and Greek heritage of political thinking, thus arguing that two kinds of republican theories existed in the early modern period.[11] Whereas Roman republican theory regarded the independence of a political community and private property and considered the empire's glory as the main objective, Greek republican theory cherished the natural ordering of the state. Consequently, this Greek tradition allowed for wealth regulations.[12] According to Nelson and other relevant research like the *Machiavellian Moment*, early modern political theory influenced by a Roman heritage was attached to Machiavelli.[13] For the Florentine, Rome had been an ideal republic, but this had not been the result of *concordia* and internal harmony, but due to the disunion between plebs, who had not wished to be governed, and the senate, who had wished to govern. All

9   Jonathan Swift, *A Discourse of the Contests and Dissensions Between the Nobles and the Commons in Athens and Rome with the Consequences They Had upon Both those States* (London: Printed for John Nutt near Stationers-Hall, 1701).

10 See especially: Hans Baron, *The Crisis of the Early Italian Renaissance*, vol. 2 (Princeton: Princeton University Press, 1955); Quentin Skinner, *Liberty before Liberalism*, (Cambridge (a.o.): Cambridge University Press, 1997).

11 Eric Nelson, "Republican Visions," in *The Oxford Handbook of Political Theory*, ed. John S. Dryzek (Oxford: Oxford University Press, 2006), 193-210. For further reading: Eric Nelson, *The Greek Tradition in Republican Thought* (Cambridge: Cambridge University Press, 2004).

12 Nelson, "Republican Visions," 193.

13 John G. A. Pocock, *The Machiavellian Moment: Florentine political thought and the Atlantic republican tradition* (Princeton: Princeton University Press, 1975).

laws in favour of freedom had been a product of this disunion.[14]

Nelson begins his narrative of early modern Greek republican theory with Thomas More, who was—as Nelson shows—one of the first scholars in England who thoroughly studied Greek.[15] According to Nelson, More recovered in his *Utopia* a political theory influenced by Greek ideology, which differed greatly from political theories influenced by a Roman heritage. The Greek ideology and early-modern theories incorporating this Greek heritage did not value freedom as non-domination but as living according to one's rational nature. However, the purpose of civic life was not glory, but happiness. As Nelson states, the most important difference between neo-Roman theory and Greek tradition was the conception of justice: Justice in a Greek sense did not concentrate on giving everyone *ius suum*, but it did esteem the rule of reason in the form of the rule of the most excellent men.[16]

Although I do not confine my sources exclusively to so-called early modern republican theories—as Nelson did—I similarly value the Greek heritage of political thought. But instead of focusing on philosophical and conceptual issues, I rather focus on the historical example of Athens in seventeenth-century political discourse. In order to do this, I will draw on the observations I exemplified at the beginning of this article: I mentioned the awareness of a period of florescence and ruin in Athens and a focus on governmental issues. This observation leads me to four further questions I want to pursue: First, when had this period of flourishing taken place according to the authors mentioned above? Second, what had constituted in their view this period of glory? Third, how did they interpret Athens' downfall, or rather, what causes did they allege for Athens' downfall? Finally, with view on the Attic history: How did they conceive of a citizen's role within a commonwealth? (Those four questions will structure the following sections). Thus, the first part will focus on the relationship between civil government and florescence. The second section will address civil law and participating citizens. In the third section, I will concentrate on integration and inclusion/exclusion of citizens. Finally, I will draw some conclusions for today's concepts of citizenship. Furthermore, my observations of the reception of the

---

14   Nelson, "Republican Visions," 201-202.
15   Ibid., 204.
16   Ibid., 203-205.

polis in seventeenth-century political discourse will lead me to the thesis that—with regard to the question of citizenship—we are dealing with a discourse of integration of participating individuals in contrast to a discourse of inclusion and exclusion of civic groups within a certain commonwealth.

1. Athens' "Golden Age"

In this section I will consider two main items: First, I will analyse when the above introduced writers located Athens' Golden Age; and second, whether they assumed a connection between a certain political regime and Athens' prosperity.

Francis Rous, an admirer of Athens' culture, discovered a connection between civil government and the dedication to art, literature and philosophy:

> I conjecture that first it was called Athens, when the people began more seriously to addict themselves to civill government, and study of good literature; knowledge and art being ascribed to Minerva [...].[17]

He assumed that the political community of Athens had obtained its name by means of two elements: civil government, and dedication to literature and knowledge. Rous traced Athens' name from the "Chaldy tongue" where Athens had been derived from the verb to study or to learn, signifying "the most learned." Rous rejected all other explanations of Athens' beginnings: The *polis*' origins lay in the dedication to civil government and study of good literature and art. Also, Marchamont Nedham stated rather clearly:

> It is wonderful to consider, how mightily the Athenians were augmented in a few years, both in Wealth and Power, after they had freed themselves from the Tyranny of Pestratus.[18]

———————

17   Rous, *Archaeologiae Atticae Libri Septem*, 5.
18   Nedham, *The Excellencie of a Free-State*, 19.

Nedham assumed a connection between the liberty of a state and its power and success. Athens had only flourished after the repulsion of the monarchy and the gain of liberty by instituting a popular government, which had not been identical with a direct-democracy, but rather had included representative elements.[19] In this sense, popular government as described by Nedham can be used synonymously with civil government, since the people consisted of free citizens and not slaves or subjects.

Guillet de Saint-George also connected popular government with prosperity: He stated that after "liberty being restored to the Athenians"—referring to the popular government, established by Solon and regained after Peisistratos' "usurpation"—the Republic had flourished, which had made possible the victory over the Persians in the naval battle at Salamis:

> After the victory of Salamis, the Republick of Athens was in its highest elevation: Its greatest Captains, its greatest Philosophers, and its most Ingenious Artists were living in that time; and never was any City so fertile in Illustrious Men.[20]

These were the "happy times" of which he wrote enthusiastically:

> I should write of nothing but what was new of a Town so universally famous, and reputed the Mother of Arts, and the Theatre of Valour and Policy.
>
> The happy times in which this City flourished, were so fertile in wonders, and we have had so few Ages since that have produced such Eminent Men, that I do not doubt your excuse, if I give you a particular specification of those memorable years that remain stille Sacred by so great and so glorious Events: [...] Of all the Ancient Cities in Greece, none has preserved its name with better success than this City of Athens.[21]

---

19   Ibid., 7.
20   Guillet de Saint-George, *An account of a Late Voyage to Athens*, 129.
21   Ibid., 127.

Guillet de Saint-George assumed that the popular government had produced these "Eminent Men" who had been responsible for Athens' cultural success, and so did Jonathan Swift: In the course of his work, Swift told us that there had been "absolute unlimited power" in a government, "which naturally and originally seems to be placed in the whole body, wherever the executive part of it lies." [22]

Furthermore, Swift exemplified that a free people had met together, "whether by compact or family government," creating a civil society and dividing themselves into three powers: The first power had consisted of men of "eminent spirit," the second of men who had acquired large possessions and the last of the "body of the people, whose Part of Power is great and undisputable, whenever they can unite either collectively or by Deputation to exert it."[23]

Swift derived these theoretical assumptions from Athens' political history: after the abolition of the monarchy, the free people of Athens, under the rule of the great law-giver Solon, had chosen four hundred men, a hundred from each tribe, as a body representative. The people collectively had reserved a share of power for themselves. According to Swift it had been under these institutions that the *polis* of Athens had "bred up" great men.[24]

Although these authors did not explicitly speak of citizens in these passages, they did tell us something about the people, civic government and periods of florescence. They spoke of the liberty of the state or of a free state, and they defined the free state historically with the abolition of the monarchy and the ending of servitude. The state was free by virtue of the self-determination of its people. Could this not be rephrased to say that a state was free, when the people of a given state govern themselves? So the people were identical with a community of citizens. Consequently, "the people" was not synonymous for "the masses." However, this is nowhere explicitly defined, nor did the authors show particular interest for the concrete exclusive regulations or restrictions of citizenship for foreigners and women as they had existed in the Attic *polis*.

"The people" evolved first of all quite simply as an incorporation of different citizens. For the seventeenth-century writers, popular gov-

---

22   Swift, *A Discourse of the Contest and Dissensions*, 3.
23   Ibid., 4-5.
24   Ibid., 15.

ernment was identical with civil government, but not necessarily with (direct-) democracy. According to Nedham, popular government meant that power and sovereignty were in the people's hands, which implied that they determined their own laws and decided their own government:

> If a People once conceive they ought to be free, this conception is immediately put in practice; and they free themselves. Their first care is to see, that their Laws, their Rights, their Deputies, their Officers, and all their Dependents, be setled in a state of freedom. This becoms like the Apple of the eye; the least grain, atome, or touch, will grieve it: it is an espoused virgin; they are extreme jealous over it.[25]

Furthermore, only in the case of popular government, Nedham spoke of "citizens" instead of "servants." If it had been a civil government that had produced the effects of greatness and glory of Athens, we have to ask what elements (of civic government) had produced this greatness according to these seventeenth-century authors? This will be the leading question for the following section.

2. Civil Law and Participating Citizens

After having stated a connection between civil government and Athens' period of florescence, we have to ask what had constituted this period of prosperity in the writers' views and which elements of civil government had determined Athens' prosperity. Rous provided us with some details on the Attic civil government. According to him, "any citizen" had had the right to "declare his mind either for, or against" the civil laws.[26] Consequently, all decisions had been tied to the people's will. Furthermore, he considered the Athenian written law to have included two objectives: mutual commerce and the citizens' appropriate and good behaviour toward the state:

---

25 Nedham, *The Excellencie of a Free-State*, 2.
26 Rous, *Archaeologiae Atticae Libri Septem*, 101.

> To these Lawes two ends were proposed, mutuall com-
> merce and direction of behaviour towards the state. To
> curb wickednesse, and injustice; & to punish offenders
> that they might be bettered. And although they were the
> ordinances of Draco and Solon, yet may we sitly call the
> Athenian Civill Law.[27]

According to Rous' interpretation, it had been the civil law that had
brought about the citizen's correct behaviour for the benefit and well-
being of a state. This had also meant the well-being of the citizens, since
the latter had decided the laws and had chosen their representatives for
the benefit of the whole *polis*, neglecting headstrong interests:

> However, I must confesse they had so much care still
> of the Common-wealth, notwithstanding their private
> pleasures, as not to give a voyce to one whom they knew
> to be guilty of so much Mollities.[28]

In accordance with Rous, Nedham considered the citizens' participation as pivotal for the well-being of a state. He assumed that the civil
government had produced this period of florescence because the citizens had given their consent only to laws which had been beneficial and
advantageous for the community:

> [...] for we see, that both in Athens and Rome, the Great
> Ones were by this means kept in awe from Injustice; the
> Spirits of the people were kept warm with high thoughts
> of themselves and their Liberty (which turned much to
> the inlargement of their Empire.)
>   And lastly, By this means they came off always with
> good Laws for their profit, (as in the case of the Law of
> twelve Tables, brought from Athens to Rome) or else
> with an Augmentation of their Immunities, and Priv-
> iledges (as in the case of procuring the Tribunes, and
> their Supreme Assemblies and afterwards in the fre-

---

27   Ibid., 97.
28   Rous, *Archaeologiae Atticae Libri Septem*, 153.

quent confirmation of them against the Incroachments of the Nobles.[29]

George Guillet de Saint-George particularly emphasized the civic harmony in Athens. He further accentuated the function of culture for the education of the people, especially with respect to theatre and architecture.[30] In this way, civil government had provided occasion for "Eminent Men" who contributed to the harmony and well-being of the state. He exemplified what single citizens could contribute to the common well-being in the person of Philo, the great architect of public buildings:

> It was not enough for Philo, like an admirable Architect, to regard the just symmetry and proportions of parts, and to make one side and the other, the upper and lower part of the Building suitable and concurrent; but as well as in Architecture, he shew'd great judgment both in Musick and Physick, and indeed there was a kind of necessity for it [...].[31]

Philo had materialized the civic harmony in his buildings, so much that Guillet de Saint-George stated that "to his care for improving the harmony to the people, he added his care for their healths."[32]

For the subject of citizenship, we can conclude that according to these seventeenth-century authors, a citizen was defined as being able to shape the laws of the political community he lived in and who could opt for them. For his consent he did not necessarily have to be virtuous. It was the law that created the right behaviour towards the state, mutual commerce and internal harmony. Civil law and self-determination had the effect of producing artistically and philosophically successful citizens who in turn contributed to the advancement and the well-being of the commonwealth. However, it was also the law of the state that created the conditions for freedom, harmony and cultural production. Harmony meant harmony for the whole of the community, avoiding dissensions and factions amongst the people.

---

29   Nedham, *The Excellencie of a Free-State*, 110.
30   Guillet de Saint-George, *An account of a Late Voyage to Athens*, 307-309.
31   Ibid., 308.
32   Ibid., 309.

These observations lead us to our last questions: Why had this time of glory according to these authors not lasted? Why had it ended in ruin? Which causes did these writers allege to Athens' downfall?

3. *Civic Integration versus Civic Inclusion*

After having illustrated the state-transformations outlined by Polybius, Francis Rous employed this pattern on Athens.[33] He considered the downfall of Athens a result of Pericles' *Ochlocratie*, the rule of the masses:

> But the vulgar for the most part strangely insolent, prone to wrong, & ready to trespasse against the Lawes, bring in by a miserable proceeding, the worst kind of government an Ochlocratie, the rule of Rascality. All these in their times did Athens feele [...].[34]

The problem of an *Ochlocratie* had been that single citizens gained too much power within the *polis* and created parties, hence had been destroying the civic harmony and causing civic dissensions.

According to Nedham, this state of greatness had not lasted because the *polis* of Athens had degenerated from its "pure principles," for "they were drawn into Parties by powerful Persons, and so made the Instruments of Division among themselves."[35]

---

33 "But the grave Historian hath observed changes in such government [a Democracy—author's annotation], as they use to be, inclining to the worst Monarchies being turned into Tyrannies; as when the people are led away by the perswations of some pleasing popular man, and are as it were willingly constrained to take the yoke that his usurping authority shall lay on them [...]. But all are accounted and called Tyrants, who have perpetuall authority in that City, which formerly had enjoyed liberty. The deprivation of which causing murmuring & rebellion, brings forth an Aristocratic, or government of the best men, such as are well brought up, and exercised in vertue. The end of an Aristocratic being, as Aristotle hath it, Vertue which of no long continuance doth soon degenerate [...] naturally inclining to an Ologarchie, or rule of few. These few being chosen according to their riches And because that many of a state cannot be wealthie, therefore the number of them cannot be great. [...] Such dominion is taken away by the people set on a rage, and not bearing [...] the injuries of their rulers. Hence comes in a Democratie [...] the power of a multitude; whose end is freedome; when all can equally partake of the same priviledges & immunities, who are true citizens: whence Terence stiles it aequam libertatem: for which the Greek Oratours have properly used the word πολετεία, as Ulpian observeth." Rous, *Archaeologiae Atticae Libri Septem*, 28-29.

34 Ibid., 29.

35 Nedham, *The Excellencie of a Free-State*, 90.

For Guillet de Saint-George, the end of Athens' glory had been brought about by Lysander, when he had established the rule of the thirty tyrants. Guillet de Saint-George assumed that this had been the incident when servitude returned and decline began.[36] This decline had been followed by a decrease of "Eminent Men" such as philosophers, who had attracted for their part other excellent men: "After this Desolation, it had continued a most deplorable solitude, had not the same of its Philosophers invited thither most of the Learned Men in the World [...]."[37]

Like Rous, Swift considered the rule of the masses and the dissension of the Athenian people as the real cause of Athens' downfall. According to his analysis, first of all the body representative had become a body of tyrants, then the people detesting this rule of the few, had constituted a tyranny of the masses, impeaching all great men.[38]

> To speak of every particular Person impeach'd by the Commons of Athens, within the compass designed, would introduce the History of almost every great Man they had among them.[39]

And further:

> Thus was the most powerful Commonwealth of all Greece, after great Degeneracies from the Institution of Solon, utterly destroyed by the rash, jealous, and inconstant humour of the People, which was never satisfied to see a General either Victorious or Unfortunate; such ill Judges, as well as Rewarders, are Popular Assemblies, of those who best deserve from them.[40]

"Eminent Men" had been thus hindered to participate in politics, and harmony had been destroyed by the creation of parties that had further

---

36   Guillet de Saint-George, *An account of a Late Voyage to Athens*, 131.
37   Ibid., 133.
38   Swift, *A Discourse of the Contest and Dissensions*, 22-23.
39   Ibid., 17.
40   Ibid., 21.

disunited the people.[41] These dissensions had led to an external dominion of the Athenians, which ended the "production" of "famous" men:

> For from the time of Alexander's Captains, till Greece
> was subdued by the Romans (to the latter part of which
> this Description of Polybius falls in) Athens never pro-
> duced one Famous Man either for Councils or Arms, or
> hardly for Learning.[42]

According to these seventeenth-century authors, the "sin" of a
citizen was to interfere with the harmony of the whole by allowing too
much power to fall in the hands of the few, or of single citizens, creating
disuniting parties, which disturbed the community's balance. According
to their interpretation, the people of Athens had not protected their
liberty as they should have, which had led to the *polis*' ruin.

In short, the political language of these writers incorporated the
idea that a citizen was always conceived of as an individual and not as a
member of a specific political group. Consequently, citizens should act
as singles and not by affiliating or acting as a group. If citizens acted
in corporations and groups in the whole, they risked destroying civic
harmony by pursuing particular interests and thereby disturbing the
balance and the power of the whole body politic. Consequently, civic
integration meant integration of the individual citizen and not of corporative groups.

4. Conclusion and Further Considerations

What does the seventeenth-century reception of the ancient Greek *polis*
tell us about citizenship? How can we summarize the assumptions of
that time concerning citizenship?

1. The early-modern authors assumed a connection between the
liberty of a political community (liberty defined as self-government
and as liberty from external domination), civil government and florescence of a state. Civil government creates civil law that promotes

---

41   Ibid., 43.
42   Swift, *A Discourse of the Contest and Dissensions*, 23.

good behaviour of the citizens and therefore provides space for eminent citizens who contribute to the advancement of the state.

2. A citizen is consequently conceived of as a participant who gives consent to the civil laws (not as a plebiscitary engaged citizen, but rather as an enfranchised and represented citizen).

3. This consent of single citizens appears as a kind of stronghold against particular interests and tyranny, which are defined as the disruption of civic harmony and *equilibrium*.

4. The citizen is understood as an individual and not as a member of a corporative group. Only single citizens can contribute to the well-being of the whole.

5. Accordingly, the "sin" of a citizen consists of fragmenting the whole.

Considering this political language, it seems that the reception of the ancient *polis* in seventeenth-century political discourse was about integration, and not (liberal) inclusion or exclusion—a discourse of integration in the sense that it was about the incorporation of the single citizen into a whole, as the origin of the word shown in "integration." Integration stems from the Latin word *integer* and means originally unspoilt, unaffected, intact and complete. In this sense, integration denotes the creation of an entity. In contrast, inclusion stems from the Latin word *inclusio*, which means embedding, involvement or membership. Considering that the creation of an entity is an active concern, the term integration leaves more space for an active designing of the political community by its citizens.

In the context of political and religious dissensions in sixteenth and seventeenth century England and France, this discourse may have generated new prospects and opportunities for the creation of a body politic with the participation of individual citizens, that neglected antagonizing and dissenting civic groups. Considering this perspective that brings together both a focus on the whole body politic and on individual citizens, I am curious if this could be a perspective for current civic dialogue in light of today's problems of integrating minority groups. After the analysis of the reception of the ancient *polis* in seventeenth-century political discourse, I think we should rather focus on the integration of individual citizens. I wonder whether a liberal discourse of inclusion, however necessary, is not perhaps insufficient to solve current challenges; also, whether we need a new perspective on individual citizens in Europe in order to integrate our numerous immigrants. Could it be a perspective to promote a certain pride in the success and the performance of these immigrant-citizens, rather than looking at them simply as (minority-) group members?

Were the Republics Able to Handle the Challenge? Commerce as a Driving Force Behind Changing Role Models in Eighteenth-Century Political Discourse

Urte Weeber

When in 1705 the English poet and statesman Joseph Addison (1672-1719) published *Some Remarks on Several Parts of Italy,* based on his journey through that part of Europe in the years 1701, 1702 and 1703, he came to the following judgement on the commerce of the republic of Venice:

> Their Manufactures of Cloth, Glas and Silk, formerly the best in Europe, are now excelled by those of other Countries. They are tenacious of old laws and customs to their great prejudice, whereas a trading Nation must be still for new Changes and Expedients, as different Juncturs and Emergencies arise.[1]

Addison names different reasons for the fact that the Venetian commerce was "far from being in a flourishing condition." He states:

> The Duties are great that are laid on the Merchandise. Their Nobles think it below their Quality to engage in Traffick. The Merchants that are grown rich, and able to manage great Dealings, buy their Nobility, and generally give over Trade.[2]

These remarks, referring to the commercial decline and lacking flexibility of the Venetian commonwealth, as well as a missing engagement of its citizens, are first of all an expression of personal judgement. That

---

1   Joseph Addison, *Some Remarks on several parts of Italy &c. in the years 1701, 1702 and 1703* (London: Printed for Jacob Tonson, 1705), 83-84.
2   Ibid.

Addison focuses on economical issues is not surprising when looking at his subsequent career, during which he held, amongst others, the office of royal commissioner of trade.[3] These remarks are also typical for the early eighteenth century, where the interdependence of politics and economy emerged as a central topic. Concerns about the compatibility of good government and profitable trade bred new discussions and ideas about how to organize and form a (modern) state. Political theorists, but also statesmen, diplomats, and travellers all over Europe searched for adequate models of this "modern state." It stood to reason that they also paid attention to the existing republics of their time—especially to Venice and the United Provinces—which were identified with liberty and, most notably, commercial success in the previous century. Whereas the Venetian commonwealth was mainly associated with beauty, religiousness, a just and stable constitution as well as rich and free citizens,[4] the United Provinces were praised for their high level of technological achievement, their welfare system, the commercial acumen, inventiveness, and diligence of their citizens, and their politics of religious coexistence.[5]

Addison's remarks let us assume that these commonwealths were no longer the undisputable shining examples of their time. Around 1700, the discourse on these republics obviously underwent profound changes and discontinuities. New statements had become possible and led to a more differentiated or at least manifold perspective on the republics. And aligned to this, the language of this discourse changed. It was less the paradigm of Civic Humanism than arguments of state interest

---

3   For the life of Joseph Addison see Peter Smithers, *The Life of Joseph Addison* (Oxford: Clarendon Press, 1954).

4   As for the myth of Venice, see Achim Landwehr, *Die Erschaffung Venedigs: Raum, Bevölkerung, Mythos 1570-1750* (Paderbon et al.: Schöningh, 2007), 327-408; David Rosand, *Myths of Venice: The figuration of a state* (Chapel Hill and London: University of North Carolina Press, 2001); Myron Gilmore, "Myth and reality in political theory," in *Renaissance Venice*, ed. John Hale (London: Faber & Faber, 1973), 431-444; Frederik C. Lane, *Seerepublik Venedig* (München: Prestel, 1980).

5   For the picture of the United Provinces in foreign reception see Julia Bientjes, *Holland und die Holländer im Urteil deutscher Reisender 1400-1800* (Groningen: Wolters, 1967); C.D. van Strien, *British travellers in Holland during the Stuart period. Edward Browne and John Locke as tourists in the United Provinces* (Leiden: Brill, 1993); Karel Davids and Jan Lucassen, eds., *A Mircale Mirrored: The Dutch Republic in European Perspective* (Cambridge: Cambridge University Press, 1995); Anja Charles de Beaulieu, *Deutsche Reisende in den Niederlanden: Das Bild eines Nachbarn zwischen 1648 und 1795* (Frankfurt a.M. et al.: Lang, 2000); for Venice see Brigitta Cladders, *Französische Venedig-Reisen im 16. und 17. Jahrhundert: Wandlungen des Venedig-Bildes und der Reisebeschreibung* (Genf: Droz, 2002).

and commercial success that hence had a normative impact on this discourse.[6]

This is the initial point of this article: I will present some examples of the discussion that took place in Europe on the contemporary republics in the first half of the eighteenth century. Furthermore, I will argue that this discussion, initiated by commercial arguments, was consequently part of a greater reform discourse on modern states, and as such can be interpreted as part of a beginning liberal discourse. At least, it must be understood as a place where a new language took its bearings.[7]

In *Utopia and Reform in the Enlightenment,* Franco Venturi presented the research on the "republican tradition" in the eighteenth century as a central key for an understanding of state-building and the history of ideas in the enlightenment.[8] He advocated the idea to look at the experiential background of the sources—the contemporary republics of the eighteenth century—rather than focussing on references to the republics of antiquity within these sources.[9] Being challenged as small states by emerging and powerful monarchies, the eighteenth century republics generated discussions on different strategies of survival. In the course of this exchange of arguments, new ideas of statehood, liberty and citi-

---

6   John Pocock accentuated the myth of Venice as paradigmatic example for the language of Civic Humanism. John Pocock, *The Machiavellian Moment: Florentine political thought and the Atlantic republican Tradition* (Princeton et al.: Princeton University Press, 1975), 271. It is therefore consequently presumable that, with the deconstruction of the myth of Venice, a different language emerged which we also have to name differently.

7   This does not mean that elements of the former language could not have been subsisted. More recently there have been some scholarly attempts to point out this integration of the language of virtue into the language of rights. One example of the argumentation that liberalism can not be thought of without the traditional elements of classical republicanism is in Andreas Kalyvas and Ira Katznelson, *Liberal Beginnings: Making a Republic for the Moderns* (Cambridge: Cambridge University Press, 2008).

8   Franco Venturi, *Utopia and Reform in the Enlightenment* (Cambridge: Cambridge University Press, 1971), 17.

9   Ibid., 18: "The republican tradition which the eighteenth century inherited and made fruitful sometimes had a classical colouring. More often it was born from a direct experience, and one not so distant in time!" Some research followed Venturi's appell recently. See for example Manuela Albertone, ed., *Il Repubblicanesimo Moderno. L´idea di repubblica nella riflessione storica di Franco Venturi* Istituto Italiano Per Gli Studi Filosofici XXXI (Napolis: Bibliopolis, 2006); The Review essay of Koen Stapelbroek in this volume: "The problem of the republics: Venturi's republicanism reconsidered," *History of European Ideas* 35 (2009): 281-288; David Wootton, ed., *Republicanism, Liberty, and Commercial Society 1649-1776* (Stanford: Stanford University Press, 1994); or articles like Wijnand W. Mijnhardt, "The limits of present-day historiography of Republicanism," *De Achttiende Eeuw* 37 (2005): 75-89. Concerning Mijnhardt's article see also Wyger Velema's critical answer in Wyger Velema, "Wijnand Mijnhardt on the Historiography of Republicanism: A Reply," *De Achttiende Eeuw* 37 (2005): 193-202.

zenship evolved. This article focuses on this European discussion, which intensified in the last third of the seventeenth century, not only within the republics themselves, but even more within the large scale monarchies that clashed increasingly in areas of commerce.[10] Characterized by a feeling of a feasible future and led by pragmatic interests, these monarchies looked at the republics to filter possibly positive and transferable aspects as well as negative ones, which they could avoid in their own process of state-building. In doing this, monarchic authors focused mainly on the—in their understanding—most influential republics of their time: Venice, the United Provinces, and the Swiss Republic. Keeping the hypothesis in mind that we can find parallel statements on all three republics, in discussions throughout Europe, concerning how commerce as a decisive argument overcame national borders—if we can speak of such borders at all—the following analysis is grounded on a rather heterogeneous corpus of sources. It covers different genres, mainly political treatises and travelogues, from different confessional and territorial backgrounds—mainly England, France, Germany, the Swiss Confederation, and the United Provinces.[11]

1. The Deconstruction of Venice

Joseph Addison was not the first, and not the only, theorist who criticized Venice, the erstwhile glorious Serenissima. Since the 1670s, the myth was deconstructed by identifying single defects of the constitution and—to a lesser extent—its citizens.[12] In doing so, Venice critics continued using a distinctly republican verbage. Amelot de la Houssaie (1643-1706) for example, in 1669 secretary of the French ambassador in Venice, whose *Histoire du gouvernement de Venise* of 1676[13] became formative for the whole evolving discourse, was at the same time

---

10 Richard Whatmore has recently pointed to this small-states debate within the European Context as well, see Richard Whatmore, " 'Neither Masters nor Slaves': Small States and Empire in the Long Eighteenth Century," *Proceedings of the British Academy* 155 (2009): 53-81.

11 A far more detailed and differentiated analysis can be found in the PhD thesis of the author (not yet published).

12 Concerning the deconstruction of the myth of Venice, see David Wootton, "Ulysses Bound? Venice and the Idea of Liberty from Howell to Hume," in *Republicanism, Liberty, and Commercial Society 1649-1776*, ed. David Wootton (Stanford: Standford University Press 1994), 341-367; Landwehr, *Erschaffung Venedigs*, 408-480.

13 Amelot de la Houssaie, *Histoire du Gouvernement de Venise* (Paris: chez Frederic Leonard, 1676).

a translator of Tacitus and Machiavelli.[14] The defects he accuses, as he calls them "maladies of the state,"[15] fit for the most part in a republican tradition of thought. But besides missing or wrong virtues of the citizens, corruption and inexperience of the office holder and wrong military approaches,[16] there are new elements he discusses, new "maladies," which he judges as "incurable."[17] Suggesting the possibility of a needed reform, a more careful English translation of Amelot's Text of 1677 states the existence of "maladies of the state" which "cannot be conveniently remedied."[18] For Amelot, it is above all the lack of legal certainty, provoked by the institution of the Council of Ten,[19] that is leading Venice to—as he calls it—"decline."[20] Consequently, he comes to the following conclusion, unmasking the topos of Venice as the model for true liberty as a farce:

> They believe the Government of Venice a Model for all the World, and no Nation under Heaven so happy as themselves, though perhaps they are (as Tacitus saith) Magis sine Domino, quam in libertate; Rather without a Master than at Liberty.[21]

These statements did not go unnoticed: first of all, in Venice itself. The Venetian government officially disposed their French colleagues to arrest Amelot de la Houssaie for a certain time. This query however, was not successful. The book was not banned and reception took its course—be it in

---

14 Niccolò Machiavelli, *Le Prince*, transl. A. N. Amelot (Amsterdam: 1684); *Tacite, avec des notes politiques et historiques*, trans. Amelot de la Houssaie, 2 vols. (La Haye: 1692); See also David Wootton, "The true origins of republicanism: the disciples of Baron and the counter-example of Venturi," in Albertone, ed., *Il repubblicanismo moderno*, 271-304, 299; Jacob Soll, "Amelot de la Houssaye (1634-1706) Annotates Tacitus'," *Journal of the History of Ideas* 61 (2000): 167-187; Jacob Soll, *Publishing the Prince: History, Reading, and the Birth of Political Criticism* (Ann Arbor: University of Michigan Press, 2005), 59-71.

15 Houssaie, *Histoire*, 90-100.

16 Ibid., 9-22, 331.

17 Ibid., 90-100.

18 Amelot de la Houssaie, *History of the government of Venice* (London: printed by H. C. for John Starkey, 1677), 72.

19 Houssaie, *Histoire*, 193-204; 350f.

20 Ibid., Dedication (o.P.).

21 Houssaie, *History*, 270. (Houssaie, *Histoire*, 335: "Ils croient que le Gouvernement de Venise doit servir de règle & de modèle à tous les autres, & qu'il n'y a qu'eux de Gens-libres dans le monde, bien que véritablement ils soient sans Maître plûtost qu'en liberté. (magis sine domino quam in libertate. Tac. Ann.2.)").

France, in England, in the Holy Roman Empire, or the United Provinces.[22]

Additionally, it was less the lack of virtue of the Venetian citizens that was being discussed as an eroding force of a declining commonwealth, but rather, again, legal arbitrariness and commercial decrease, which were in the very center of the discussion. The assessment of these defects, though, turned out differently. Alexandre de Saint-Didier (1630-1689), successor of Amelot in the French embassy in Venice, also came to the conclusion that the argument of greater liberty in this republic was simply a "chimera."[23] The Huguenot refugee Casimir Freschot deals in his treatise on Venice with nearly every single argument of Amelot, mostly neglecting or at least relativising these arguments in defence of the Venetian citizens.[24] Even though he also states a Venetian decrease in the field of commerce,[25] he strictly rejects Amelot's statement of decline of the republic.[26] He finally justifies his position by insisting that

---

22 In three years there were twenty-two editions of his work and numerous translations (see Zera S. Fink, *The Classical Republicans: An Essay in the recovery of a pattern of thought in seventeenth-century England* (Evanston: Northwestern University Press, 1945), 143. Different authors dealt with it in affirmative and arguing ways. See for example: Casimir Freschot, *Nouvelle Relation de la Ville & Republique de Venise* (Utrecht: chez Guillaume van Poolsum, 1709); Heinrich Gude, *Einleitung zu den Europäischen Staaten und derselben Beschluß* (Franckfurt und Leipzig, 1708), vol. 1, 35; Paul Sarpi, *The Maxims of the Government of Venice in an Advice to the Republick. Done into English from the Italian* (London: Printed by J. Morphew, 1707), xiv. Concerning Amelot de la Houssaie and his ideas see Wootton, *Ulysses Bound?*, 340-367; Terence Allot, "'Undermining Absolutism': The Disguised Critique of Amelot de la Houssaye (1634-1706)," *The Seventeenth Century* 7 (1992): 71-81; Koen Stapelbroek and Antonio Trampus, "Commercial reform against the tide: Reapproaching the eighteenth-century decline of the republics of Venice and the United Provinces," *History of European Ideas* 36 (2010): 192-202, 195.

23 Alexandre Toussaint Limojon de Saint Didier, *La Ville et la Republique de Venise. Troisiéme Edition revenüe & corrigée par l'Autheur* (Amsterdam: chez Daniel Elsevier, 1680), Au Lecteur (o.P.), 326: "lorsque l'autorité du Gouvernement n'y est, à parler proprement, un libertinage politique, avantageux à la Republique, commode à la Noblesse, & agréable au Peuple, qui ne s'apperçoit pas que la liberté qu'il pretend avoir au dessus des Peuples qui vivent dans un estat Monarchique, n'est qu'une pure chimere."

24 Casimir Freschot, *Nouvelle Relation de la Ville & Republique de Venise, divisée en trois parties dont la premiere contient son Histoire Generale, la seconde traite du Gouvernement & des moeurs de la Nation, et la troisieme donne connoissance de toutes les familles patrices, employées dans le Gouvernement* (Utrecht: chez Guillaume van Poolsum, 1709).

25 Ibid., 393-394: "On ne dira rien ici du commerce de la Ville de Venise, qui lui a autrefois fait donner le surnom de Riche. Il est aujourd'hui tout a fait diminué, & il ne consiste guerre que dans quelques marchandises qu'elle donne & reçoit des Allemans & des Turcs. On a touché ailleurs la premiere & principale cause de sa décadence, qui a été le passage des Portugais & des Hollandois dans les Indes par delà le Cap de Bonne Esperance, & qui a fait prendre la même route aux marchandises & aux richesses de ce pays là, qui venoient autrefois toutes au Golfe Persique, ou dans la Mer rouge, d'où elles passoient par terre à Ale de Syrie & à Alexandrie d'Egypte, où les Venetiens les alloient prendre, & les distribuoient en suite par toute l'Europe."

26 Ibid., 299: "Encore une fois la durée de la Répub. pendant tant de siècles prouve au contraire

most of the defects should and could be criticized in a monarchy, but
that they are sometimes necessary in the reality of a republic:

> [...] the maxims of leading in a republic are different to
> those of ruling a state subordinated to an absolute sov-
> ereign. The republics are young women, as once said a
> noble Venetian of common sense to me, and the monar-
> chies are young men. Though as for guarding the honour
> of a girl you have to use means of care a lot more exact
> than for guarding a young man. In the same manner for
> keeping the honour and the liberty of a republic you have
> to use different and much more severe maxims than for
> keeping the authority of a prince to whom the subjects
> obey whatever command he gives to them, they have it
> already arranged: This shows, most of the injustices that
> Amelot reproaches with regard to the Venetians are ow-
> ing to means necessary for the welfare of the state, and
> the others, owing to precautions against corruption and
> disorder, which would infallibly lead to ruin.[27]

Hence, not all authors agree on the degree of fatal developments on
Venice, but they all started at least to argue in a critical manner.

2. The Critical Discourse

At the beginning of the eighteenth century, these authors competed for
the best form of state and the criteria to find and define this form. In

---

que les desordres y sont rares, & qu'on sçait y remedier par des voyes qui contribuent plus à son
affermissement qu'à sa ruine à laquelle une conduite telle que la décrit Monsieur Amelot, l'auroit
depuis long-temps precipitée."

27   Ibid., 268-269: "...c'est que les maximes de conduite dans une Répub. sont autres que celles du
Gouvernement d'un Etat soumis à un Souverain absolu. Les Républiques sont filles, me disoit
autrefois un Noble de sort bon sens dans Venise, & les Royaumes sons mâles. Or comme pour
garder l'honneur d'une fille il faut employer des soins beaucoup plus exacts, que pour garder un
jeune homme, de même pour maintenier l'honneur & la liberté d'une Rép. il faut d'autres & de plus
séveres maximes que pour maintenir l'autorité du Prince, à qui les sujets doivent obeïr, quelques
commandement qu'il leur fasse, les y ayant déja disposés: Cela étant, la plus part des injustices que
M. Amelot reproche aux Venetiens, devienent des soins nécessaires au salut de l'Etat, & les autres,
des précautions contre la corruption & la desordre, qui en entraineroit infailliblement la ruine."
(Translation in the text UW) See also ibid., 296.

which fields does a republic need to modify itself to cope with a new reality? Is the constitutional form of a republic maintainable at all? Political theorists, diplomats and travellers did not only discuss these questions in view of Venice. The discussion on the other two famous republics of the time, the United Provinces and the Swiss Confederation, developed under the same premises. Embodying as federative entities an alternative way of state formation, these two republics became increasingly spotlighted.

Statements on the alleged moral decay of the citizens can be found frequently in this discourse. The observers criticize an increasing addiction to luxury entailing corruption and political anergia. This complaint about the moral decline is a typical, and maybe the most dominant, element of Early Modern narratives of decline[28]—especially of republican, cyclical narratives of rise and fall, as it is well-known. But as the debate on luxury changed over the course of the eighteenth century, discussing more the amenities of "unregulated" or "well-ordered" luxury than condemning luxury per se as the virtue corrupting force,[29] the discourse presented in this article also does not remain within this type of argumentation. In an increasing manner—a new development that emerged around 1700—the decline of the existing republics was explained by their commercial decay. This commercial decay was ascribed to high duties and taxes, and especially to the encroachment upon individual liberties and rights regarding trade and property.

This was indeed the tenor of the critics of Venice, as we have seen in the beginning. It was also the tenor of Abraham Stanyan (1669-1732)—English legate in the Swiss Confederation from 1705-1713—in his *Account of Switzerland* of 1714. He states:

> As to the Citizens of the Aristocratical Cantons [...] they may be divided into Three Classes, the Trades-men and Merchants, the Pen-men, and the Military Men. The first are generally esteemed to be proud and lazy; which

---

28 On early modern ideas of decline see especially Peter Burke, "Tradition and Experience: The Idea of Decline from Bruni to Gibbon," *Daedalus* 105/3 (1976): 137-152; John G.A. Pocock, *Barbarism and Religion.* vol. 3: *The First Decline and Fall* (Cambridge: Cambridge University Press, 2003).

29 See Istvan Hont, "The early Enlightenment debate on commerce and luxury," in *The Cambridge History of Eighteenth-Century Political Thought*, ed. Mark Goldie and Robert Wokler (Cambridge: Cambridge University Press, 2006), 379-442.

Qualities chiefly proceed from two Privileges they enjoy. One is, their Right of being chosen into the Government by Virtue of their Burgership, which makes them proud; and the other is, that of hindering any but a Citizen, from exercising any Trade within the Cities, which makes them lazy. From whence two Inconveniencies naturally flow: One that Inhabitants pay very dear for their Goods; and the other, that the Workmen are bad; for where there is no great Choice of Artificers, one must be contented not only with bad Work, but to pay such a Price for it, as they please to impose.[30]

With a view to the United Provinces, we also find some complaints about too strictly regulated market conditions. In the wake of William Temple's (1628-1699) influential analysis of the United Provinces of 1673 and his tending pessimistic forecast for the Dutch commerce, the economic potential of the small republic was more and more discussed.[31] In the second half of the eighteenth century, the phrase of Dutch commercial decline became even more topical. For the Scottish Enlightenment, it virtually functioned as a test-case, considering the correlation of new market conditions and the decline of states.[32] In the Holy Roman Empire as well, authors started to criticize the Dutch economic policy. Anton Friedrich Büsching (1724-1793) for instance in his *Neue Erdbeschreibungen* from 1760 complained about the "far too high taxes" that had led the Dutch to commercial decline.[33] Nevertheless, in

---

30 Abraham Stanyan, *An Account of Switzerland* (London: Printed for Jacob Tonson, 1714), 140-141.
31 William Temple, *Observations Upon the United Provinces of the Netherlands*, ed. George Clark (Oxford: Clarendon Press, 1972). See especially Chap. VI "Of their Trade," which concludes with the sentences: "So as it seems to be with Trade, as with the Sea (its Element), that has a certain pitch, above which it never rises in the highest Tides; And begins to ebb as soon as it ever ceases to flow; and ever loses ground in one place, proportionable to what it gains in another." Ibid., 126.; For Temple and his ideas of the United Provinces within a changing structure of international trade see Istvan Hont, *Jealousy of Trade. International Competition and the Nation-State in Historical Perspective* (Cambridge, MA and London: Harvard University Press, 2005), 194-201. Concerning a discussion on "Dutch Decline" in general see the recently published issue of History of European Ideas with the title "Dutch Decline in Eighteenth Century Europe" (36/2, 2010).
32 Iain McDaniel, "Enlightened history and the decline of nations: Ferguson, Raynal, and the contested legacies of the Dutch Republic," *History of European Ideas* 36 (2010), 203-216.
33 Anton Friedrich Büsching, *Neue Erdbeschreibung. Vierter Theil, welcher die vereinigten Niederlande, die Eidgenossenschaft samt denen derselben zugewandten Orten, Schlesien und Glatz enthält* (Hamburg: bey Johann Carl Bohn, 1760), 19.

contrast to treatises on the other two republics, we mainly find positive judgements on the Dutch commerce in the first half of the eighteenth century. Authors strongly endorse a great exemption from duties and taxes as an essential basis for a still-flourishing economy. And above all they praise toleration with regard to religious refugees as a possible column of survival. In the treatise *A Description of Holland* from 1743, the anonymous author states as an example:

> Holland is as industrious to receive Strangers from all Parts, as other Countries are to get rid of them. It is Maxim with the Dutch, that no Nation can be too populous, provided it be industrious. They admit all Strangers that come to settle amongst them, and immediately grant them all the Privileges of the Natives. [...] And this conduces exceedingly to the Wealth, Trade and Strength of the State. No country perhaps stands more in need of fresh Supplies of People than this.[34]

Another factor emerged in conjunction with the argument of commerce, as we can see here: the right of citizenship. Being the precondition of political participation, but most notably in this context of participation in trade, market and guild-organized handicraft, it is—according to the authors—assigned too exclusively and too restrictively. Especially with regard to the Swiss Confederation, this point was often made. The Huguenot refugee de Blainville, for example, who accompanied two young English noblemen on their travels through Europe, in his travelogue from the years 1705 and 1707, criticised the practice of citizenship assignment in Basel and Zurich. He calls it a "bad maxim of state, that they accord their right of citizenship only one person in hundred years. And beyond that this person has to be born or at least originally come from the respective canton."[35]

---

34   *A Description of Holland. Or, the Present State of the United Provinces* (London: Printed for J. and P. Knapton, 1743), 96; see also Jacques Basnage de Beauval, *Annales des Provinces-Unies*, Tome 1 (la Haye: chez Charles le Vier, 1726), 121.

35   *Des Herrn von Blainville ehemaligen Gesantschaftssekretärs der Generalstaaten der vereinigten Niederlande an dem Spanischen Hofe Reisebeschreibung durch Holland, Deutschland und die Schweiz besonders aber durch Italien aus des Verfasssers eigener Handschrift in englischer Sprache zum erstenmal zum Druck befördert von Georg Turnbull der Rechten Doktor und Wilhelm Guthrie Ritter nunmehr in das Deutsche übersetzt, erläutert und hin und wieder mit Amerkungen versehen von Johann Tobias*

An enhancement of the group of citizens resulting in additional rights being granted in regard to commercial activities is one of the main postulations we can detect in this discussion on the existing republics of the eighteenth century.

Associated with this core aspect was a demand for freedom of speech and, above all, a higher degree of legal certainty. The latter finds its expression in many critical judgements on the Council of Ten in Venice. This institution leads to the fact, as Amelot puts it, that in legal affairs, "shadow is to be taken for substance and possibility for matter of fact."[36]Abraham Stanyan states similarly for the Swiss Confederation: "I wish I could as easily justifie them of another Crime laid to their Charge, which is the Corrupt Administration of Justice. But that Vice is too palpable to be denied."[37]

In these statements, we still find the citizens in a way reproached for their corrupt behaviour. But in the first instance these sources admonish the arrangement of the political system of the republics. Unsurprisingly, another main point of critique is the alleged lack of flexibility to be found in these commonwealths. Especially with a view to the federal republics of the Dutch and the Swiss, authors complain about the slowness and complexity of decision making processes. Stanyan indicates this problem, discussing the "Helvetick Union" as an "artificial body" that is "far from making but one sovereignty."[38] The Huguenot refugee Jacques Basnage (1653-1725), in his 1726 published *Annales des Provinces Unies*, recommends that the Dutch form such a sole sovereignty in order to become more effective:

> It seems to me that the government would be much more closed and more handy, if the seven provinces provide not more than one sole and same sovereignty. The decision-making processes would be quicker, if they derive from one same court which is always assembled; and the execution would be more forceful, if it depends on one same head.[39]

Köhler, Bd.1, 1. und 2. Abtheilung (Lemgo: gedruckt von Georg Turnbull, 1746), 363.

36 Houssaie, *History*, 156.
37 Stanyan, *Account of Switzerland*, 151.
38 Ibid., 120.
39 "Il semble que le Gouvernement seroit beaucoup plus ferme & plus commode, si les sept Provinces-

Likewise, the anonymous published treatise *A Description of Holland: Or the Present State of the United Provinces* from 1743 elucidates this "enormous defect" in differentiation with the English model of a limited monarchy:

> Thus this Assembly [The States General], which is called Sovereign, only represents the Sovereignty, and essentially differs from the Parliament of Great Britain, of which the Members are in a manner Principals, and may act independently of the Counties that deputed them [...] This is an enormous Defect in this Constitution [...] For at present the Corruption of any small Town may put the publick Affairs into great, and even fatal Disorder.[40]

The English Constitution increasingly emerged as the new point of reference, as the new positive model in the beginning eighteenth century—as it is well-known not least from the writings of Montesquieu.[41] While the discourse in England itself was primarily affected by party considerations within the politics of the day, the continental discourse on the English Constitution developed under more general constitutional premises. Around 1700 it was—as was the discourse on the republics—highly influenced by writings of Huguenot refugees, like Jacques Abbadies *Defense de la Nation Britannique* (1692), or Paul Rapin de Thoyras' *Dissertation sur l'Origine du Gouvernement d'Angleterre* (1717).[42] In the first instance they generated a confessional dualism, dis-

---

Unies ne faisoient qu'une seule & même Souveraineté. Les Délibérations seroient plus promptes, si elles émanoient d'un même Corps toûjours assemblé; & l'éxécution plus vigoreuse, si elle dépendoit d'une même tête." Basnage de Beauval, *Annales*, 13.

40 *A Description of Holland: or the Present State of the United Provinces* (London: printed for J. and P. Knapton, 1743), 68-73.

41 See among others Simone Zurbuchen, "Republik oder Monarchie? Montesquieus Theorie der gewaltenteiligen Verfassung Englands," in *Die Natur des Staates: Montesquieu zwischen Macht und Recht*, ed. Karlfriedrich Herb and Oliver Hidalgo (Baden-Baden: Nomos, 2009), 79-98; Hans Christof Kraus, *Englische Verfassung und politisches Denken im Ancien Régime: 1689-1789*, Veröffentlichungen des deutschen Historischen Instituts London 60 (München: Oldenbourg, 2006), 169-178.

42 Jacques Abbadie, *Defense de la Nation Britannique, ou Les droits de Dieu, de la Nature, & de la Societé clairement établis au sujet de la révolution d'Angleterre, contre l'Auteur de l'Avis important aux Refugiés* (London: chés la Vesve Mallet, 1692); Paul Rapin de Thoyras, *Dissertation sur l'Origine du Gouvernement d'Angleterre, et Sur la Naissance, les Progrès, les Vûës, les Forces, les Intérêts, & les Caractères des deux Partis des Whigs & des Torys* (La Haye: 1717); again printed in Paul Rapin de

tinguishing the protestant-liberal constitution of England and the catholic-despotic one of France. But the confessional argument was fading quickly. The Constitution that emerged from the Glorious Revolution became a symbol for an institutional arrangement that could guarantee stability and effectiveness as well as the liberty of its citizens by balancing the political actors and promoting the rule of law.[43]

Hence it is not surprising that in many of the examined treatises and travelogues dealing with the republics of Venice, the United Provinces and Switzerland, this ideal of the English Constitution as a "Just Mixture of Prerogative and Liberty," as Onslow Burrish puts it in his 1728 published treatise *Batavia Illustrata*,[44] embodied the norm of reference, as well.[45]

Aside from this new ideal, and following Rousseau, another model was developed in the second half of the eighteenth century: the idea of a small, self-sustaining and democratically organized republic, embodied for some in small agricultural cantons of the Swiss Confederation. The German writer Johann Michael Afsprung (1748-1808), for instance, praises the canton Appenzell as a place where citizens were "totally free" primarily due to freedom of trade, freedom from guild organization and the democratic political structure.[46] With regard to an increasing competition of expanding territorial states, this ideal had a more or less utopian character.

3. How to Make the Republic Competitive?
The Inner-Republican Discourse

Nevertheless, not all contemporaries wanted to refuse the republic as such and abandon the existing ones. The citizens of these republics themselves, who also took notice of the discussion on their commonwealths,

---

Thoyras, *Histoire d´Angleterre. Seconde édition*, Vol. XI (Den Haag, 1749), 47-107.

43 See Kraus, *Englische Verfassung*.

44 Onslow Burrish, *Batavia Illustrata: or, a View of the Policy, and Commerce of the United Provinces, in three parts* (London: Printed for William Innys, 1728), ii.

45 In the anonymously published treatise "*A Description of Holland: or, the Present State of the United Provinces*" from 1743 for example, we even find a schedular comparison of the British king and the Dutch stadholder (84-92).

46 Johann Michael Afsprung, *Reise durch einige Cantone der Eidgenossenschaft* (Leipzig: Weidman und Reich, 1784), 99: "Hier ist der Bürger, was er in jeder Republik seyn sollte, und fast in keiner ist,'vollkommen frey in allem, was den' andern nicht schadet" [sic]. Dieses Volk gibt den stärksten Beweis von der Nützlichkeit der GewerbeFreyheit und völligen Befreyung vom Zunftzwange; denn wo ist eine Strecke Landes in der Welt, die eine solche gesunde, starke, wohlgenährte, arbeitsame und erfindsame Volksmenge zählt, wenn auch gleich die Polizey noch so viel dichtet und trachtet?"

especially reacted. An increased awareness of a needed reform can be attested for the United Provinces, starting by the 1660s with the brothers de la Court. They paved the way for a discussion revolving around the relationship of republican citizenship and the economic interest of the Dutch commonwealth.[47] In Venice, we also find reform-oriented treatises, like Scipione Maffei's (1675-1755) *Consiglio Politico* of 1736.[48] Ascertaining the decline of Venice due to the evolving force of other European states, and mainly the loss of important trade routes, he recommends a reform of the commonwealth targeting an enlargement of power without an expansion of the territory. He advocates major political participation by the Venetian citizens, making their self-interest useful for the whole commonwealth. The United Provinces and Switzerland as well as England provide positive examples for him in this sense.[49]

Swiss reform-debates in the eighteenth century also referred to the Dutch case as a close model of a European federal republic, debating on strategies of adapting republican values and institutions to changed commercial realities.[50] They also referenced the critical discourse that

---

47 See E.H. Kossmann, *Political Thought in the Dutch Republic: Three Studies* Verhandelingen der Koninklijke Nederlandse Akademie van wetenschappen, Afd. Letterkunde, Nieuwe Reeks 179 (Amsterdam: Koninklijke Akademie van Wetenschappen, 2000), 53-83. For the Dutch discussion in the eighteenth century see: Wyger R. E. Velema, *Republicans. Essays on Eighteenth-Century Dutch Political Thought* Brill's Studies in Intellectual History 155 (Leiden and Boston: Brill, 2007); and especially on Dutch decline and the historiographic debate on that point see: Koen Stapelbroek, "Dutch decline as a European phenomenon," *History of European Ideas* 36 (2010): 139-152.

48 Scipione Maffei, *Consiglio politico finora inedito presentato al Governo Veneto nell'anno 1736* (Venezia 1797) (Reprint Napoli: Bibliopolis, 1977). An approach to explain the political thought of Scipione Maffei can be found in Eluggero Pii, "Il pensiero politico di Scipione Maffei: dalla Repubblica di Roma alla Repubblica di Venezia," in *Scipione Maffei nell'Europa del settecento*, ed. Gian Paolo Romagnan (Verona: Consorzio Ed. Veneti, 1998), 93-117; Lena Maurach, *Scipione Maffeis politisches Werk im Kontext seiner Zeit. Der Suggerimento—eine Schrift des venezianischen „Anti-Mythos"?*, (Heidelberg: unpublished MA thesis, 2010). For the broader view on the reform-debates in Venice in the eighteenth century see Franco Venturi, "'Venise et, par occasion, de la liberté'," in *The idea of freedom. Essays in honour of Isaiah Berlin*, ed. Alan Ryan (Oxford et al.: Oxford University Press, 1979), 195-210; Piero del Negro, "Introduzione," in *Storia di Venezia. Dalle origini alla caduta della Serenissima, Tomo VIII. L'ultima fase della Serenissima*, ed. Piero del Negro and Paolo Preto (Roma: Istituto della Enciclopedia Italiana, 1998), 1-80; Stapelbroek and Trampus, "Commercial reform," 192-202.

49 Maffei, *Consiglio politico*, 84-111.

50 Béla Kapossy has shown this convincingly in Béla Kapossy, "Republican Futures: The Image of Holland in 18th-Century Swiss Reform Discourse," in *The Republican Alternative: The Netherlands and Switzerland compared*, ed. André Holenstein, Thomas Maissen and Maarten Prak (Amsterdam: Amsterdam University Press, 2008), 279-298; Béla Kapossy, "Neo-Roman Republicanism and Commercial Society. The Example of 18th Century Berne," in *Republicanism: A Shared European Heritage*, Vol. 2, ed. Quentin Skinner and Martin van Gelderen (Cambridge: Cambridge University Press, 2002), 227-247.

was promoted in Europe on the republics by foreign observers.

One example is the treatise *L´Etat et les Delices de la Suisse*, published by an anonymous—presumably Swiss—author in Amsterdam in 1730.[51] In this treatise the editor combines, confronts, and comments on the script of Abraham Stanyan and a treatise of the Swiss author Abraham Ruchat (1680-1715), whose work *Les Délices de la Suisse* was published in 1714, the same year as Stanyan's treatise.[52] In doing so, the editor picks up many relevant aspects already known from the outside perspective on the existing republics. He puts these aspects into perspective, but does not deny their relevance completely. Hence, this treatise does not present itself as a glorification of the Swiss Constitution, but consciously points out defects that are to be resolved.

The issues of commerce are located in the center of this argumentation, too. In this context the editor consistently points to the part of religious refugees and their integration as an opportunity for commercial improvement. Some cantons had lost their chance by refusing Huguenot refugees.[53] In writing this, the author is absolutely aware of the problems of citizenship that are related to this issue. According to which criteria should the right of citizenship be awarded? Who should be taken into account?[54] Conventional criteria of inclusion and exclusion are questioned in this treatise, and the commercial factor gains weight in these considerations.

The lack of legal security is mentioned by the author as well. Again, he does not deny the criticism of Abraham Stanyan, but contests the claim in its universal validity.[55] This source thus attests to an existing awareness of a needed (constitutional) reform. As in every republic—

---

51 *L´Etat et les Delices de la Suisse, en forme de Relation critique, par plusieurs Auteurs célèbres. Enrichi de Figures en Taille-douce, dessinées sur les Lieux mêmes & de Cartes Géographiques très-exactes en IV. Volumes* (Amsterdam: chez les Wetssteins et Smith, 1730). For information concerning the possible author of this compilation see Edgar Bonjour and Richard Feller, *Geschichtsschreibung in der Schweiz vom Spätmittelalter zur Neuzeit*, vol. 2 (Basel and Stuttgart: Schwabe, 1962), 616-617, and Thomas Maissen, "Als die armen Bergbauern vorbildlich wurden. Ausländische und schweizerische Voraussetzungen des internationalen Tugenddiskurses um 1700, " in *Reichtum und Armut in den schweizerischen Republiken des 18. Jahrhunderts* (Travaux sur la Suisse des Lumières XII), ed. André Holenstein et al. (Genf: Slatkine, 2010), 95-119, 113-114.

52 Abraham Ruchat, *Les Délices de la Suisse (1714)*, avec une introduction de Marcus Bourquin (Genève: Slatkine, 1978) (Réimpression de l´édition de Leide 1714).

53 *L´Etat et le Delices de la Suisse*, 446f.

54 "Enfin, comment donner le droit de Bourgeoisie aux uns, sans causer de la jalousie aux autres?" (Ibid., 260).

55 Ibid., 351f.

the author reveals—there are defects in the Swiss Confederation which need to be resolved:

> It is for the same reason, that there is no republic where there is nothing to correct. People have criticized the republic of Platon, the system of Hobbes, the Oceana etc. Why do we not change for the better in the republics which exist the failures you can detect; because, I think, that in the whole world no man is blind enough to argue that the form of constitution of his mother country is absolutely perfect.[56]

Statements like this are accompanied by the confidence that such a reform would be possible and successful. The author points explicitly to a positive vision of a stable, not expansive commonwealth which guarantees the rule of law and the protection of property. [57] But this ideal is located in the future. The author does not accept the English Constitution as a better one. In addition, he regards democratic commonwealths as only coming close to this ideal when they are very small.[58] It is more a vision the Swiss should attach themselves to and strive for. They need to do so—that is his clear position—otherwise they have no chance to continue surviving in a world dominated by absolutist powers.

4. A European Discourse of Reform

The critical voices from outside the republics and the inner-republican discussions that stuck to these critics are evidence of a commerce-oriented reform discourse in Europe. Most of the treatises functioned as

---

56   "C'est aussi par cette même raison, qu'il n'y a point de République, où il n'y ait quelque chose à corriger. On a critiqué la République de Platon, les Systêmes de Hobbes, d'Océana, &c. Pourquoi ne reprendroit on pas dans les Républiques, qui sont existentes, les défauts que l'on y apperçoit; car je ne crois pas, qu'il y ait au monde une Homme assés aveugle pour soutenir, que la forme du Gouvernement de sa Patrie soit absolument parfaite." (Ibid., 283).

57   Ibid., 230: "La meilleure forme du Gouvernement étant, sans contredit, celle où l'on jouït en sûreté de ce que l'on a, où l'on ne craint point une Domination Tyrannique, où l'ambition des Grands, & le pouvoir de celui qui gouverne, ne cherchent point à se satisfaire par des Guerres éternelles; mais sous laquelle on peut jouïr, en toute sûreté, de son bien; où celui, qui seroit troublé, est certain de trouver un Juge équitable."

58   Ibid., 226 and 281-282.

a mirror of defects in their respective home countries.[59] Throughout Europe, people faced the trend that the public good was substituted by class interests of merchants and manufactures. In France, authors argued about the impact of Colbert's economic politics, trying to bring together wealth and virtue.[60] The English struggled with the Whig Regime, which provided a greater extent of stability, an expansion of trade, and the growth of military power of the English commonwealth, but their influence was based on a system of aristocratic dependencies. Thus, the growth of commercial success was associated with an oligarchic regime, provoking critical treatises on alternative ways of providing a lawful state that could at the same time bear the challenge of an international order, ruled by commerce as decisive factor with regard to military and political survival.[61]

Speaking of a "reform" discourse, it is important to bear in mind that this discourse bears strong connections to a new concept of time that emerged around 1700.[62] In the examined treatises, the authors no longer argue in a cyclical manner like many had done before them, following Polybios or Machiavelli, nor do they refer to any programmed decline imposed by any kind of natural necessity, nor to a salvific history

---

59   Some of the treatises do this explicitly as for example Onslow Burrish, who dedicates his 1728 "Batavia Illustrata: Or a view of the Policy, and Commerce, of the United Provinces. Particularly of Holland" to Robert Walpole, and discusses the Dutch system of "treating bankrupts" with regard to an English need for a "further Reformation." Burrish, *Batavia Illustrata*, 67.

60   See among others for the debate in Eighteenth-Century France: John Shovlin, *The political economy of Virtue: Luxury, Patriotism, and the Origins of the French Revolution* (Ithaca and London: Cornell University Press, 2006); Michael Sonenscher, "Republicanism, State Finances and the Emergence of Commercial Society in Eighteenth-Century France—or from Royal to Ancient Republicanism and Back," in *Republicanism*, ed. Skinner and Van Gelderen, vol. 2: *The values of republicanism in Early Modern Europe*, 275-291.

61   See among others Hont, *Jealousy of Trade*; John G. A. Pocock, "Cambridge Paradigms and Scotch philosophers: a study of the relations between the civic humanist and the civil jurisprudential interpretation of eighteenth-century social thought," in *Wealth and Virtue: The Shaping of Political Economy in the Scottish Enlightenment*, ed. Istvan Hont and Michael Ignatieff (Cambridge et al.: Cambridge University Press, 1985), 235-252.

62   For the complex of time conceptions around 1700 see for instance Reinhart Koselleck, *Begriffsgeschichten: Studien zur Semantik und Pragmatik der politischen und sozialen Sprache* (Frankfurt a.M.: Suhrkamp, 2006), 170–173 and 328; Reinhart Koselleck, *Vergangene Zukunft. Zur Semantik geschichtlicher Zeiten* (Frankfurt a.M.: Suhrkamp, 1988); Winfried Schulze, "Die Wahrnehmung von Zeit und Jahrhundertwenden," *Jahrbuch des Historischen Kollegs* (2000): 3-36, 20-29; Landwehr, *Erschaffung Venedigs*, 429-431; Lucien Hölscher, *Die Entdeckung der Zukunft* (Frankfurt a.M.: Fischer, 1999), 9 and 34-46; Jochen Schlobach, *Zyklentheorie und Epochenmetaphorik: Studien zur Bildlichen Sprache der Geschichtsreflexion in Frankreich von der Renaissance bis zu Frühaufklärung* (München: Wilhelm Fink, 1980), 270-331.

in the Christian tradition. On the contrary: this discourse is rather designed as a discourse of an open decision, which constitution guarantees its citizens the highest degree of liberty, and what kind of liberty? And above all: which kind of constitution and state order may best adapt to the new political and economical structures in Europe?

The frame of reference is no longer located in the past, as could have been the case with the republics of antiquity or the Italian renaissance. The new ideal is located in the present, embodied by the new English state with its principle of the rule of law, or it is located in a now thinkable and feasible future, embodied by the vision of a small, stable, federative and economically successful republic.[63] "Reform" in this sense does not mean a return to old ideals, but in fact a departure to a modern state, adjusted to new (commercial) developments.

This modern state seems to be associated with a new understanding of liberty as well. Being on the one hand a necessary prerequisite of commerce, and on the other hand its necessary political consequence, liberty is more and more defined as an individualistic value than as a collective one.

This paradigm shift in speaking about the republic in general provoked by commerce as the crucial argument at the beginning of the eighteenth century has already been pointed out by historians of political thought, namely John Pocock and Istvan Hont.[64] The sources presented in this article indicate this shift on another level: in relatively short political treatises mainly by diplomats and other active statesmen and even in travelogues as well, it was not the abstract idea of any republican model or the republics of Antiquity or the Italian renaissance that shaped new visions of a modern state, but rather the real existing republics of their time—mainly Venice, the United Provinces, and the Swiss Confederation—that functioned as no-longer-model, as negative foil, in fact as "midwives of a new republicanism."[65]

---

63   The aspect of federation was highly disputed. Especially with Montesquieu the positive aspects of it gain ground within the discussion. See Charles-Louis de Montesquieu, "De L'Esprit des Lois," in *Œuvres complètes de Montesquieu* (Bibliothèque de la Pléiade 26), ed. Roger Caillois (Paris: Gallimard, 1951), 225-1117, Livre IX, Chap. I, 369.

64   Pocock, *Machiavellian Moment*; Pocock, *Cambridge Paradigms*; Hont, *Jealousy of Trade*; See also Donald Winch, "Commercial Realities, Republican Principles," in *Republicanism*, ed. Skinner and van Gelderen, Vol. 2, 293-310.

65   Wijnand Mijnhardt interprets Franco Venturi's perception of the eighteenth-century republics in this way. Wijnand Mijnhardt, "Franco Venturi's Dutch republic and the crisis of the historiography

If we should label this republicanism a "commercial republicanism," or in fact no longer republicanism, but liberalism, is hard to say; and finally, labelling is not that decisive. Probably, this new republicanism is something in between. Accentuating the rule of law and individual economical liberty as well as property rights, this discourse bears liberal traits. In contrast to former republican arguments, the authors demand an enlargement of the circle of citizens. The ideal citizen is no longer the one who engages himself in the defence of his patria and excels in active political participation, but rather the one who contributes to the welfare of the commonwealth by using his commercial capacity. What differs is the intention, the regulative aim the authors had in mind: for some it is the welfare and the growth of the whole commonwealth, and for others it is the individual welfare and personal happiness. In the view of the latter, the constitutional state then should only guarantee this personal aim. Thus, this discourse fluctuates between different statements, maybe even between different languages.

In either case, this discourse was not so much triggered by a an optimism based on and aiming for moral improvement, but rather by one which was pragmatic and open-ended in its character and above all oriented to efficiency.

To conclude, we can sum up the following results:

1. The discussion on the existing republics at the beginning of the eighteenth century remained embedded in a republican ductus of language, and criticized different single defects of the three commonwealths that have been examined here. Next to aspects like virtue of citizens and office holders, new elements like legal certainty and above all commercial liberties gained weight in the authors' considerations.

2. The commercial issue turned out to be the decisive argument in this discussion, provoking a need for action in other fields like that of citizenship and institutional design. Expanding personal liberties and citizenship rights in the realms of commerce and property became instrumental for the flourishing of the commonwealth as a whole.

3. Since the 1670s, the republics of Europe no longer functioned as

---

of republicanism," in *Il Reppublicanesimo Moderno*, ed. Albertone, 407-429, 412.

positive models, but rather as (negative) foils, which authors probably often used to expose the needed reform of their own commonwealths. Whereas the United Provinces was the only republic which—
due to its commercial system—was still seen as relatively positive
until the mid-eighteenth century, the other two contemporary republics were displaced by new models: the English Constitution, the
small, democratic and self-sustaining republic, or the future vision of
a stable, not expansive commonwealth guaranteeing legal and pos-
sessory certainty.

4. The discussion on the existing republics was therefore part of a
greater reform discourse on modern states, which featured a new
conception of time and was pragmatic and open-ended in its character.

5. Can Early Modern Ideas Address Current Affairs?

Such a debate could definitely fit in our post-nation-state time. Efficiency,
pragmatism and adaptability as leading aspects of discourse are familiar to us. But could the knowledge of the discussion on the existing republics at the beginning of the eighteenth century be of any use to our
understanding of today's European and/or Israeli problems? Such an approach is definitively disputable: but reading, for example, an article of
Gershon Shafir and Yoav Peled, titled "Citizenship and stratification in
an ethnic democracy,"[66] one can find some interesting parallels. Trying
to analyse the transformation of the structure of ethnic relations in
Israel by using citizenship discourses as an instrument of their analysis,
they came to the conclusion that there was a "gradual replacement of
the republican citizenship discourse by a liberal discourse" in the 1990s
and that this shift was decisively provoked and provided by an economic
boom.[67] Commerce became a crucial argument in questions of citizenship—as in Europe as well, where the criteria of inclusion and exclusion
have been determined by commercial interests from the beginning of
the project of the European Union. As Bo Stråth has argued recently,
the economic category has always been the crucial one in defining a

---

66   Gershon Shafir/Yoav Peled, "Citizenship and stratification in an ethnic democracy," *Ethnic and
     Racial Studies* 21/3 (1998): 408-427.
67   Ibid., 408.

European identity, leaving social aspects within the frame of the nation-state. To keep Europe capable of acting in the future, he rather pleads to make the willingness to social responsibility and political commitment the main criteria of inclusion into the European Union.[68] Facing these two statements, one can question if now—facing the Global Financial Crisis with all its consequences—the shift to a more liberal discourse is again reversed? Are discourses on citizenship and state interest now (again) debated in a different language? And could we label this different language as being part of any kind of "republicanism"? Early modern discussions can at least address the notion that it is worth looking at these questions.

---

[68] Bo Stråth, "Europe and the Other and Europe as the Other," in *Selbstbilder und Fremdbilder: Repräsentation sozialer Ordnung im Wandel* Eigene und fremde Welten 1, ed. Jörg Baberowski, Hartmut Kaelble and Jürgen Schriewer (Frankfurt and New York: Campus, 2008), 191-202.

Beyond the Republican Synthesis:
Biblical Republicanism and the American Revolution

ERAN SHALEV

Historians of the American Revolution spent much of the final decades of the twentieth century arguing about the nature of the American Revolution: was it an attempt by American colonists to restore English-born rights, or a drive to restore civic virtue and fight monarchic corruption? That is, they were debating whether the American Revolution (hence the American nation that it begot) was liberal or republican. Synthetic attempts to reconcile the polar ideologies were followed by assertions as to the wholly inadequate conceptual contours of the disputation; eventually this so-called liberal-republican debate faded out inconclusively in the 1990s. In this essay I wish to revisit the intellectual landscape that the debate shaped, from the perspective of more than a decade since its conclusion. The insights of the recent scholarly branch dubbed Political Hebraism, I will argue, provide ways to better understand what republicanism meant to late eighteenth century Americans, and how that austere ideology became meaningful to a people renowned for its pursuit of happiness.[1]

1. The Republican Synthesis

It would be an understatement to aver that republicanism had been a major analytical concept for understanding the ideological and intellectual universe of early America since at least the 1970s. It would also be a platitude; there are few topics in American history upon which so much ink has been spilt. After the paradigm shift during the late 1960s and early 1970s that shattered the hegemony of the Consensus History school of thought, which stressed the lack of ideological conflict

---

1   Robert Shalhope's synthetic articles are "Toward a Republican Synthesis: The Emergence of an Understanding of Republicanism in American Historiography," *William and Mary Quarterly* 29 (1972): 49–80; and "Republicanism and Early American Historiography," *William and Mary Quarterly* 39 (1982): 334–56.

in American history, the "republican synthesis" replaced the Consensus paradigm as the leading interpretive mode. The domination of Consensus interpretations of American history were first shaken by the early works of Caroline Robbins, Douglass Adair, and Edmund Morgan, all of whom disputed Louis Hartz's influential contention that America was forged in a Lockean mold and was based solely upon rights and consent. Soon after came three epoch-making works that severely impaired the Consensus foundation: *The Ideological Origins of the American Revolution* (Bernard Bailyn, 1967); *The Creation of the American Republic* (Gordon Wood, 1969); and *The Machiavellian Moment* (J.G.A Pocock, 1975).[2]

Bailyn was the first to render a full-blown reading of the revolutionary generation that was not just non-Lockean, but forcefully anti-Lockean. The aggravated reaction to the relatively modest British attempts to tax the colonies, followed by the neurotic and inflated American rhetoric and political behavior could not easily fit into a Lockean scheme, if at all. Two years later Bailyn's student Wood illuminated and articulated the uniqueness, importance, and radicalism of American republicanism. Again, the focus in explaining the creation of the United States was not on Locke but on a republican ideology. A few years later Pocock unveiled a rich intellectual cosmos of Civic Humanism that stretched back from classical antiquity to the Early American Republic.

It did not take long for a "liberal" reaction to gather and defend the significance of Lockean principles as a key for understanding America's founding. Heretofore historiographic wars had raged between "liberals" and "republicans," each camp asserting the precedence of its intellectual idols for a better understanding of American history. While liberals took rights and liberties, and their pursuit, as the drivers of the dynamism of American history, Republicans underscored the priority of the duty to the commonwealth, deriving from the fear of its imminent dissolution. Those vigorous debates between *Gesellschaft* and *Gemeinschaft* interpretations of American history began waning after the appearance of major synthetic statements about the state of the field, but not before Daniel T. Rogers voiced an influential statement questioning altogether the usefulness and aptness of the concept of "republicanism" for under-

---

2   Louis Hartz, *The Liberal Tradition in America,* Second Edition (Mariner Books, 1991); Douglass Adair, *Fame and the Founding Fathers* (New York: W. W. Norton, 1974); Caroline Robbins, *The Eighteenth-Century Commonwealthman* (Indianapolis: Liberty Fund, 2004); Edmund Morgan, "The Puritan Ethic and The American Revolution," *William and Mary Quarterly* 24 (1967): 3-43.

standing American history. Suddenly it seemed unfruitful to commit to "liberalism" and "republicanism," modern conceptual constructions in which late eighteenth-century contemporaries were not versed. Further, late eighteenth century Americans seem to have found creative ways to conciliate these apparently conflicting ideas about the political world. Thereafter, historians attempted to sidestep a debate that seemed to have reached a dead end. Many also may have conceded that although classical republicanism was probably an important impulse in shaping early American political minds, civic humanism was a stern ideology that could not be reconciled with the permissive tendencies that the colonists had manifested since the early days of settlement, and also contradicted the American democracy that would emerge soon after the Revolution was over. Classical republicanism, in short, could not sustain the full brunt of the ideology of the American Revolution; in societies as radical and centrifugal as the British North American colonies and the young United States, liberalism, or the pursuit of happiness, seemed like a perfectly valid ideological explanation for resistance, rebellion, independence and state-building, perhaps more than republicanism.[3]

Nevertheless, throughout that debate scholars identified various ways in which religion reinforced and served as the handmaid of republicanism. Historians recognized the conceptual similarities between reformed Protestantism and republicanism, hence the influence of the sacred and Christian upon a doctrine rooted in pagan classicism. For example, Edmund Morgan revealed how Puritanism and its eighteenth century legacy were related to the harsh and demanding world of the American revolutionary ideology. More than a decade later, Nathan Hatch published a provocative monograph that revealed the pervasiveness of "civic millennialism," a coherent body of thought that for revolutionary New Englanders imparted a new religious significance to the function of man as citizen. This theo-republican dialect reflected perceptions of the polity as a Christian commonwealth, of Roman virtue

---

3   Daniel T. Rodgers, "Republicanism: The Career of a Concept," *The Journal of American History* 79 (1992): 11-38. For a leading voice among Liberal historians see Joyce Appleby, *Liberalism and Republicanism in the Historical Imagination* (Cambridge, MA: Harvard University Press, 1992); James T. Kloppenberg, "The Virtues of Liberalism: Christianity, Republicanism, and Ethics in Early American Political Discourse," *The Journal of American History* 74 (1987): 9-33; Jack P. Greene, *Pursuits of Happiness: The Social Development of Early Modern British Colonies and the Formation of American Culture* (Chapel Hill: University of North Carolina Press, 1988).

as religious piety and benevolence, and of political corruption as sin. By pointing out a unique revolutionary mixture of grace and fortune (or *fortuna*), Hatch effectively demonstrated how a republican eschatology crystallized around the most evocative puritan religious forms. The historical vision of both Puritanism and millennialism was premised on the dynamic struggle between cosmic moral forces, so the apocalyptic battle against the antichrist could be understood as similar, if not identical to the Whig struggle of freeborn men against tyranny. The darker side of both mentalities was expressed in exaggerated fears of moral decline and the organic concept of the state. Hatch was not the only scholar to point out the significance of religion for republican and revolutionary consciousness. Others similarly indicated the significance of millennial ideas for the formation of revolutionary consciousness. Scholars seemed to agree that Reformed Protestantism and classical virtue, Christianity and republicanism went hand in hand as revolutionary tensions tore the British North American Empire apart.[4]

2. Hebraic Republicanism

For decades then, scholars recognized that the "republican rhetoric of corruption formed an alliance with the jeremiad," and that fervent Protestants "identified the American republic with the advent of the millennial period." However, this fateful merging of civic humanism and millennialism was only the tip of the iceberg of late eighteenth century American intersections of the language of republicanism and of Protestantism. An overlooked and similarly powerful alliance between the sacred and the political was the Bible with republicanism, or rather the Old Testament with civic humanism. Examining this under-explored biblical republicanism might help us understand more fully the intellectual and ideological universe of the revolutionary Americans. Further, by recognizing how far the Old Testament served as a rich source for republican teachings, or for the biblicization of civic humanism, we may come to realize how revolutionary Americans, and following them gen-

---

4   Nathan O. Hatch, *The Sacred Cause of Liberty: Republican Thought and the Millennium in Revolutionary New England* (New Haven: Yale University Press, 1977); Ruth H. Bloch, *Visionary Republic: Millennial Themes in American Thought, 1756-1800* (New York: Cambridge University Press, 1985). Mark Noll, *America's God: From Jonathan Edwards to Abraham Lincoln* (New York: Oxford University Press, 2002),

erations of politically conscious citizens of the United States, absorbed, adhered to, and co-opted the demanding and unyielding doctrine of classical republicanism.[5]

While the importance of millennial ideas has subsequently been generally recognized, since the 1990s historians have been offering new religion-related explanations of the revolutionary American embrace of republicanism. This relatively recent strand of interpretation is part of a larger trend, where scholars have begun to appreciate the extent to which Europe, for a century and a half after the Protestant Reformation "between Bodin and Locke, with Machiavelli as a significant Predecessor," experienced the efflorescence of the analysis of the Hebrew Bible as a political text. Michael Walzer's renowned book *Exodus and Revolution* conveys the importance of the Exodus and the flight of the Israelites to the wilderness as a recurrent theme in American history. In the words of Sacvan Bercovitch, the Exodus provided America with a "typology of mission" from the early days of settlement and beyond.[6]

Consequently, the study of religion and religious discourse in revolutionary America has produced some of the richest and most impressive scholarship in American history. It is amply documented how revolutionary discourse in America consisted of a "resilient intermixture of religious and republican vocabularies" which culminated in a novel American "Christian republicanism." Yet regardless of the breadth and depth of that scholarship, in studies ranging from intellectual to social, and from institutional to theological, Americanists have yet to take advantage of the scholarly field that defines itself as "Hebraic political studies." This new field aims to analyze readings of the Old Testament "in a political context, whether or not the authors read those texts in the original Hebrew." Its students insist that such readings, increasing dramatically after the Renaissance, were intimately concerned with

---

5   Dorothy Ross, *The Origins of American Social Sciences* (New York: Cambridge University Press, 1992), 24.

6   Nathan Perl-Rosenthal, "'The Divine Right of Republics': Hebraic Republicanism and the Debate over Kingless Government in Revolutionary America," *William and Mary Quarterly* 66 (2009); Eric Nelson, *The Hebrew Republic: Jewish Sources and the Transformation of European Political Thought* (Cambridge, MA: Harvard University Press, 2010). Fania Oz-Salzberger, "The Political Thought of John Locke and the Significance of Political Hebraism," *Hebraic Political Studies* 1:5 (2006): 568-592, quote on 569. Sacvan Bercovitch, "The Typology of America's Mission," *American Quarterly* 30:2 (1978). For an Atlantic, confessional-crossing context of typology see Jorge Canizares-Esguerra, *Puritan Conquistadors: Iberianizing the Atlantic, 1550-1700* (Stanford: Stanford University Press, 2006); Michael Walzer, *Exodus and Revolution* (New York: Basic Books, 1986).

the political questions of the time, and manifested a remarkably wide spectrum of predominantly Christian interpretations of the Hebrew Bible. Rather than a particular ideologically coherent reading of scripture, they insist, political Hebraism should be seen "as a common mode of discourse [rather] than as a defense of a specific political position," and should thus "take its place of honor among other [contemporary] languages or paradigms." The potential benefits of such an approach to early American history should be evident. Nowadays this history is conceived as Atlantic due to its ongoing intellectual exchange with the Old World, but it is also clearly defined through the common, if not universal, self-conceptions of that historical society as a chosen nation on a God-sanctioned mission. But students of the political uses of the Bible habitually conceive their historical field as flourishing both geographically and temporally remote from the American Revolution. This field of erudition is currently not only self-consciously Eurocentric (at least in its early modern interest), it also understands its zenith as being reached at least a full century before the start of the Age of Democratic Revolutions.[7]

The fact is that regardless of the centrality of religion in America, as well as the vigor and extent of religious American studies, political Hebraism has to date been surprisingly under-employed by early American historians. If there were sporadic, eclectic, and, by now, dated attempts to unveil *The Biblical Origins of American Democracy* or the role of *Hebrew and the Bible in America*, historians certainly did not provide the lead. Rather, it was political scientists such as the late Daniel Elazar and Donald Lutz who produced the most innovative work in the field by ana-

---

7   Mark Noll, *America's God*, 54. See also Patricia U. Bonomi, *Under the Cope of Heaven: Religion, Society and Politics in Colonial America* (New York: Oxford University Press, 2003); James T. Kloppenberg, "The Virtues of Liberalism: Christianity, Republicanism, and Ethics in Early American Political Discourse," in James T. Kloppenberg, *The Virtues of Liberalism* (New York: Oxford University Press, 2000), 21-37; Jon Butler, *Awash in a Sea of Faith: Christianizing the American People* (Cambridge, MA: Harvard University Press, 1992); Harry S. Stout, *The New England Soul: Preaching and Religious Culture in Colonial New England* (New York: Oxford University Press, 1986); Bloch, *Visionary Republic*; Hatch, *The Sacred Cause of Liberty*; Kalman Neuman, "Political Hebraism and the Early Modern 'Respublica Hebraeroum': On Defining the Field," *Hebraic Political Studies* 1:1 (2005): 57-70, quote on 59, 63, 57. For a good introduction see David Armitage and Michael J. Braddick, *The British Atlantic World, 1500-1800* (New York: Palgrave Macmillan, 2002). On the differences in perceptions of "chosenness" between New England and Mid-Colonies clergymen see Keith Griffin, *Revolution and Religion: American Revolutionary War and the Reformed Clergy* (New York: Paragon House, 1994). R. R. Palmer, *Age of Democratic Revolutions: A Political History of Europe and America, 1760-1800* (Princeton: Princeton University Press, 1970).

lyzing the importance and the role of the Hebraic notion of Covenant and Compact in the American constitutional tradition. Only recently we have benefited from a few works dedicated to unveiling the Atlantic dimensions of political Hebraism.[8]

Although the origin and the historical model of classical republicanism were Greece and Rome, only a small part of late eighteenth century American society could have been versed in the history and teachings of those remote societies. The vast majority of the American population did not receive a university education, still less, one with an emphasis on Greek and Latin. As in all societies to which the Old Testament, in the words of Perry Miller, was "like the air they breathed," they could easily relate to the Bible and its teaching. Biblical republicanism added a sacred aura to the republican cause, but it also potentially enabled every American to identify with a doctrine which otherwise would have less than a universal appeal.[9]

3. Early American Biblicism

It is hardly surprising that the Bible, as the historian Paul Gutjahr states, was the "most printed, most distributed, and most read written text in North America up through the nineteenth century." This dominance of the Book of Books over printing in America gave rise to countless shared "idioms, metaphors, narrative themes" in colonial British North American and the early United States. Bibles were the chief source for school-age children's reading and writing, together with a few other heavily doctrinal texts such as catechisms and the New England Primer, that shaped the form and content of education in early America. The prevalence of the Bible in a Protestant world was

---

8 Abraham Katch, *The Biblical Heritage of American Democracy* (New York: Ktav, 1977); Shalom Goldman (ed.), *Hebrew and the Bible in America: The First Two Centuries* (Hanover, NH: University Press of New England, 1993). On the centrality of the concept of Covenant in political thought see: Daniel J. Elazar, *The Covenant Tradition in Politics*, 4 vols. (New Brunswick: Transaction, 1995-1998); and Delbert R. Hillers, *Covenant: The History of a Biblical Idea* (Baltimore: Johns Hopkins University Press, 1969). See also Donald S. Lutz, *The Origins of American Constitutionalism* (Baton Rouge: Louisiana State University Press, 1988), and *Publius: The Journal of Federalism* 10.4 (1980), "A Special Issue on Covenant, Polity and Constitutionalism." See *Hebraic Political Studies* 4 (2009), "Hebraic and Old Testament Politics in Colonial America," special issue.

9 Caroline Winterer, *The Culture of Classicism: Ancient Greece and Rome in American Intellectual Life, 1780-1910* (Baltimore: Johns Hopkins University Press, 2002). Miller quoted in Nathan O. Hatch and Mark A. Noll, "Introduction," *The Bible in America* (New York: Oxford University Press, 1982), 5.

of course no accident, but the consequence of a Reformed theology that emphasized a direct relationship with the word as an essential component of spiritual life and ultimately a path to salvation. In stark contradiction to centuries of Catholic practice, early in the history of Protestantism vernacular, Anglophone Bibles asserted that they were meant for everyone:

> all manner of persons, men, women, young, old, learned, unlearned, rich, poor, priests, laymen, lords, ladies, officers, tenants, and mean men, virgins, wives, widows, lawyers, merchants, artificers, husbandmen, and all manner of persons of what estate or condition soever they be, may in this book learn all things that they ought to believe, what they ought to do, and what they should not do.

Sola scriptura eventually raised the readership of the Bible in America to unprecedented, if not universal, levels.[10]

The ubiquity of Bibles in early America, combined with the book's central place in early Americans' cosmologies, underscores its potential for becoming an immeasurably useful facilitator of early modern ideologies, particularly of civic-humanism. One may justifiably wonder how a literate (and significantly biblically literate), yet for the most part not classically educated people might absorb a harsh, pagan and in more than one sense foreign ideology such as civic humanism. By turning our attention to the animated and overlooked ways in which late eighteenth century Americans read, analyzed and communicated the Old Testament as a republican text we may gain a clearer sense of the manner in which the ideas of the doctrine we have come to call "classical republicanism" became accessible to the revolutionary generation and succeeding Americans. The republicanization of the Old Testament, or the predilection to interpret the Hebrew Bible, its narratives and protagonists, as if they reflected the ideological sensibilities of revolutionary America, enables us to understand better the American Revolution, an event that even contemporaries recognized

---

10 Paul Gutjahr, *American Bible: A History of the Good Book in the United States, 1770-1880* (Stanford University Press, 1999), 2. Preface to *Cranmer's Bible* (London, 1540).

was not merely an imperial war, but a battle for the "minds and hearts of the people."[11]

4. Exodus

The best-known republican use of a biblical narrative in America is of the aforementioned Exodus, a narrative that reverberated from the Puritans of the seventeenth century Great Migration to the Civil Rights Movement of the twentieth century and beyond. American historians have long recognized the central role of that story, and have consequently explored how the struggle of the Israelites—going out from Egyptian bondage, led by a charismatic and God-inspired Moses to win over Pharaoh and his minions, wandered in the desert for forty years, and eventually conquered Canaan and settled in the Land of Milk and Honey inspired Americans and contributed to their theo-historical consciousness. By the time of the Revolution, the Exodus had already a long history in the colonies, especially in the New England colonies where it had been read typologically since the early seventeenth century. Although British North Americans found little use for that trope through most of the eighteenth century, once the imperial conflict between Britain and its American colonies gained momentum American writers across the colonies revived the story of the Israelites' resistance and escape from a mighty and oppressive captor, a narrative told and told again by New Englanders in earlier generations. Once more, the Exodus became a central theme for contemporaries' typological imagination and historical understanding of their conflict with the "Egyptian" British Empire. [12]

During the years leading to independence, the presumption that "[t]he miraculous deliverance of the children of Israel from the Egyptian Bondage" was "a very signal instance of God's appearing in favour of liberty, and frowning on tyrants" became prevalent. The God of Israel was a republican God, who showed "how much he regards the rights

---

11   John Adams, *The Works of John Adams, Second President of the United States: with a Life of the Author, Notes and Illustrations, by his Grandson Charles Francis Adams* (Boston: Little, Brown and Co., 1856). In 10 volumes. Vol. 10: "To Dr. J. Morse"; http://oll.libertyfund.org/title/2127/193567/3102868 (accessed on December 12, 2010).

12   Walzer, *Exodus and Revolution*; Avihu Zakai, *Exile and Kingdom: History and Apocalypse in the Puritan Migration to America* (New York: Cambridge University Press, 1992).

of his people, and in how exemplary a manner, hard hearted tyrants, and merciless oppressors," such as Pharaoh and George III, "feel his vengeance." Preachers chose the Exodus as the typological plot around which to construct their view of the American situation, a theme most elaborately developed by Nicholas Street in *The American States Acting over the Part of the Children of Israel in the Wilderness, and thereby Impeding Their Entrance into Canaan's Rest* (1777). This remarkable typological reading lengthily juxtaposed "[t]he history of the children of Israel in Egypt, their sufferings and oppression under the tyrant Pharaoh, their remarkable deliverance by the hands of Moses out of the state of bondage and oppression, and their trials and murmurings in the wilderness" with the Americans, "acting over...the children of Israel in the wilderness, under the conduct of Moses and Aaron, who was leading them out of a state of bondage into a land of liberty and plenty in Canaan."[13]

As the Revolution advanced, however, it became clear that the Exodus was not a model that applied merely to New England, or one that was used only by New Englanders. Indeed, historians have been aware of the process through which the American nation, in the words of Mark Noll, "was engrafted onto the New England special destiny." This graft included the typological relevance of the Exodus to the young United States. Americans outside of predominantly Congregationalist New England, particularly in the middle colonies-turned-states, were too becoming accustomed to think that although they, like the Israelites in Egypt, were enslaved in foreign bondage, with "a wilderness still be before us," they should expect soon to "have crossed the Red Sea of our difficulties." We may note that although "crossing the Rubicon" would arguably be a more apt simile for the circumstances before declaring American independence than crossing the Red Sea, the biblical metaphor seems to have been more popular at that time. Even the most deist of revolutionaries such as Thomas Jefferson and Benjamin Franklin imagined the revolution as a Exodus-like deliverance from slavery, as evident from their proposals for the American Great Seal in 1776. The numerous references to the tyrannical English "Pharaoh" and his Israelite-American subjects-turned-enemies during the Revolution

13   Gad Hitchcock, *A Sermon Preached at Plymouth, December 22, 1774* (Boston, 1775), 20. Nicholas Street, *The American States Acting Over the Part of the Children of Israel in the Wilderness and Thereby Impeding their Entrance into Canaan's Rest* (Boston, 1777), 3, 9.

were brought to a dramatic climax by Timothy Dwight's epic poem *The Conquest of Canaan* (1785), dedicated to Washington, the American Moses, with the ending of the War.[14]

5. Beyond Exodus: Biblical Civic Humanism

Our close focus on the centrality and evident importance of the story of the Mosaic Exodus for the political discourse of the American Revolution may have obscured the presence of other key biblical narratives in the revolutionary discourse. As the remainder of this essay aims to demonstrate, the intense use of biblical idioms beyond Exodus reveals the depth of the commitment to present the revolutionary situation in biblical terms. These "other" biblical tropes represented anti-monarchical sentiments and the striving for freedom, just like the Exodus. However, their message to American revolutionaries was also significantly distinct. While the Exodus expressed "republican" notions of deliverance from slavery to freedom, it was not necessarily a civic-humanist narrative. Much of the revolutionary biblical language, unlike the account of the Exodus, reveals a recognizable cosmology of corruption and stern virtue, of relentless striving for power and disinterestedness. In other words, that language unveils a world of biblical civic humanism.

6. Corruption

Corruption is the negative force that propels the civic humanist creed. While early modern republicans wished to preserve the health of their polity through active and disinterested citizenship, they knew that since the time of Greece and Rome humans were too weak to preserve free societies, which depended on their citizens' and magistrates' virtue, indefinitely. The civic humanist worldview, which idealized self-sacrifice and disinterestedness and dreaded the advance of personal or sectional interests at the expense of the public good, saw "corruption" as a vicious and potent force; men could hardly be expected to withstand the

---

14   Harry S. Stout, "Rhetoric and Reality in the Early Republic: The Case of the Federalist Clergy," in Mark A. Noll ed., *Religion and American Politics: From the Colonial Period to the 1980s* (New York: Oxford University Press, 1990), 67; see also Sacvan Bercovitch, "How the Puritans Won the American Revolution," *Massachusetts Review* 17 (1976): 597-630; "From the Pennsylvania Packet," *Continental Journal*, July 18, 1776.

temptations of power-grabbing and self-aggrandizement. Corruption was thus believed to be incessantly at work to undermine virtue, hence to harm the innately frail republic.[15]

Contemporary understandings of corruption tend to denote moral perversions, often relating to greed and sexual depravity. Although such "modern" debaucheries were in no way unrelated to the early-modern civic humanist world-view, they seemed to contemporaries more like the consequences than the causes of corruption; avarice and lust were symptoms, not factors, of moral turpitude. Civic humanist corruption was fundamentally a political concept, concerned with the ability and will of men's (men indeed completely dominated that political world) to control the temptations of power: on the one hand a citizen should preserve at all costs his in-dependence (hence the classical and neo-classical belief that only economically self-sufficient yeomen were truly independent and politically autonomous), and on the other hand control the temptation to dominate others by usurping power. This worldview, which originated in the classical world and was revived and transformed in Renaissance Italy and the seventeenth- and eighteenth-century Anglophone world, shared, as historians have long noted, the assumptions of reformed Protestantism, especially its Calvinist branches. The assumed potency of sin or corruption, and the frailty of piety or virtue, constructed parallel and similar republican and reformed Protestant sensibilities, centered on corruptible human beings. Neither the reformed Protestant nor the civic humanist political man could be expected to withstand temptation, whether religious or political, and was thus corrupt, or at least corruptible, in a most fundamental sense. Those who beat the odds and prevailed were respectively deemed "saints" and "virtuous." While not all late eighteenth-century Americans held the pessimistic Calvinist belief that humanity was irrevocably corrupt, they did believe, according to the historian John Murrin, "that humankind [was] highly corruptible and that a surrender to corruption had destroyed nearly every republic before their day." Hence, Murrin concluded, the classical dread of corruption had "a genuine affinity" to orthodox Christian values.[16]

---

15 Bernard Bailyn, *The Ideological Origins of the American Revolution* (Cambridge, MA: Harvard University Press, 1967), 55-60.

16 Morgan, "The Puritan Ethic and The American Revolution"; Hatch, "The Sacred Cause of Liberty." John Murrin, "Religion and Politics in America from the First Settlements to the Civil War," in Noll, *Religion and American Politics*, 35.

As similar as the Christian and classical republican views about man and corruptibility might have been, the inhabitants of the early modern Anglophone world (indeed, Europeans in general) who tried to understand why republics had failed in the past, and how—if at all—they could be constructed to endure, drew far more directly on civic humanist sources than on Christian theology. The histories of past republics were the common sources demonstrating the ways in which corruption occurred and spread. Corruption was an inherent characteristic of the historical process, ensuring an unending flux in human events that perpetuated the recurrence of cycles of rise and decline in the lives of political entities. Free republics fell prey to the destructive forces of corruption, and were quick to disintegrate into anarchy or coalesce into tyranny once their citizens preferred to indulge their desires and yield to their vices (options that ironically became available through the riches pouring in from foreign conquests which were possible through virtuous conduct in the first place). Preoccupied with self-indulgence, corrupt citizens rapidly lost their autonomy to ambitious men who were quick to encroach on their freedom. Unfortunately, this process was true not only on the personal level, but also on larger social scales, since historical communities were dependent on their citizens' virtue, hence lack of corruption. For millennia, early modern Europeans believed the advance of individual corruption signaled the immanence of decay of virtuous government. Tyranny, or anarchy, were soon to follow.

The inimical forces of corruption that have been at work throughout history raised time and again the painful sight of virtuous republics' decline and consequent fall. There was however one grand example of this process that towered over all others in the West's historical imagination: the virtuous Roman republic, rising from rustic and small beginnings, expanding immensely and consequently transforming into an autocratic imperial principate, thus conveying the whole gamut of civic-humanist beliefs regarding political rise and fall, and the relation of that processes to corruption. Many historians, including the Roman Tacitus, the Greek Polybius and more recently the English Gibbon, had described the transformation of the Roman polity from republic to a perverse and eventually faltering empire. But how would Americans engaged in an eighteenth century revolution make a classical narrative relevant to their own experiences? Could corruption, a central building block of the civic humanistic creed, be explained and become relevant through a more accessible and intimately familiar history?[17]

Although many revolutionary-age Americans found the decline of Rome useful for understanding corruption and its working in history, most were more biblically than classically-literate, and more psychologically invested in the Bible than in the annals of Rome. Historians seem to have overlooked the significant republican way in which much of the civic humanist corruption during the years of the War of Independence (1775-1783) was rendered through remarkable representations and analyses of biblical Israel. A war-time sermon by John Murray (1742-1793) demonstrated this biblical republicanism: a characteristic analysis of the dangers of corruption, "prosperity frequently becomes a poison in disguise—the sweeter in taste, the more fatal in effect: nations, as well as individuals, are generally intoxicated by it," was followed by an Old Testament verse telling how Jeshurun, a poetic and metonymic name for Israel, indicating an uprightness now bygone, "have waxed and fat and kicked at the hand by which they were nourished." Waxing fat and kicking were, to American readers, the way in which the biblical author rendered civic corruption.[18]

Early moderns on both sides of the Atlantic commonly understood polities as "bodies politic," in which monarchs typically functioned as the head, while the other organs stood for discrete governmental branches and social classes. Eighteenth-century British opposition writers adapted this idiom to their needs, representing the commonwealth as a living organism that experienced youth, maturity and eventually decline into old age. Revolutionary Americans, who continued to use this metaphor for their own purposes, absorbed that trope into their biblical cosmology. In a sermon preached at Coventry, Connecticut, Joseph Huntington (1735-94) offered a revolutionary sermon steeped in the Bible. He aptly titled this elaborate discourse *On the Health and Happiness, or Misery and Ruin, of the Body Politic, in Similitude to that of the Natural Body* (1781). In it he asserted that the healthy body politic, like a salubrious human body being "perfect in every part, and enjoy[ing] perfect health," needed "no man, no angel, no creature" to mend it. Huntington had in mind a particular, perfect, body politic: The "ancient plan

---

17 J. G. A. Pocock, *Barbarism and Religion: The First Decline and Fall* (New York: Cambridge University Press, 2005), 3, passim.
18 J. Murray, *Nehemia, or the Struggle for Liberty Never in Vain, when Managed with Virtue and Perseverance* (1779), 11.

of civil policy, delineated for the chosen tribes of Israel," had a "divine constitution" that rendered "the most perfect form of civil government." Those "united states or tribes of Israel"—biblical Israel was commonly seen as constituting a federacy—referred to an Israelite "republicanism" to which Huntington and his contemporaries could easily relate. Huntington thus envisioned, for example, Hebrew officers, like their counterpart American magistrates, "elected by the people at large," as well as a Hebrew "general congress" appointed "with a president at their head." Nevertheless, if the Hebrew polity was a body, as perfect as it may be, like every living organism it was bound to decay. Hence, its successful constitutional arrangement prevailed only until "the days of Samuel, when the constitution was subverted" as the Hebrews requested, and got, a king. Like Rome, the Hebrew republic turned into a dynastic autocracy of unelected, and often inapt and sinful, rulers.[19]

Huntington's identification of the Hebrew republic with civic-humanist decline was common, and so was the postulate of an original virtuous era, a golden age of political perfection. Indeed, even before the war between Britain and the American confederacy had dragged on and brought with it anguish and pessimism, the Congregationalist clergyman Samuel Langdon (1723-1797), in a corruption-fixated sermon, revealingly titled *Government Corrupted by Vice* (1775), reflected on the reasons for what he perceived as the Hebrew republic's dissolution. However, to render that process as a history of decline, Langdon needed to portray a pre-lapsarian moment of political virtue, in which, in Langdon's words,

> the public good engage[d] the attention of the whole; the strictest regard [was] paid to the qualifications of those who held the offices of the state; virtue prevail[ed]; every thing [was] managed with justice, prudence, and frugality; the laws [were] founded on principles of equity rather than mere policy; and all the people [were] happy.

---

19   Antoine De Baecque, *The Body Politic: Corporeal Metaphor in Revolutionary France, 1770–1800*, trans. Charlotte Madell (Stanford, CA: Stanford University Press, 1997). For eighteenth-century biopolitical metaphors in America, see Drew McCoy, *The Elusive Republic: Political Economy in Jeffersonian America* (Chapel Hill: The University of North Carolina Press, 1996), 33. Joseph Huntington, *A Discourse Adapted to the Present Day, on the Health and Happiness, or Misery and Ruin, of the Body Politic, in Similitude to that of the Natural Body* . . . (Hartford: 1781), 8-10.

Langdon went so far as to profess that the Hebrew polity was a "perfect republic," endowed with a Godly constitution. Other patriots held similar views of the Hebrews' early virtuous beginnings: "Israel," David Jones asserted, "when first planted in the land of Canaan, were a brave, heroic and virtuous people, being firmly attached to the true worship of God." Like other past virtuous polities the Hebrews "were both formidable and invincible: when their armies went forth to battle, thousands and tens of thousands fell before them." Like others, Jones believed that the Israelites were uniquely "clothed with the majesty of virtue and true religion."[20]

Yet even so perfect a republic as the Israelite's might have been, this happy, virtuous condition could not, and would not, last. Explanations for this dramatic reversal often took on the guise of standard accounts of republican decline. The advance of vice in Israel was the fault of the increase in the "riches and glory of an empire," which in turn corrupted the Hebrew constitution, and "in time [brought] on it dissolution." And as in the anxiety-ridden histories of past republics, the Israelite commonwealth's annals proved that "if the people in general are not engaged to promote the strength and honor, wealth and happiness of a nation...all must fall to the ground." Hence, during the final period of the Hebrew republic and on the verge of its becoming a monarchy, "when vice and immorality became prevalent," the Israelites "lost their martial spirit, and were soon enslaved." Throughout the revolutionary era, the political axiom, that while "pride and luxury predominate, we cannot expect such a nation to be long happy," would not be seriously contested.[21]

Corruption was not exclusively manifested during the "republican" period of Israel's biblical history. Under the Davidic monarchy, as perhaps under every monarchy, Americans saw corruption raise its head,

---

20   Langdon, *Government Corrupted by Vice* (Boston: 1775), 12, 3-4; David Jones, *Defensive War in a Just Cause Sinless* (Philadelphia: 1775), 3-4. The Israelites were also deemed virtuous during other eras. William Gordon, for example, believed that "[t]he Jewish state flourished amazingly under the reign of Solomon, whose court was the resort of the wise and noble ... his subjects enjoyed not only plenty, but security: Judah and Israel dwelt safely, every man under his vine and under his fig tree, from Dan even to Beersheba"; "The Separation of the Jewish Tribes, after the Death of Solomon ... a Sermon, delivered on July 4th, 1777," in *The Patriot Preachers of the American Revolution*, ed. Frank Moore (New York: 1860), 161.

21   Huntington, *A Discourse*, 20; Langdon, *Government Corrupted by Vice*, 12; Jones, *Defensive War*, 4, 3.

due to the "the bad policy that prevailed under the reign of [King Solomon's] successor," Rehoboam, David's grandson. "Solomon's funeral is scarce closed, before fatal dissensions arise: The Jewish tribes separate, through the imprudence and tyranny of Rehoboam, and the empire is suddenly divided into two independent states." While corruption and decline could thus be interpreted in relation to imprudent policy, or bad personal choices made characteristically by egotistical rulers such as Rehoboam, they could not have occurred, as American public speakers seemed to agree, without the loss of republican virtue by the community as a whole.[22] Similarly, revolutionary expounders of the Bible noticed that political corruption also characterized later periods of Jewish history, for example during the encroachments of the Seleucid tyrant Antiochus Epiphanes, who applied "chicanery and flattery" in an attempt to cause the Jews "to favor and assist him in his wicked practices." Antiochus was at least partly successful, as he was able, in a direct reference to George III ("his Antitype in England") to build a "corrupt party" of "minions and vassals."[23] That tyrant's corruption was firmly answered, however, by the resurgence of the virtuous Maccabees whose rebellion would culminate in re-founded Jewish independence.

Nevertheless, it was Rome that would continue to serve as the most common and important source and reference for understanding biblical corruption. To demonstrate the remarkable extent to which contemporaries understood the Bible through the prism of Roman-like corruption, it is worth citing at length the following account in which Robert Langdon described ancient Israel in the language of Sallust. For Langdon and his readers, the Israel he described was identical to first-century B. C. Rome, a decadent republic on the verge of becoming a *principate*:

> The whole body of the [Israelite] nation, from head to foot, was full of moral and political disorders without any remaining soundness. Their religion was all mere ceremony and hypocricy, and even the laws of common justice and humanity were disregarded in their public

22   Gordon, *Separation of the Jewish Tribes*, 161-164.
23   Peter Powers, *Tyranny and Toryism Exposed, Being the Substance of Two Sermons* (Westminster, VT: 1781), 5-6.

courts. They had Counselors and Judges, but very different from those at the beginning of the common wealth.
Their Princes were rebellious against God, and the constitution of their country, and companions of thieves,
giving countenance to every artifice for seizing property
of the subjects into their own hands, and robbing the
public treasury. Every one loved gifts and followed after
rewards; they regarded the perquisites more than the
duties of their office; the general aim was at profitable
places and pensions; they were influenced in everything
by bribery; and their avarice and luxury were never satisfied, but hurried them on to all kinds of oppression and
violence.

Langdon's grim description of the Roman-like Israel concluded with
the ominous statement that "the whole body being so corrupted, there
could be no rational prospect of any great reformation in the state, but
rather its ruin."[24]

7. Biblical Corruption and Its Causes

The question contemporaries understandably asked themselves was
how such a shocking subversion could take place, since as long as
the Israelites "abode firm in this reasonable and divine constitution,
supported it, and made the best of the happy privileges contained in
it" they were "by far the happiest nation under heaven." If contemporaries could make sense of the Roman republic's decline in terms
of corruption, as Europeans had been doing for centuries, the Israelite case demanded extra effort. How could a "perfect republic" of a
chosen people decline? Were classical portrayals of corruption enough
to explain the dissolution of the Hebrew republic? They were not. To
explain the inexplicable fall of a perfect republic, American commentators appealed to the realm of Godly republicanism, an analysis of
politics in which virtue was not restricted to its civic-humanist origins
but was conceived also in theological terms. The derailment of a Godly

---

24   Langdon, *Government Corrupted by Vice*, 13.

constitution was linked to ungodly conduct.[25]

Joseph Huntington asserted, for example, that as long as "true religion and good moral principles prevail and rule, that nation is in health"; once "religion dies away," however, "morality decays, infidelity, vice and iniquity prevails among the people in general." Such theological causality had evidently little bearing on the classical pagan republics (on the contrary: Christians had to confront the opposite accusation, most recently made by Edward Gibbon, that Rome fell *because* of the spread of Christianity). Still, this reasoning struck a chord in the anxious hearts of American Protestants, especially Calvinists conditioned by the tradition of the Jeremiad. The new element in this civic-humanist account, which Huntington was in no sense the only one to adopt, was the crucial place of pious religiosity in a virtuous republic. With religion waning, these explanations pointed out, a Hebraic (or Christian) republic could not endure.[26]

So, unlike in traditional historical explanations that centered on the destructive work of the secular fury of *fortuna* to explain the ever-changing fates of republics, American revolutionary commentators believed that the transformation of the Jewish republic occurred "not only as the natural effect of vice," as in the case of the classical republics, "but a righteous judgment of heaven, especially upon a nation which has been favor'd with the blessing of religion and liberty, and is guilty of undervaluing them, and eagerly going into the gratification of every lust." Religiosity (or the lack thereof) and liberty, piety and sin, deeply corresponded with virtue and corruption. If Roman decline was conventionally told as a story of secular rise and fall, a history of civic virtue corrupted, in the case of ancient Israel it was God "in righteous judgment" that left the biblical Hebrews "to run into all this excess of vice to their own destruction, because they had forsaken him, and were guilty of willful inattention to the most essential parts of that religion which had been given them by a well attested Revelation from heaven." With their past piety and religiosity gone, in vain the Jewish nation "hoped for a change of men and measures and better times." "When the spirit of religion was gone" classical-style corruption would occur: "the infection

---

25 Huntington, *A Discourse*, 10.
26 Huntington, *A Discourse*, 18; Sacvan Bercovitch, *The American Jeremiad* (Madison: The University of Wisconsin Press, 1978); Philip S. Hicks, *Neoclassical History and English Culture: From Clarendon to Hume* (New York: Macmillan, 1996).

of vice was become universal. The whole body being so corrupted, there could be no rational prospect of any great reformation in the state, but rather of its ruin." Israel, a chosen nation that established a perfect republic lasting from Moses to Samuel, succumbed to corruption. If Israel and Rome manifested variations in the causes of such corruption, its results were painfully similar.[27]

8. Biblical Virtue

We have seen how American commentators could read classical corruption into biblical narratives and figures, aligning the Old Testament with their cause by familiarizing audiences with an ideology that drove their revolution. This was possible, however, only because a more general Whig interpretive mode prevailed, namely one that understood the larger trajectory of the Old Testament as a narrative of resistance to tyranny. The New York author "Philalethes" thus characteristically concluded, just days before the outbreak of hostilities in Lexington and Concord, that "passive obedience and non resistance" was "contrary to the word of God," a stance he proved by citing a string of Old Testament anecdotes; the Bible persuaded Philalethes that "oppression, tyranny, and unrighteous acts of government, are odious to the supreme Being." The Patriots' God emerged from such polemics as a republican deity, a God that "from the beginning...had a regard for liberty, and that tyrants, and oppressors, have been the objects of his abhorrence." This divinely-based republicanism manifested itself in history as "[o]ppression and tyranny began to work in early ages...and spread abroad its baneful influence, and pernicious effects among men." Although "injustice, tyranny, and oppression" often prevailed, the history of the Israelites indisputably demonstrated God's "favour of liberty, and frowning on tyrants; and it shews how much he regards the rights of his people, and in how exemplary a manner, hard hearted tyrants, and merciless oppressors, sometimes feel his vengeance." The Bible could thus provide readers with a store of justified rebellions against despotic domination and political repression. A "Moderate Whig" accordingly pointed out in a tract dedicated to George Washington that "the lawfulness of taking up arms to oppose all tyranny, oppression, and those who abase and

---

27   Langdon, *Government Corrupted by Vice*, 12-14.

misuse their authority" was obvious from an examination of the history of numerous despotic biblical rulers, and went on to enumerate biblical tyrants from Rehoboam to Sennacherib against whom the Israelites demonstrated such resistance.[28]

The common Whig view of liberty as a positive but fragile and ever-threatened political element, together with a traditional and common cyclical understanding of history, facilitated readings of the Bible that underscored the repetitive sequences of the Israelites' oppression by their enemies, followed by successful, if temporary resistance to tyranny. The same biblical narratives that could demonstrate classical corruption could also provide biblical instances of the polar opposite of civic decadence, namely republican public virtue. As we shall now see, the figure of the Israelite Judge Gideon presented Americans with an opportunity to merge Israel and Rome in a striking example of biblical republicanism.[29]

9. The Jewish Cincinnatus

Gideon, whom the Bible also identifies as Jerubbaal, was the fifth Judge of the Israelites, who saved his people from their enemies the Midianites and the Amalekites. Victorious on the battlefield, Gideon was renowned for his military leadership, which in itself would suffice for revolutionary Americans to discuss and mobilize a biblical figure in republican terms. However, Gideon's character was multifaceted, and was richer than mere warriors such as his preceding Judges Barak and Ehud. Beyond Gideon's military prowess, his aversion to power, epitomized in his refusal to become king, made this Israelite Judge a perfect republican model for revolutionary Americans.

Only in the months preceding independence, when the movement for severing the ties with the British Empire gained momentum, would a starkly negative discourse emerge on the institution of monarchy. It was only fitting that the man perhaps most responsible for the anti-

---

28   Philalethes, *New York Journal*, April 6, 1775. Hitchcock, *A Sermon*, 20. For an Old-Testament based defense of monarchy see "To the People of Pennsylvania," *The Virginia Gazette* (Dixon and Hunter), March 4, 1776, 1-2. A Moderate Whig [Stephen Case?], *Defensive Arms Vindicated, and the Lawfulness of the American War Made Manifest* (1783), 7.

29   For the Whig Interpretation of history in the American context see Trevor H. Colbourne, *The Lamp of Experience: Whig History and the Intellectual Origins of the American Revolution* (Indianapolis: Liberty Fund, 1998).

monarchical sentiment in America, Thomas Paine, would introduce Gideon's example into the American discourse through his epoch-making tract. The significance of *Common Sense* for understanding the shift to anti-monarchical sentiment in early 1776 is little-disputed among historians, and continues as a fruitful source for fresh insights into the political imagination of the era. For instance, we have learned just recently about the importance of the Hebraic republican ingredient in Paine's reasoning.[30] Surprising as it may seem, elements of that intensely examined tract have yet to be noted and contextualized: such is the significance of the Israelite Judge Gideon's appearance in that most important of revolutionary pamphlets, as well as his meaning in the American republican vocabulary more generally.

After the Israelites were hard pressed by the Midianites, the Book of Judges tells of God's choosing the young Gideon, a seemingly unremarkable man from a marginal family, to lead his people. The Bible tells of Gideon's insecurity and skepticism, and his initially reluctance to assume the leadership of his people. Only after God performed repeated miracles was he able to persuade Gideon to undertake the task. Gideon went on to destroy the pagan altars and rally the Israelites to fight their enemies. With a miniscule band of 300 warriors (perhaps reminding Americans of another band of 300 warriors, the admired Spartans led by King Leonidas to repel the Persians in Thermopylae) Gideon defeated Israel's enemies. Thereupon the Israelites appealed to the Judge in a dramatic gesture to become their king and establish a dynastic monarchy. Gideon refused, and maintained his judgeship until his death in old age.

Algernon Sidney, the seventeenth century English republican martyr, is best remembered for his magisterial and rambling *Discourses Concerning Government* (posthumously, 1698). Americans, in the words of Caroline Robbins, a leading historian of English politics of opposition, made a "textbook of revolution" out of this work; Perhaps Sidney's mention of Gideon caught Paine's attention. Sidney briefly acknowledged that "Gideon was indeed much pressed by the Israelites to be their king ... [but they] desisted when [the] offer [was] refused." A century later, across the Atlantic, Thomas Paine further developed this theme in *Common Sense*. Interpreting the Biblical story of Gideon's rejection of dynastic monarchy within the conceptual world of civic-humanism,

---

30   Perl-Rosenthal, *The Divine Rights of Republics*.

Paine pointed out that the Israelites, so elated with their rescue by Gideon's small army, "proposed making him a king, saying, Rule thou over us, thou and thy son and thy son's son." Paine identified this as the most dangerous moment, when the corrupting lust for political power, "temptation in its fullest extent," surfaced. Gideon, however, "in the piety of his soul," could not accept such an offer. Paine then went on to cite the Judge's reply in the words of the Bible: "I will not rule over you, neither shall my son rule over you, THE LORD SHALL RULE OVER YOU." "Words," Paine concluded, "need not be more explicit."[31]

As Paine noticed and other American revolutionary exegetes realized, Gideon performed what could be constructed as the ultimate republican deed of disinterested political action. Consequently, revolutionary writers would interpret the Israelite Judge's conduct as equivalent to that of one of the most of commendable heroes of the Roman republic, Lucius Quinctius Cincinnatus. Cincinnatus (519-438 B.C.) was a rather obscure figure from the early history of Rome about whom we know mostly from Livy's writings. The retired senator was known for the episode that followed his being called from working his field to save Rome: Cincinnatus returned his dictatorial powers to the Senate shortly after winning a battlefield victory, to return to his oxen and plow. In the early modern pantheon of civic humanist heroes, Cincinnatus would become the embodiment of republican ideals in America.[32]

John Murray in *Jerubbaal* (1784), a thanksgiving sermon preached with the ending of the war, articulated the Cincinnatian trope in a remarkable and telling fashion. Murray's sermon took Gideon's (Jerubbaal's) typological relevance to revolutionary America as its subject. However, the Patriot minister's civic humanistic interpretation of Gideon not only demonstrates the bearing of the Israelite Judge on the American situation; it also exemplifies how the worlds of the Bible and classical republicanism, hence of the American Revolution, could be conflated into an amalgam of a novel biblical republicanism.

Murray emphasized Gideon's aversion to power and his negative response to "the ambition which would prompt some men to court so

---

31 Algernon Sidney, *Discourses on Government*, 3 vols. (New York, 1805), 3: 92; Thomas Paine, *Common Sense* (Mineola, NY: Dover Publications, 1997), 10.

32 Garry Wills, Cincinnatus: *George Washington and the Enlightenment* (Garden City, N.Y.: Doubleday, 1984); Eran Shalev, *Rome Reborn on Western Shores: Historical Imagination and the Creation of the American Republic* (Charlottesville: University of Virginia Press, 2009), 217-240.

high an honor—or to grasp the nomination to office." Indeed, when first approached by God's angel as a young man and told about God's selecting him to lead his people, "the judge-elect," Murray pointed out,

> modestly declines the appointment—remonstrates the smallness of his tribe—the obscurity of his family—and his own inferiority in it—represents himself as the last person, of the last family, of the last tribe, from which a commander in Israel should be expected—and persists in his doubts.

To revolutionary readers such as Murray the young Gideon was not manifesting timidity or weakness, a plausible interpretation of the biblical text. Rather, Gideon was seen as acting the virtuous role of self-effacement, of avoiding the slightest appearance of the pursuit of power for its own sake, or of personal gratification and ambition. Contemporary classical republicans, Murray's Gideon included, would accept political power only to serve the common good, and no less importantly, they would vigorously emphasize that they assume that power reluctantly.[33]

In light of Murray's interpretation of Gideon's behavior, it is striking to recall George Washington's statement to the Continental Congress on his appointment as the commander of the Continental Army, eight years earlier: "Tho' I am truly sensible of the high Honour done me, in this Appointment, yet I feel great distress, from a consciousness that my abilities and military experience may not be equal to the extensive and important Trust."[34] The Israelite Judges reluctance to lead his people ("Oh my Lord, wherewith shall I save Israel? Behold, my family is poor in Manasseh, and I am the least in my father's house") and the Virginian planter's ("my abilities and military experience may not be equal to the...Trust") seemed to revolutionary-era Americans to have sprung from the same republican conceptual world.

Sure enough, Murray went on to construct George Washington, the

---

33   John Murray, *Jerubbaal, or Tyranny's Grove Destroyed, and the Altar of Liberty Finished. A Discourse on America's Duty and Danger*...(Newburyport, Mass: 1783), 13.

34   George Washington, June 16, 1775, in: *http://www.loc.gov/teachers/classroommaterials/ presentationsandactivities/presentations/timeline/amrev/contarmy/accepts.html* (accessed October 28, 2010).

master of classical politics of virtue, as a latter-day Gideon. The Israelite Judge valiantly won a war, saved his people and was consequently, in Murray's words, "crowned with the blessings of his rescued country— and loaded with laurels."[35] Students of republics knew that it was at that dangerous moment of victory that military leaders throughout history capitalized on their battlefield successes to consolidate and perpetuate their personal power. At that critical moment the Children of Israel invited Gideon "to ascend a throne." Not only were the Israelites "ready to receive him as Monarch in Israel," they also implored Gideon "to settle the crown upon his issue-male, as their hereditary property in lineal succession." Like the Romans who awarded Julius Caesar, their republic's destroyer, a dictatorship for life, the Israelites "consent tamely to surrender to their General, those precious liberties with which heaven had made them free." It is significant that Murray presented Gideon at this point not as a judge but as a general, a military chieftain, thus emphasizing that he could now apply his power over the polity for his personal gratification. Gideon's act was opposed to that of another chieftain, Julius Caesar, who was remembered for insincerely rejecting the diadem offered to him—thrice!—to appear as a sincere republican before the Roman crowds, only to become the *de facto* monarch of the republic he had ruined. Gideon's "patriotic greatness of soul" on the other hand obliged him to "positively refuse the unadvised present" of a king's throne. Gideon thus declined perpetual sovereignty and refused "rewards which none ever did better deserve." Not only did he "accept no pay for his laborious services" he did not even accept "any pension to himself or family."[36]

Yet again the American author must have been alluding to George Washington, who famously asserted on becoming the Continental Army's commander: "As to pay, Sir, I beg leave to assure the Congress, that, as no pecuniary consideration could have tempted me to have accepted this arduous employment, at the expence of my domestic ease and happiness, I do not wish to make any proffit from it." The classical disinterestedness of both the Israelite Judge and the American leader culminated in Murray's ultimate description of Gideon as "greatly retir[ing] to his farm … while he withdraws from the command." The

---

35   Laurels themselves are however of classical and pagan, not biblical, origin.
36   Murray, *Jerubbaal*, 21.

archetypal trope that he appealed to was obvious: Gideon was "the Jewish Cincinnatus."[37]

This assimilation of the Roman dictator Cincinnatus, who left his field to assume absolute power in order to save Rome from its enemies only to retire victorious days later and return to his oxen and plow, to an Israelite Judge is remarkable. This parallel reading, which aligned two important figures in the remote worlds of the Bible and classical antiquity, was not accidental or fleeting but a theme that Murray thoroughly explored. Even the vocabulary of classical republicanism was applied to describe Gideon, who was repeatedly referred to as "Israel's Dictator," a term not associated in the early Roman republic with tyranny but with absolute powers limited in time and granted to a military leader to confront severe emergencies. Gideon's self-effacement, his modesty, his military prowess as well as his disinterestedness, all fed into the Israelite's Cincinnatian image. However, Murray's careful representation of Gideon as a Cincinnatus was more than an exercise in historical comparison; rather, it was meant to link the most famous American Cincinnatus, the now retired general George Washington, with the biblical Jerubbaal.[38]

"We," Murray exclaimed, "were blessed with a Gideon too." "Like Gideon," George Washington was "singularly qualified" for his mission. Further, "the American Gideon, with scarce that number of men, equally destitute of every military advantage," was able to beat a superior enemy; and "Like Israel's Dictator, the American Gideon rose—like him he conquered—and like him too, he retires." George Washington, already widely renowned among Americans as a retired Cincinnatus who, after winning the War returned his commission to Congress to withdraw to his Mt. Vernon farm, was now part of a virtuous, self-effacing, power-averse triangle of a classical Roman, a biblical Israelite and an American leader. The three seemed in fact inseparable: "[a]s Jerubbaal, when his work is done, returned to his native city," Murray asked his compatriots to "behold the AMERICAN CINCINNATUS greatly retiring to his beloved privacy!" After winning the war speculation indeed ran high about whether Washington could, or would indeed become king; upon hearing

---

37 George Washington, June 16, 1775, *op. cit.* Perhaps Murray too was addressing the Continental Army's soldiers' disgruntlement regarding the lack of pay after the long hardships of war. Murray, Ibid.

38 Murray, *Jerubbaal*, 11, 43.

about the American general's retirement George III was said to say that if that was true Washington would be "the greatest man in the world." While Washington of course indeed willingly retired, Murray assured his audience that even if Americans had "copied the weakness of Israel"— and one may add, the weakness of the Romans—"and rashly invited him to a throne," Washington's "past conduct affords unequivocal proof, that the offer would have met the deserved repulse." Murray fantasized Washington's answer to so vile an offer in Cincinnatian fashion and Gideonic language: *"I will not rule over you;—neither shall my son rule over you:—the Lord alone shall be king in* AMERICA."[39]

10. Conclusion

This chapter has examined significant political categories and tropes from the Old Testament that Patriots mobilized to interpret and use as republican texts during the American Revolution. Such uses in no sense ceased after the War of Independence. Biblical republicanism remained a central interpretive mode for Americans well into the nineteenth century, as even occasional students of Antebellum America realize. The republican Bible was a dynamic and responsive text, which Americans were able continuously to adapt to their changing situations for decades. While episodes such as Gideon's rejection of monarchy became less relevant after the establishment and solidification of the American republic, the Cincinnatian interpretation of Jerubbaal did not lose its appeal. Political commentators continued to portray Gideon during the nineteenth century in the most Cincinnatian form of representations, as a modest, self-effacing "perfect able young farmer, [who] was called to lead the army of Israel, while he was threshing wheat." Americans in the early decades of the nineteenth century kept on thanking both the biblical Gideon and their own versions for not setting "a yoke of iron" on the Israelites' (and Americans') "tame and submissive necks," although they could easily have done so by becoming monarchs. Rather, those Gideons respectively said to the people of Israel, the Old and the New, "I will not rule over you, neither shall my son rule over you." The ties binding

---

39   Murray, *Jerubbaal*, 38-39, 47. George III quoted in William M. S. Rasmussen, Robert S. Tilton, *George Washington, The Man Behind the Myths* (Charlottesville: The University of Virginia Press, 1999), 155.

Jerusalem and America, or rather the construction of Americans as a Chosen People, were intensified and consolidated through the ideology forged in the tyranny hating, duty-bound Roman republic.[40]

Biblical republicanism adds a heretofore overlooked strand of biblico-republican exegesis to the growing scholarship of Hebraic republicanism, an endeavor still conceived mostly in Eurocentric terms. This American biblical republicanism was part of a wider and dynamic contemporary political Hebraism, which was especially appealing to an American nation that would conceive itself as a "second Israel." While such biblical republicanism, namely the interpretation of Old-Testament narratives and protagonists through a civic-humanist reading, did not render novel solutions to contemporary problems, it greatly expanded American patriots' ability to communicate, discourse and express their political beliefs. It also brought scriptural authority, and approval, hence coherence and legitimacy, to bear on their late eighteenth century political predicaments.[41]

---

40   "The Ingratitude of the Hebrew Republic toward the Family of Gideon," *Jenk's Portland Gazette*, November 19, 1804; see also Junius, "For the Washington Whig," *The Washington Whig*, September 20, 1828.

41   For the articulation of notions of America as a Second Israel see Eran Shalev, "'Written in the Style of Antiquity': Pseudo-Biblicism and the Early American Republic, 1770-1830," *Church History* 79:4 (2010): 800-826. My understanding of "language" is indebted to John Pocock's definition and usage of that term. For a theoretical exposition of political languages see "Introduction: The State of the Art," in J. G. A. Pocock, *Virtue, Commerce and History* (Cambridge: Cambridge University Press, 1985), 1-36; and Pocock, *Politics, Language and Time: Essays on Political Thought and History* (Chicago: University of Chicago Press, 1989).

Toleration, Liberty, and Rights:
or, What Hobbes Knew, Others Feared, and Hohfeld Figured Out

GORDON SCHOCHET

Of the many books I read in 1959 as a second-year graduate student, two in particular have remained with and continue to motivate if not haunt me: Howard Warrender's *The Political Philosophy of Hobbes: His Theory of Obligation* (1957),[1] and Wesley N. Hohfeld's *Fundamental Legal Conceptions as Applied in Judicial Reasoning* (1919 and 1946).[2] Neither of them is well-known today, but Hohfeld, who had an enduring impact on thinking about rights and duties, especially among lawyers, even though his name may have been forgotten, is making something of a comeback.[3]

Warrender, as the title suggests, purported to be about Hobbes' treatment of what was once regarded as the central problem in political philosophy, why people should—or are obliged to—obey political authority. Indeed, when Warrender wrote, the problem of political obligation was treated as the question around which all else in Hobbes could be gathered. Few were satisfied with Hobbes' apparent discussion of the subject, but we were at least taught to be fully persuaded that Hobbes

---

1   Howard Warrender, *The Political Philosophy of Hobbes: His Theory of Obligation* (Oxford: Oxford University Press, 1957).

2   Wesley N. Hohfeld, *Fundamental Legal Conceptions as Applied in Judicial Reasoning*, ed. and introduction by Walter Wheeler Cook (New Haven: Yale University Press, 1919, reprinted with a new Forward by Arthur L. Corbin, 1964). This Work was a reprinting with editorial introductions of two articles of the same title from the *Yale Law Journal* 23 (1913) and 26 (1917). A new edition was published in 2001 with an introduction by Nigel E. Simmonds and edited by David Campbell and Philip Thomas (Burlington, VT: Ashgate, 2001).

3   The most important and influential recent jurisprudential reliance on Hohfeld is H.L.A. Hart, "Bentham on Legal Rights," in *Oxford Essays on Jurisprudence*, 2nd series., ed. A.W.B. Simpson (Oxford: Oxford University Press, 1973), 171-201, reprinted as "Legal Rights" in his *Essays on Bentham, Jurisprudence, and Political Theory* (Oxford: Oxford University Press, 1982), 162-193. For an extensive discussion of Hohfeld, see Hamish Ross, "Hohfeld and the Analysis of Rights," in *Introduction to Jurisprudence and Legal Theory: Commentary and Materials*, ed. James Penner, et al. (London: Butterworths, 2002), 595-648. See also Ronan Perry, "Correlativity," *Law and Philosophy* 28 (2009): 537-584, for a survey of much of the literature on Hohfeld and for a valuable bibliographic guide to the recently renewed interest.

was *about*—as we put it then—political obligation, and the interpreta-tive grail after which we quested was a definitive reading of *Leviathan* (which was pretty much all the Hobbes we read, for the achievement of a properly *historicized* history of political thought, while burgeoning, was some years in the future).

Political philosophy was still closely allied with ethical theory; ty-pology rather than history was all the rage in those days; and Hobbes' theory constituted perhaps the archetypical example of what was called the "instrumental- [or sometimes 'mechanistic-'] force" theory of obli-gation.[4] We were not so much interested in what Hobbes himself was up to as we were in what could be made of his arguments. The problem was that by basing the presumptively *moral* duty to obey an *immoral* force, Hobbes had violated one of the cardinal principles of political philoso-phy: he *presumed* and did not *derive* the validity of authority and of the duty to obey it, thereby extracting the *ought* of obligation from the *is* of existent authority. There was simply no room for the insertion of mo-rality into that self-interested, force-based account of politics. And yet there *had to be* obligation. Where could it possibly have come from? (The would-be pundit wag—likely to be labeled a smart-ass today—who had the audacity to respond that this puzzle suggested either that obligation was not a problem addressed by all political philosophers or that politi-cal—and, hence, legal as well as perhaps other social—duties were not rooted in ethics was quickly silenced.)

Warrender stepped into this breach and wrote a book that, as it turned out, was not about Hobbes at all but, brilliantly and perversely, about the ethical natural law and about Kant (who was never men-tioned), from whose perspective Warrender had read Hobbes.[5] In the

---

4   See, for instance, T. D. Weldon, *States and Morals: A Study in Political Conflicts* (London: J. Murray, 1962), and E.F. Carritt, *Ethical and Political Thinking* (Oxford: Oxford University Press, 1947), for accounts of theories of political obligation from radically different perspectives—Weldon was on his way to becoming the somewhat logical positivist author of *The Vocabulary of Politics*, and Carritt was one of the last of the intuitionist-idealists—that employed the same general framework. While Hobbes on obligation often merited a mention, Warrender's was the first extensive treatment of the subject.

5   The general contours of Warrender's reading of Hobbes had been advanced some years earlier, as Warrender fully acknowledged, in much briefer compass by A.E. Taylor in "The Ethical Doctrine of Hobbes," *Philosophy* 13 (1938): 406-424, reprinted in *Hobbes Studies*, ed. Keith C. Brown (Cambridge, MA: Harvard University Press, 1965), 35-55. The "Taylor Thesis," as it came to be called, and of which Warrender's interpretation was an extended instance, and was examined in that volume. See also some of the papers reprinted in *Hobbes' Leviathan: Interpretation and Criticism*, ed. Bernard A. Baumrin (Belmont, CA: Wadsworth, 1969), and *Hobbes and Rousseau:*

process, however, Warrender provided a general account of political obligation that went beyond anything in the obligation literature. Here, from an analytic perspective, was a theory worthy of taking its place in the company of J.L. Austin's *How to Do Things with Words* (1962) and H.L.A. Hart's *Concept of Law* (1960).[6] Distinguishing among the *grounds* (or bases) of political obligation, the *conditions* under which such obligations bind, and the *reasons* there are political obligations in the first place—as well as our reasons for fulfilling them—Warrender offered to restructure subsequent discussion of the subject. Although that was not his stated intention, his presentation of Hobbes, in many respects, was a case-study in the application of his conception of political obligation. But his focus on Hobbes, and even his novel interpretation, deprived him of the attention to which he was entitled: Warrender had the misfortune to publish his book just as contextualism was beginning to dominate the history of political thought, especially the study of seventeenth-century England,[7] and conceptual and "historical" were being separated as the field divided itself into political theory or philosophy and the history of political thought.[8]

In terms of Hobbes scholarship, perhaps Warrender's greatest achievement was to lay bare and then to clarify the structure of the Hobbesian state of nature, to show both why it was the calamitous condition depicted by Hobbes and therefore could not work and what

---

A Collection of Critical Essays, ed. Maurice Cranston and Richard Peters (Garden City, NY: Anchor Books, 1972).

6   J.L. Austin, *How to Do Things with Words* (Oxford: Oxford University Press, 1962), and H.L.A. Hart, *The Concept of Law* (Oxford: Oxford University Press, 1960; 2nd ed. with new Postscript, 1994).

7   See *Political Philosophy of Hobbes*, 124, for Warrender's dismissive indifference toward history. Explaining his interpretation, Warrender wrote that he arrived at "the thesis of this book. . . on the strength of reading the *Leviathan* a number of times until its argument assumed some coherence." He concluded, "I have attempted to construct an interpretation of Hobbes' theory of obligation out of his various writings, and have been concerned entirely with his statements and their inner coherence. No explanation is offered, therefore, of the place of this doctrine in the history of political thought. . . . I have been less concerned with the problem of how Hobbes' theory originated or how it is to be explained than with the prior question of what his theory is." Preface. vii and viii-ix.

8   The analytic, conceptual approach to political obligation as part of a general theory that characterized Warrender's analysis was beginning to fall out of academic fashion as well; that mode of analysis was ultimately superceded by more substantive examinations of specific obligations and questions about the relationships of broad categories of people—women, racial minorities, and the economically disadvantaged—to the political order. The neglect of Warrender and other works published about the same time—and earlier—can also be ascribed at least in part to the impact of computer-based research. By the time *The Political Philosophy of Hobbes* showed up in retrospective databases, the field had moved on.

was required to remedy its deficiencies. Warrender provided a compelling and comprehensive interpretation of the differences Hobbes drew between obligations *in foro interno* and *in foro externo*,[9] explaining that in the absence of "sufficient security," the obligations of the law of nature were not to be acted on (*in foro externo*) but nonetheless continued to bind in conscious and intention (*in foro interno*).[10] I will return to this important distinction, but first, an account of Hohfeld.

Hohfeld is best known for having established the correlative relationship between rights and duties. The starting point of this analysis was a legal contract, most fundamentally but not exclusively of exchange, in which Spenser recognizes Katherine's *right* to something—an identifiable object (possession) or an ability to act in a particular way—and thereby acquires the *duty* to provide the object, not to interfere with Katherine's enjoyment or use of it, and/or to do what is necessary to enable the actions in which Katherine has a right to engage. Hohfeld did not claim to have invented or even to have discovered what has come to be known as the "correlativity" thesis[11] with which his name is associated; quite the contrary, for he provided rich details about the uses of correlativity in cases and earlier texts in jurisprudence.[12] His interest

---

9   Warrender, *Political Philosophy of Hobbes*, 52-79, passim.
10   In Hobbes' formulation in *Leviathan: or The matter, Forme, & Power of a Common-Wealth Ecclesiasticall and Civill* (1651), ch. 15, text from the edition by Richard Tuck (Cambridge: Cambridge University Press, 1991), 110: "The Lawes of Nature oblige *in foro interno*; that is to say, they bind to a desire they should take place: but *in foro externo*; that is, to the putting them in act, not always. For he that should be modest, and tractable, and perform all he promises, in such time, and place, where no man els should do so, should but make himself a prey to others, and procure his own certain ruine, contrary to the ground of all Lawes of Nature, which tend to Natures preservation. And again, he that having sufficient Security, that others shall observe the same Lawes towards him, observes them not himselfe, seeketh not Peace, but War; & consequently the destruction of his Nature by Violence."
11   For a comprehensive discussion of correlativity that remains helpful, see David Lyons, "The Correlativity of Rights and Duties," *Nous* 4 (1970): 45-55. Hohfeld set forth eight dyadic relationships, not just that between rights and duties; his argument was far more complex than this summary suggests, but it is only the simple and relatively straightforward rights-duties correlation that is relevant here.
12   See *Fundamental Legal Conceptions*, 35-50, passim. The correlativity of rights and duties was appreciated by Hugo Grotius (otherwise, not part of this analysis) who spoke of a "perfect right" as one in accord with which (citing Aristotle, *Nicomachean Ethics*, V, 5) "I have the Right to demand Restitution of my Goods, which are in the Possession of another," implying a corresponding and presumably enforceable duty of the holder of the goods to return them, which, Grotius was quick to point out, is a matter of justice, not contract: "it is not by vertue of any *Contract*, and yet it is the Justice in question that gives me such a Right." *The Rights of War and Peace*, ed. Richard Tuck, from the edition by Jean Barbeyrac, trans. John Morrice (1738), I, 1, §8 (Indianapolis: Liberty Fund, 2005), 3 vols., I, 142. More ambiguously, an earlier note to the text, not by Grotius, called "that

seems to have been not merely to demonstrate the long-standing recognition of correlativity, almost as if he were codifying the notion, but
to suggest that the discussions in the writings of his predecessors were
often confused and contradictory.

Beyond that clarification, the novelty of Hohfeld's position as he
himself appears to have understood it was the establishment of the
distinction between rights and privileges, which his juridical forebears
apparently missed. A right as he conceived it appears to have been one's
strong entitlement to do or receive something; it was always matched by
someone else's duty (to provide or refrain from interfering) and enjoyed
legal protections. A privilege, by contrast, was either an exemption from
regulations or restrictions or a conferred ability to act or possess that
was specifically granted, a distinction that will be important later in this
analysis.

Hohfeld's analysis of the rights-duty correlation is rooted in the
law and is especially pertinent to contract law, for it is in the reciprocity of agreements of exchanges that characterize contracts that
he and his predecessors found what would today be characterized as
the paradigm instance of correlativity. A contract in many respects
is a formal and structured form of promise. In the least complicated
kind of agreement, Spenser agrees to or promises Katherine that he
will do something or deliverer some goods or benefits that she wants;
Spenser is thereby obliged or *duty-bound* to act or deliver as promised,
and Katherine also thereby acquires a *right* to Spenser's behaving as
promised. Prior to the agreement, Katherine might have *desired* that
Spenser act in the specified way and may even have thought, from
the perspectives of "justice," "morality," or convention, that Spenser
should have done what she wished, but in strictly legal terms, she was
not fully entitled to Spenser's actions prior to his actual agreement.
By promising or contracting, Spenser imposed a duty on himself, and
because he made the promise to or contracted with Katherine, she
acquired a right to his fulfillment of that duty. Had Spenser not made
the promise, Katherine would have had no right.[13]

---

which we may assert by Force" a "perfect right" (ibid., §4, n. 21, vol. I, 138) for which there is no
readily apparent corresponding duty. What the two notions have in common is that they conceive
of rights, at least "perfect rights," as irreducible and unassailable *entitlements*, an understanding
to which I shall return.

13 My thinking about these matters reflects the strong influence of H.L.A. Hart, especially his "Are

In this simplistic instance, the duty is parent to the right—no-duty, no right—which, in a general sort of way is how promising and contracting actually work. Had Katherine offered Spenser some compensation or other return for his actions, then she would have had that contractual duty and he the corresponding right; but he would have been bound to do whatever he had agreed to be compensated for, and she would have a right to that performance.

Most contracts, in fact, are about that kind of exchange, with at least paired rights and duties: Spenser's contractual duty to Katherine to act in a specified way gives rise to Katherine's right to Spencer's acting *and* to Katherine's duty to Spenser to act herself in the agreed-upon way in exchange for his acting; Spenser's right to Katherine's reciprocating action is as strong as her right to his performance. What makes the reciprocal exchange-agreement more interesting than the simple promise to act is the shift in perspective from Spenser's duty to Katherine to his right to her corresponding performance. And in that respect, the correlativity thesis goes considerably beyond the law and reveals much about the notion of rights in general.

As a way of turning to that subject that will take us back to Hobbes, let me further complicate this picture. Let us suppose that there is no formal contract or overt agreement between Spenser and Katherine, but that Katherine nonetheless believes that she has a right (or *rights*)—is entitled—to certain statuses, benefits, possessions, and even "liberties"; Spenser, in consequence, is seen by her as a member of a class of persons who have a duty—are obliged—to assist her (by acting in particular ways) in achieving and protecting them and/or not to interfere with her exercise and enjoyment. Without a set of stipulated and corresponding responsibilities and legitimate expectations, and in the absence of the legal mechanisms that enforce contracts, what are the statuses of Katherine's right(s) and her beliefs about it (them)?

Let me illustrate all this with a pertinent and familiar but contentious example from contemporary United States jurisprudence. The Supreme Court held in the well-known, landmark case of *Roe v. Wade* (410 U.S. 113 [1973]) that there is a constitutionally-protected right to abortion in

There any Natural Rights?" *Philosophical Review* 64 (1955): 175-191, and "Legal Rights," and visibly lurking behind them is Austin, *How to Do Things with Words*.

the first trimester of a pregnancy.[14] That "right" has been circumscribed by subsequent decisions, and some fear that it will be removed by a decision that overrules *Roe*. Should that happen—should "abortion *rights*" lose their *legal* status—many people will continue to assert that those rights continue to exist. Such claims could not be about legal rights but about, let us call them, moral and/or political rights, the proponents of which, *vis-à-vis* the law, believe should receive legal protection, just as they argued in the period before the *Roe* decision. And, in fact, people will act *against the law* in furtherance of that right, as they did before 1973, following the examples of Martin Luther King, Jr., the civil rights protestors of the 60s and 70s, and even Antigone, opposing the *might* of the state with the *rightness*—moral correctness—of their actions[15] and often invoking the protective doctrine of civil disobedience. Structurally, such a claim amounts to the following:

1. There is a "higher," moral law or order having to do with justice and the entitlements of people that transcends the positive law of the state, and all human actions should be based on and in accord with justice.

2. We have a right to do this thing even though it is not legally recognized but should be because it is derived from that "higher" standard of justice.

3. There is a corresponding duty to permit our actions or to assist us; and despite the fact that this duty is also not recognized, in consequence of the recognition of the right, it should be.

4. We will continue to engage in these "illegal" actions because they are just and right—and, it might be repeated, all of us are obliged to do the right and just.

5. A possible but not necessary further assertion could claim that we are also acting in protest against injustice as a means of calling its existence to the attention of both our governing officials and our fellow citizens in order to motivate them to change.

---

14   An equally pertinent example is so-called "assisted suicide," which has never been generally legal in the United States but which has supporters who act in accord with what they regard as a right.

15   Just to clarify and to avoid confusion, *rightness* and its root word *right*, both meaning correct or proper, close in denotation to the notion of the *good*, and derived from the German *richtig*, have nothing to do with *right* and *rights*, the concepts explored in this essay, meaning entitlement, and presumably derived from the German *Recht* and possibly the Latin *rex/regina* and *regulare*.

It should now be clear that a right not matched by a corresponding duty and, therefore, to the extent that it requires support and/or
forbearance cannot be exercised, is ineffectual. Is it nonetheless *real*?
Or is it a "mere" assertion of a claim that its supporters hope will be a
successfully persuasive urging that the putative right be recognized by
others? Is it what we might call an "incomplete" right—"inchoate" is the
term lawyers, especially international lawyers, sometimes prefer—the
actualization of which is "suspended" until the supporting conditions
have been met, rather like the natural law obligations of the Hobbesian
state of nature that, without "sufficient security," bind the conscience
(*in foro interno*) but not the will (*in foro externo*)?

Hobbes understood all this: he knew how rights worked and what
work their advocates wanted them to do, and his political and philo-
sophic writings were designed to deal with both. One of his goals was to
show the dangers of rights as part of politics. Although the ground had
been prepared in his discussion of the state of nature, the weightiest
part of Hobbes' demonstration was reserved for his discussion of the
intrusion of personal (religious) conscience into politics. As part of an
attack on what would come to be seen as toleration—and later, religious
liberty—he said that the unfettered rights of judgment claimed by the
defenders of Parliament, by the Levellers, and by radical religious groups
in the English Civil War were, in fact, among the most destructive forces
at work in English politics. His strongest attacks were reserved for "the
Diseases of a Common-wealth that proceed from the poyson of sedi-
tious doctrines," especially the notions that "every private man is Judge
of Good and Evill Actions" and "whatsoever a man does against his Conscience is Sinne."[16]

What I will term a strong or robust sense of rights was a relatively
new political notion when Hobbes wrote (duty, on the other hand, was
well and clearly known). Like many emerging concepts, it was vaguely
understood and even more vaguely articulated. And it was closely related to the transformed understanding of liberty that was also emerging.
The genius of Hobbes was that he clarified both notions, not however to
celebrate but to undermine them and to reveal their dangers. Only when
rights were properly understood would their threats to society be fully

---

16 *Leviathan*, ch. 29, 223.

apparent. To subvert the doctrine of rights in this way, Hobbes first had to capture it from its radical proponents.

All this was done in the context of great political and religious stress. The appeal to rights was consequent upon the multiplicity of religious sects that were the institutional heritage of the Reformation, the perceived—or at least claimed—threats to "property" and "liberty" allegedly posed by Charles I, and the turn from a humanistic politics of counsel and virtue to a juridical politics of law and interest. Just as Hobbes had sought to capture and upend the new rights-talk, so it would be up to his successors to recapture that discourse and to pass it on to modernity as part of what we have come to call "liberalism."

It has become a commonplace assertion, but it is hardly trivial to observe that many of our fundamental political values took important shape during the tumultuous and momentous years of the English Civil War and Interregnum. One of the watchwords of the period was "liberty"—and its analogue "freedom"[17]—which was used in several different and not clearly related ways. In its political senses, it almost invariably functioned as a would-be bulwark against what was seen as the improper exercise of governmental power, especially by the monarchy. The general claim was that the "people"—however ill-defined—had legal, historic, or even natural liberties—equally ill-defined—that restricted the rulers. Not only were King Charles and his ministers guilty of overstepping the proper bounds of authority, they were violating the very liberty of the subjects that their offices bound them to protect and uphold, and that violation would ultimately be seen as the worse of the two offensives.

The core meaning of this liberty was the absence of restraints. To be free, to be at liberty, was to be able to act and to refrain from acting in accord with one's will. To violate liberty, therefore, was without sufficient warrant or entitlement, to place impediments in someone's way, thus coercing behavior and preventing a person from acting as her or his will directed. In its most elementary form, this is "negative" or even "liberal" freedom, and it means that insofar as one is not subject to the

---

17   I am persuaded that the only difference between these terms is that "liberty" is Latinate and "freedom" is Germanic. While there are specific usages that call for one or the other, I think that they are generally interchangeable and are appropriately but unenlighteningly often defined in terms of one another.

will or direction of another, she or he is free.[18] Contrary to Phillip Pettit and Quentin Skinner, I am persuaded that so-called "republican" (or "neo-classical") liberty also incorporates the absence of restraints and with the same force.[19]

In all cases, liberty is always good and valuable, and, like a Hohfeldian rights-claim, restricts those against whom it is asserted; what it restricts or limits is generally undesirable. And it is in this context that Hobbes entered the picture and attempted to "neutralize" the concept, arguing instead that liberty or freedom was a descriptive and not a prescriptive or normative notion. It pertained simply to an individual's abilities (and entitlements), "depend[ing] on the Silence of the Law," "to do, or forbear, according to his own discretion."[20] The enemy, as Skinner has pointedly demonstrated,[21] in part, was the republican notion that liberty is possible only in a "free state." But more importantly for our purposes, there was another even more dangerous set of enemies— some of whom, in a confused sort of way, may also have incorporated "republican" perspectives—those who derived liberty from natural law and a state of nature. As it turned out, they spoke the language of the politics of the future—not that Hobbes had any way of knowing that this would occur—and it was a language that, at least from 1640, he shared with them.

---

18 It is conventional, following Isaiah Berlin's *Two Concepts of Liberty* (Oxford: Oxford University Press, 1958; frequently reprinted), to limit negative liberty to the absence of *external* impediments to action, and to describe being self-willed as "positive liberty." I have argued against this distinction that there is nothing inherent in either negative liberty or the notion of being self-willed that prevents their being united. See my "The Rhetoric of Democratic Liberty," in *The Future of Democracy*, ed. Gerald M. Pomper and Marc Weiner (New Brunswick, NJ: Rutgers University Press, 2003), 91-110.

19 Which is not necessarily to deny that it exists but to insist on a basic meaning of liberty in all its guises. Cf. Quentin Skinner, "A Third Concept of Liberty," *Proceedings of the British Academy* 117 (2001): 118-172; *Liberty before Liberalism* (Cambridge: Cambridge University Press, 1998), and *Hobbes and Republican Liberty* (Cambridge: Cambridge University Press 2008); and Phillip Pettit, *Republicanism: A Theory of Freedom and Government* (Oxford: Oxford University Press, 1997), and *A Theory of Freedom: From the Psychology to the Politics of Agency* (Oxford: Oxford University Press, 2001). Also relevant are Eric Nelson, "Liberty: One Concept Too Many?" *Political Theory* 33 (2005): 58-78, which cites much of the older literature; and Efraim Podoksik, "One Concept of Liberty: Toward Writing the History of a Political Concept," *Journal of the History of Ideas* 71 (2010): 219-240.

20 *Leviathan*, ch. 21, 152. That is, where the law does not bind or oblige one to do or forbear—to act or not to act—she or he is free to choose. Although Hobbes was here talking about liberty in a commonwealth, the same would apply to the state of nature, where the absence of (binding) law would have been equivalent to its "Silence."

21 *Hobbes and Republican Liberty*.

Nature is one of those unassailable justificatory categories (that often include the standards and grounds of justice and rightness): it is difficult to argue that something rooted in nature, be it natural law, natural rights, or a conjectural state of nature, is incorrect or needs to be altered. Perhaps the most stunning polemical accomplishment of Hobbes' political philosophy was to take on precisely that category. And he did so, not in the manner of some of his contemporary critics of natural law/state of nature reasoning, who, like Sir Robert Filmer, substituted biblical history for the proffered anthropology of the state of nature, or who, like the common law lawyers, argued from English customs and established usages that may have gone back to an ancient and immemorial constitution.[22] Hobbes agreed with the starting point of the natural law devotees of state of nature theories, but insisted that they had gotten their own theory wrong. Whereas some of the Levellers and other Civil War radicals had used the natural human condition and putative anthropological origins of politics to argue for limited government, Hobbes sought nothing less than the subversion of that nascent liberal vocabulary of individual rights and liberty and its transformation into the bases of monarchical government.

But this appeal to rights was relatively new when Hobbes wrote. Apart from the discussion of the birthright of Esau, the King James Bible contains nothing about rights, and this omission was not part of the ordered removal of political content from the Bible, for the same absence occurs in the Geneva and Tyndale bibles.[23] Early English dictionaries also have little to say about rights, and what they include is usually tied to clerical entitlements to the proceeds from benefices,[24] and there is virtually no appeal to, let alone discussion of, rights in the pamphlet literature of the first twenty-five years of the seventeenth century. We first encounter rights in detail in the 1628 Parliamentary debates about the Petition of Right, where the notion of *rights* was most frequently

---

22 See, of course, J.G.A. Pocock, *The Ancient Constitution and the Feudal Law: A Study of English Historical Thought in the Seventeenth Century* (Cambridge: Cambridge University Press, 1957), 2nd ed. ("A Reissue with a Retrospect," 1987).
23 As well as in modern translations of the Hebrew Bible.
24 It is a pleasure to acknowledge the assistance of two superb Rutgers University undergraduate research assistants—both now graduated—who initially examined these dictionaries, Stephanie Horwitz and Michael Ford; I am deeply indebted to the Aresty Research Center at Rutgers for providing and funding these superlative assistants.

yoked to *liberty* and *property*.[25] In the 1640s, *rights* appeared with growing frequency, still tied to *liberty* and *property*, and increasingly became identified as "natural rights" and rooted in the law of nature. Barely 60 years after the Petition of Right, in 1689, the English Parliament, in one of its most important actions following the expulsion of James II, adopted the Declaration of Rights.[26] By 1759, rights had become commonplace. Laurence Sterne demonstrated the humanity of the Homunculus by describing it as a rights-bearing creature: "in all senses of the word, as much and as truly our fellow-creature as my Lord Chancellor of England.—He may be benefitted,—he may be injured,—he may obtain redress; in a word, he has *all the claims and rights of humanity*, which Tully, Puffendorf, or the best ethick writers allow to arise out of that state and relation."[27]

Not quite ninety years after the adoption of the Declaration of Rights, thirteen of Britain's American Colonies based their 1776 revolution on the "unalienable rights" that all people ("men") had from "their Creator."[28] The first set of amendments to the U.S. Constitution (1791), collectively known as the Bill of Rights, included the statement that "The enumeration in the Constitution, of certain rights, shall not be construed to deny or disparage others retained by the people,"[29] making it undeniably clear that there were rights beyond those enshrined in the positive law. And the French Declaration of the Rights of Man (1789) opened with the assertion:

> The representatives of the French people, organized as a
> National Assembly, believing that the ignorance, neglect,
> or contempt of the rights of man are the sole cause of

---

25 See the index to the splendid edition of those debates, which are the finest and most complete record we have of English Parliamentary debates in the early-modern period, *Proceedings in Parliament, 1628*, ed. Mary Frear Keer, et al., 6 vols. (New Haven: Yale University Press, 1983), vol. VI, "Appendices and Indexes," and especially J.G.A. Pocock, "Rhetoric, Liberty, and Valour: Ideology, Rhetoric, and Speech in the 1628 Debates in the House of Commons," in *The Political Imagination in History: Essays Concerning J.G.A. Pocock*, ed. D.N. Deluna (Baltimore: Owlworks, 2006), 231-260.

26 See Lois G. Schwoerer, *The Declaration of Rights, 1689* (Baltimore: Johns Hopkins University Press, 1981).

27 Laurence Stern, *The Life and Opinions of Tristram Shandy* (1759-67), I, ii, text from the Penguin Classics edition, ed. Christopher Ricks (London: Penguin Books, 1967, 1985, etc.), 36. Emphasis added.

28 Declaration of Independence.

29 U.S. Constitution, Amendment IX.

public calamities and of the corruption of governments, have determined to set forth in a solemn declaration the natural, unalienable, and sacred rights of man, in order that this declaration, being constantly before all the members of the Social body, shall remind them continually of their rights and duties.[30]

Works by Thomas Paine[31] and Mary Wollstonecraft[32] defending rights against Edmund Burke's attack[33] soon followed. It would not be an exaggeration to say that by the end of the eighteenth century, *rights* had acquired a secure and permanent place in a western political discourse that had been substantially altered from that of the sixteenth century and earlier.

While the contours of that history can be noted, it is impossible to say how the change occurred. One of the factors was certainly the gradual replacement of virtue as the end of political society with interest and rights and the corresponding movement from a humanistic to a juridical view of the political world.[34] Both of these changes were probably due, in part, to the growing importance of lawyers in the English court and in Parliament. The Petition of Right debates in the Parliament of 1628 were dominated by lawyers, as were those in the Long Parliament that led to the Civil Wars. The latter ultimately sprang from the legitimacy and legalistic crises that coincided with religious conflicts that were themselves consequences of the peculiar character of the English Reformation, the Protestantisms to which it gave rise, and their relationships to what would come to be called the English "constitution." In summary, what seems to have occurred is that concepts and words from the relatively stable and policed vocabulary of the law[35] were incorporated into political argument, an inherently unstable domain of rhetoric and pragmatism where meanings are loose and often contentious.

---

30 French Declaration of the Rights of Man, 1789. Text from the Avalon site at Yale University: http://avalon.law.yale.edu/18th_century/rightsof.asp
31 *Rights of Man* (1791 and 1792).
32 *A Vindication of the Rights of Woman* (1792).
33 *Reflections on the Revolution in France* (1789).
34 So far as I can determine, that distinction was first suggested by J.G.A. Pocock, who was followed by Richard Tuck.
35 Hohfeld was engaged in precisely that sort of verbal and conceptual policing in *Fundamental Legal Conceptions*.

The English Reformation was, in the eyes of many, more political than doctrinal: the established Church of England retained numerous Roman Catholic practices but with the important addition that the secular sovereign was the arbiter of religious doctrine. In addition, it was a comprehensive church, legally incorporating all English Protestants, many of whom had strong objections to what they saw as its "Papist" practices and secular impositions and wanted to "separate" from the official church. Appealing to the sacredness of their consciences, they called on the state to grant them legal toleration, often using phrases like "liberty of conscience" and even occasionally *"rights of conscience."* But the toleration they sought was requested not as a matter of rights-based liberty in the strict sense of an *entitlement* that was theirs by nature, but as a *grant* or privilege that would depend on the largess of the rulers, a distinction that is suggestive of Hohfeld's, as well as of Hobbes's notion that beyond the ambiguous right to life, the only rights and liberties people possessed in civil society were those that were conferred by the sovereign. And even though they did not themselves make this distinction, it is essential to an understanding of the religious politics of seventeenth-century England.

Hobbes fully appreciated the differences between rights and privileges, and one of the objectives of his political writings, especially *Leviathan*, was to minimize the role of rights in the political order. His discussion of liberty of conscience and the defeat of the episcopacy, and toleration—ably analyzed by Richard Tuck, Quentin Skinner, and Alan Ryan[36]—as well as his repeated insistence that in civil society, apart from the right to life, subjects have only so much liberty and so many rights as the sovereign allows all point to

---

36   See especially *Leviathan*, ch. 47, 478-81. For Tuck, see "Hobbes and Locke on Toleration," in *Thomas Hobbes and Political Theory*, ed. Mary G. Dietz (Lawrence, KS: University Press of Kansas, 1990), 153-171, and his *Thomas Hobbes* (Oxford: Oxford University Press, 1989), 78-91; Skinner's analysis and endorsement of Tuck is in *Hobbes and Republican Liberty*, 168-169. See also Alan Ryan, "Hobbes, Toleration and the Inner Life." in *The Nature of Political Theory*, ed. David Miller and Larry Siedentrop (Oxford: Oxford University Press, 1983), 197-218, "Hobbes and Individualism," in *Perspectives on Thomas Hobbes*, ed. Thomas Rogers and Alan Ryan (Oxford: Oxford University Press, 1988), 81-105, and Ryan, "A More Tolerant Hobbes?" in *Justifying Toleration*, ed. Susan Mendus (Cambridge: Cambridge University Press, 1988), 37-59. While they are fully aware of Hobbes'—and the Church of England's—Erastianism, all three of these authors, in my opinion, fail to grasp its importance as a limitation on the "Christian liberty" and free conscience endorsed by Hobbes, and none of them sees the significance of Hobbes' having restricted the role of conscience in political affairs in ch. 29 of *Leviathan*.

privileges and grants, not to rights and entitlements.

No part of Hobbes' writings is better known than his account of the state of nature in chapter 13 of *Leviathan*, a description that does not require repeating. Suffice it to say for present purposes, Hobbes' description amounted to a denial of correlativity. Everyone has natural rights—the same rights to all things including one another's bodies—and no one has the corresponding duties to respect those rights, either by forbearing or by cooperating; therefore, no rights are protected: "Covenants, without the Sword, are but Words, and of no strength to secure a man at all."[37] The only duties are those having to do with seeking peace, but even they are suspended in the absence of "sufficient security," that is, they oblige *in foro interno* but not *in foro externo*. It is, nonetheless, a radical conception that attributes rights equally to all adult, rational persons, male and female, but the absence of correlative duties meant that the exercise of one's rights would always be unprotected and perilous. Hobbes' remedy, no less familiar than the dilemma he presented, was that in exchange for the protections afforded by living under the rule of a strong sovereign, everyone had to surrender all her and his rights[38] but the right to life.

It was a superb analysis—all the more so given Hobbes' aims of subverting the emerging state of nature / natural rights theory—that left little room for response, at least in terms of the argument Hobbes presented. In the short run, he had captured the doctrine in a way that was true to what Hohfeld would figure out more than 250 years later.

Hobbes, like Hohfeld and those on whom Hohfeld drew, going back to Jeremy Bentham, was a legal positivist, and he turned the right of nature to his positivist purposes: the only rights and liberties available to subjects (apart from the right to life) were those afforded by the sovereign. The means of commodious living that were conspicuously missing from the state of nature—industry, agriculture, building, time, property, arts, letters, and all the rest[39]—required the cooperation and forbearance of others, and none of that was possible without sovereign

---

37 Hobbes, *Leviathan*, ch. 17, 117. Thus, in the state of nature, even a proper Hohfeldian contract would be worthless.

38 The formulations are complex, and there are distinctions among transferring and setting aside one's rights and conquest. I have discussed this in "Intending (Political) Obligation: Hobbes on the Voluntary Basis of Society," in *Thomas Hobbes and Political Theory*, ed. Dietz, 55-73

39 *Leviathan*, ch. 13, 89.

superintendence and enforcement. Life in civil society for Hobbes rested on contract and exchange, but there was no natural or spontaneous comity. Humans without the socializing benefits of civil society were too self-interested and oriented to short-term advantage to be other-regarding or even to appreciate the value to themselves of cooperation. And the deteriorated social life left behind by civil war had eliminated even that learned cooperation. The remedy for Hobbes was the return of strong rule that would restore stability and order, and that would never be found in the natural freedoms and rights advocated by so many of his compatriots who had shown their inability to understand the implication of their own doctrines. It was precisely the rampant freedoms called for by the champions of religious liberty and toleration and the defenders of natural rights that had destroyed society, and Hobbes put forth what is probably the best and most coherent argument against them.

If, as I have claimed, the tenor of political discourse was changing when Hobbes wrote, and if, as I implied, Hobbes was almost alone in recognizing that change, and if, as Hobbes himself seems to have implied, the older, humanistic and republican ways of understanding the world no longer worked and the world had indeed been turned upside down,[40] the only possible response to Hobbes would have had to be in his own terms.

We can say with the benefit of hindsight that the appeals to rights and liberty would eventually triumph, that they would be rescued from their Hobbesian strictures. I would argue that the principal goads to that triumph were both contained in Hobbes' view of the world: experientialism and religious diversity, both of which were defining features of late early-modernity. Not that Hobbes was the one to exploit them: that remained for those who came later, and the major figure here was to be John Locke. It is not simply that Locke *saw* the world differently from Hobbes and that he used many of the same conceptual building stones to construct the bases of "liberal" political theory. It is more that Locke *experienced* the world differently from Hobbes.

Because of fears about the loss of social control and the vindictive an-

---

40 What we loosely think of, retrospectively, as the growth of science, changes in philosophy and theology—including and abetted by Protestantism—economic shifts, the loosening of traditional forms of social control, and growing demands for wider political participation are all part of what made the world of the seventeenth century seem topsy turvy.

ger of Parliament at the religious dissidents who had been so powerful during the Commonwealth and Protectorate and were blamed for the Civil Wars, and the continuing fear that Roman Catholics would have to be included in any toleration, even the limited toleration of the 1650s was not in the picture at the Restoration. But the refusal to grant toleration—to permit so called "dissenters" to worship as their consciences dictated but without weakening the structural dominance of the established Church of England—increased resentments and tensions. What began as requests for the *privilege* of toleration would become calls for the recognition of the *right* of religious liberty.

Having witnessed the ability of people with radically different faiths to cooperate with one another,[41] Locke became a thoroughgoing advocate first of toleration in 1667 and then, in his *Letter Concerning Toleration* of 1690, a subtle advocate of religious liberty and of the disestablishment of the Anglican Church.[42] Almost as if he were speaking to the future, Locke resolved Hobbes' Hohfeldian dilemma. Diverse peoples, even those who differ over something as fundamental as religious beliefs, can learn to get along with one another, he believed. And he also argued in the "Second Treatise" that "truth and keeping of faith belongs to men as men, and not as members of society."[43] While he did not question the correlativity thesis—indeed, it is doubtful that he even would have understood it, for Locke was hardly the juridical thinker that Hobbes was—he said that we do not need the coercive power of the state to teach us to keep our word.

Not only are these lessons that Locke himself learned from his experience, they are lessons that we ourselves should learn from him. They are lessons that in an ever more diverse world become ever more vital. And whether they come to us from "liberalism" or "republicanism" is of no moment.

---

41   See Locke's very important letter from Cleves to Robert Boyle, 12/22 December 1665, *The Correspondence of John Locke*, ed. E.S. de Beer (Oxford: Oxford University Press, 1976–), I, 228, and my "Toleration, Revolution, and Judgment in the Development of Locke's Political Thought," *Political Science* 40 (August, 1988): 84-96.

42   See my "John Locke and Religious Toleration," in *The Revolution of 1688-89: Changing Perspectives*, ed. Lois G. Schwoerer (Cambridge: Cambridge University Press, 1992), 147-64, and "From Persecution to 'Toleration'" in *Liberty Secured? British Freedom before and after 1688*, ed. James Jones, The History of Modern Freedom, vol. II (Stanford: Stanford University Press, 1992), 122-57.

43   John Locke, *Two Treatises of Government*, II, §14; text from the edition by Peter Laslett (Cambridge: Cambridge University Press 1960).

Cooperation and the recognition that what we have in common is more important than what divides us are undoubtedly slender reeds to support society, but they are almost all we have, and without them, we have nothing.

Old and New Justifications for War:
Just Wars and Humanitarian Interventions

Marco Geuna

1. Introduction

Can early modern concepts address current affairs? This was the question put forward by the organisers of the conference on which this book is based. I would like to answer this question by examining the way in which two modern concepts—the concept of just war and the concept of human rights—have been reformulated and used over the last two decades to justify armed conflicts, and to legitimate wars in the most diverse geopolitical contexts.

I therefore choose to concentrate on two key concepts which can be traced back to the wide tradition of natural law, and not on concepts belonging to the republican tradition. The historiographical rediscovery of the republican tradition has undoubtedly offered many starting points for reconsidering contemporary problems. Many scholars have reformulated concepts from that tradition to address current problems. It is sufficient to mention the names of Quentin Skinner and Philip Pettit, in the Anglo-Saxon world, or of Claude Lefort, in France. But the concepts which have been re-examined and reformulated have been mainly concepts—such as freedom and citizenship—which referred to internal politics, to politics within the borders of the *respublica*.[1] From Machiavelli to Harrington, classical republicans referred to the Roman model, to the republic which expands and which builds an empire. Change occurred when the generation of Commonwealth-men, at the end of the seventeenth century, radically challenged the Roman model. In its place this generation put forward the ideal of a small republic, which involved a clear critique of large empires.[2] For a variety of reasons, neither of these models seems to

---

1   For a recent assessment of the republican revival in political theory, see Frank Lovett and Philip Pettit, "Neorepublicanism: A Normative and Institutional Research Program," *Annual Review of Political Science* 12 (2009): 11-29.

2   See Quentin Skinner, *Liberty Before Liberalism* (Cambridge: Cambridge University Press 1998), 65-66; David Armitage, "Empire and Liberty: A Republican Dilemma," in *Republicanism: A Shared*

have attracted the interest of contemporary commentators.[3]

In order to face contemporary challenges, scholars have chosen instead to reconsider and reformulate late medieval and early modern ideas about war and the theorizations of human rights developed in the context of the tradition of natural law. These contemporary reformulations will be the focus of my paper, in which I will try to stress the limitations and the questionable aspects of these approaches.

2. Wars and Their Justifications in Our Time

2.1. In the last decades, globalization has come together with war. As many others, I take 1989—the withdrawal of the Soviet army from Afghanistan and the fall of the Berlin Wall—as a turning point.[4] With the end of the Cold War and the collapse of the bipolar structure in international relations, a new type of war has emerged and imposed itself. It is definitely a conventional war—it is neither an atomic war, nor the threat of it—but a war of a new kind. To refer to this unprecedented form of conventional war, some scholars, following Mary Kaldor, use the expression "new wars,"[5] others prefer to speak of "global war."[6] The

---

European Heritage, ed. Martin van Gelderen and Quentin Skinner (Cambridge: Cambridge University Press 2002), 29-46; Guido Abbattista, "Imperium e libertas. Republicanesimo e ideologia imperiale all'alba dell'espansione europea in Asia (1650-1780)," in *Ideali repubblicani in età moderna*, ed. Fiorella De Michelis Pintacuda and Gianni Francioni (Pisa: ETS, 2002), 193-234.

3   For contemporary attempts to apply republican concepts to issues of international politics and global justice, see, for example, Mortimer N.S. Sellers, "The Republican Foundations of International Law," in *Legal Republicanism: National and International Perspectives*, ed. Samantha Besson and José L. Martí, (Oxford: Oxford University Press, 2009), 187-204, and Samantha Besson, "*Ubi Ius, Ibi Civitas*: A Republican Account of the International Community," ibid., 205-237. See also the proceedings of the Symposium on "Republicanism and Global Justice," in particular Philip Pettit, "A Republican Law of Peoples," *European Journal of Political Theory*, 9, no.1 (2010): 70-94 and C. Laborde, "Republicanism and Global Justice. A Sketch," ibid., 49-69.

4   Among recent studies on 1989, see: Mary E. Sarotte, *1989: The Struggle to Create Post-Cold War Europe*, (Princeton: Princeton University Press, 2009); Jeffrey A. Engel, ed., *The Fall of The Berlin Wall: The Revolutionary Legacy of 1989* (Oxford: Oxford University Press, 2009).

5   See Mary Kaldor, *New and Old Wars: Organized Violence in a Global Era* (Cambridge: Polity Press, 1999). Mary Kaldor points out that most of these new wars originate in contexts which are characterized by a crisis of the state and that in most cases these new wars are waged neither by public nor institutional subjects. In this paper, I will focus exclusively on one specific category of the new wars: the asymmetric wars waged by western countries against the so called rogue states. On new wars, see also, for example: Herfried Münkler, *Die neuen Kriege* (Hamburg: Rowohlt, 2002); Mark Duffield, *Global Governance and the New Wars* (London: Zed Books, 2002); Marco Deriu, *Dizionario critico delle nuove guerre* (Bologna: EMI, 2005).

6   The expression was introduced by William R. Thompson, *On Global War. Historical-structural Approaches to World Politics* (Columbia: University of South Carolina Press, 1988). Among Italian

main feature of these new wars is their radically asymmetric nature: they are fought by the United States and by some other western countries against single states, each time defined for different reasons as "rogue states."[7] What characterises these new wars is a radical disproportion between the military forces of the subjects engaged in the conflict, and, therefore, a radical disproportion in terms of human losses as well. Western states fight these new wars with the aim of not suffering any loss, or a negligible number of losses.[8]

Thus, after 1989, at the historical and political level we witness a return of war, in new forms. At the philosophical and ideological level, we observe a return of the legitimisation of war, as well. What are the philosophical-political legitimisations of these new wars? It is possible to distinguish two types of justifications: (a) First, new wars are justified by reshaping ancient theories. Basically, by selectively re-proposing the fundamental notions of the tradition of just war. Many European and American intellectuals presented the first Iraq war in 1991 as a just war par excellence. b) Second, these new wars are justified by resorting, more and more over the last few years, to new theories and new forms of rhetoric: scholars have dealt with the notions of "humanitarian interventions," wars to defend human rights, wars to export democracy.

Let us return for a moment to the Cold War years, that is, to a period characterised by the confrontation between nuclear superpowers. During the 1950s and 1960s, debates about war were essentially about nuclear war. Conventional and atomic war were situated on a continuum: the threat that a conventional war may give way to an escalation by degenerating into an atomic war was apparent. Superpowers would engage in conventional wars through intermediaries—the so-called

---

scholars, see: C. Galli, *Guerra globale* (Rome, Bari: Laterza, 2002), Angelo A. D'Orsi, ed., *Guerre globali. Capire i conflitti del XXI secolo* (Rome: Carocci, 2003).

7   Anthony Lake introduced the expression "rogue states" in the international debate; see Anthony Lake, "Confronting Backlash States," *Foreign Affairs* (March-April 1994): 45; for a political science approach, see Robert S. Litwak, *Rogue States and U.S. Foreign Policy* (Washington: Woodrow Wilson Center Press, 2000); for a philosophical approach, see Jacques Derrida, *Voyous: deux essais sur la raison* (Paris: Galilée, 2003), eng. trans. *Rogues: Two Essays on Reason* (Stanford: Stanford University Press, 2005).

8   On the asymmetric character of the new wars, see Josef Schröfl et al., ed., *Asymmetrische Kriegführung—ein neues Phänomen der internationalen Politik?* (Baden-Baden: Nomos, 2004); Herfried Münckler, *Der Wandel des Krieges: von der Symmetrie zur Asymmetrie* (Weilerswist: Velbrück, 2006). Among Italian scholars, see Alessandro Colombo, *La guerra ineguale. Pace e violenza nel tramonto della società internazionale* (Bologna: Il Mulino, 2006).

"proxy wars"—from Korea to Vietnam. But the atomic war remained the center of the debates in moral and political philosophy. The atomic war appeared to most scholars as a dead-end, as a war without any legitimacy whatsoever, as a fundamentally unjustifiable war.[9] This scenario radically changes with 1989 and the end of the Cold War. War is re-legitimised on a large scale. Initially, in 1991, during the first Iraq war, such re-legitimisation took place through the reformulation of the criteria of the just war tradition, within a universalistic context that recognized the importance of the International Law as stated in the UN Charter, in the UN Declarations and later resolutions. It was this universalistic context that allowed many western authoritative intellectuals, from Habermas to Dahrendorf, from Lyotard to Bobbio, to argue that the Gulf war was a "just" war or, at least, a "justified" war.[10] Subsequently, the re-legitimisation of war took place under new terms, and within a context which seriously challenged the role of the UN and of classic international law. This happened for the first time when the NATO intervened in Kosovo, in spring 1999, and it was fully deployed as a justification of the 2003 Iraq war. Formulas such as "humanitarian intervention," "war promoting human rights," "war exporting democracy" attest that war has been re-legitimised by resorting to "high" terms and concepts of the European and Western tradition, such as humanity, rights, and democracy. Thus, creating what many recognize properly speaking as a series of oxymora. I am convinced that these restatements of ancient theories and new justifications of war should be accurately reconstructed, and their conceptual structures and premises criticised, and not simply denounced for their rhetorical effects.

2.2. Before taking a closer look at these strategies of re-legitimisation of war, I would like to add a remark concerning the global post-1989 his-

---

9   See, for example, Norberto Bobbio, "Il problema della guerra e le vie della pace," *Nuovi argomenti* (1966): 29-90, later in Norberto Bobbio, *Il problema della guerra e le vie della pace* (Bologna: Il Mulino, 1979), 21-96, in particular 60.

10 Among others, see J. Habermas, *Vergangenheit als Zukunft* (Munich: Piper, 1991); N. Bobbio, *Una guerra giusta? Sul conflitto del Golfo* (Venezia: Marsilio, 1991). Among Anglo-Saxon scholars who interpreted and discussed the Gulf war in the perspective of the just war tradition, see James T. Johnson and George Weigel, *Just War and the Gulf War*, (Washington: Ethics and Public Policy Center, 1991); David E. DeCosse, ed., *But Was It Just? Reflections on the Morality of the Persian Gulf War* (New York: Doubleday, 1992).

torical-political situation, namely, the one brought about by the fall of the Berlin Wall. An indubitable ambiguity characterised that situation, which was read and interpreted, at the time and later on, from two extremely different perspectives. (i) On the one hand, many philosophers, including Jürgen Habermas, conceived it as a first step toward the creation of a cosmopolitan order, in some way carrying out the Kantian project of perpetual peace; (ii) on the other hand, it was considered as the first step toward the realisation of a political order dominated by a single superpower, acting unilaterally, and as the beginning of the unilateral hegemony of the United States. Many scholars embracing this second perspective, whether they are political experts, internationalists, or experts in strategy, have brought into light how such hegemony or unilateral imperial power has been carefully conceived and planned. They have pointed out that, behind the political choices which lead to this new type of war, there is a whole new culture, mainly the Neo-conservative culture, aiming at subverting many of the prevalent political principles, as well as the fundamental assumptions of classical international law.

3. Contemporary Reformulations of Just War Theory

There have been a variety of reformulations of just war theory over the last two decades, which may be situated at different levels of discourse.[11] We can distinguish at least two levels: (i) a strictly philosophical one; (ii) a level of discourse more directly engaged in actual questions, what we may address as a political-ideological level.

From a strictly philosophical point of view, if we start from the Anglo-Saxon debate, we may refer to the most influential and debated political philosophers of the last decades, John Rawls. In essays such as *Fifty Years after Hiroshima* (1995),[12] and especially in the book *The Law of Peoples*,[13] he takes over and reformulates some of the key notions of

---

11 See Richard Falk, "Legality to Legitimacy: The Revival of the Just War Framework," *Harvard International Review* 26 (2004): 40-44.

12 John Rawls, "Fifty Years after Hiroshima," *Dissent* (Summer 1995): 323-327, now in John Rawls, *Collected Papers*, ed. Samuel Freeman (Cambridge: Harvard University Press, 1999), 565-572.

13 John Rawls, *The Law of Peoples with "The Idea of Public Reason Revisited"* (Cambridge: Harvard University Press, 1999), 89-105. For a discussion of the conceptual tensions in Rawls' book, see Rex Martin and David A. Reidy, ed., *Rawls's Law of Peoples: A Realistic Utopia?* (Oxford: Blackwell, 2006). Among the vast number of critical studies, see for example: Rex Martin, "The Just War

the just war tradition. In the first essay, Rawls sets out six principles and assumptions which govern the conduct of war, the *jus in bello*, for democratic peoples. He can therefore claim, in a classic mode of expression, that "the norms of the conduct of war set up certain lines that bound just action. War plans and strategies, and the conduct of battles, must lie within their limits (The only exception [...] is in times of extreme crisis)."[14] From these premises, Rawls has no difficulties in reaching the conclusion that both the firebombing of Japanese cities in spring 1945 and the subsequent dropping of atomic bombs on Hiroshima and Nagasaki were "great evils."[15]

These principles, which refer to the *jus in bello*, are reworked and put forward in *The Law of Peoples* as part of an attempt to extend the principles of justice from the national to the international context; therefore, as part of a theory of international justice. The theory of just war reappears in Rawls' work when he must examine, in the context of what he calls "the non-ideal theory," the possibility that "liberal and decent peoples" are forced into war against those he calls "outlaw states" or "outlaw regimes."

We cannot follow here the details of the ways in which he works out his theories. I only want to mention a significant change of wording, related to what he previously defined as situations of extreme crisis, in which it is possible to violate the constraints set down by the principles and norms of the *jus in bello*. These are now defined, following the terms used by Michael Walzer, as situations of supreme emergency. In these cases, civilians are no longer protected by a rigorous status of immunity and they may be subject to military attacks. We are not going to pursue any further the discussion of Rawls' project. Suffice it to be said that it has been the object of many discussions and criticisms, and that in the last decade literature on international justice, cosmopolitan justice, and global justice has vastly grown, following paths quite different from those proposed by Rawls.[16]

Theory of Walzer and Rawls," *Southwest Philosophy Review* 19 (2003): 135-146; Perry Anderson, "Arms and Rights. Rawls, Habermas and Bobbio in the Age of War," *New Left Review* 31 (2005): 5-40.

14 Rawls, "Fifty Years," 567.

15 Ibid., 570.

16 See for example Thomas Pogge, *World Poverty and Human Rights: Cosmopolitan Responsibilities and Reforms* (Cambridge: Politiy Press, 2002); Thomas Nagel, "The Problem of Global Justice," *Philosophy and Public Affairs* 33 (2005): 113-147; Joshua Cohen and Charles Sabel, "Extra

On the political-ideological level, a series of reformulations of the theory of just war has come to the fore over the last two decades, among which the most famous and well-constructed are probably those proposed by Michael Walzer in *Just and Unjust Wars*[17] and, more recently, in *Arguing about War*.[18] Walzer opposes political realism, according to which *inter arma silent leges*, and argues persuasively that the reality of war is not beyond any moral judgement. He describes just war theory as an intermediate theory which avoids both the assumptions of the realists, and those of the pacifists (which were formulated in the paradigmatic manner by early Christians). In his renewal of the *jus belli*, Walzer starts from the assertion of the existence of moral laws, of "those general principles that we commonly acknowledge, even when we can't or won't live up to them."[19] He does not, however, move on to clarify the foundations of these principles or of these moral laws. Indeed, he argues that in a first moment we may consider "practical morality detached from its foundations." Moving from these premises, followed by a complex discussion of historical cases, he illustrates the conditions of legitimacy and legality of armed conflicts. He then examines what he calls "the dilemmas of war," and especially the issue of supreme emergency situations, in which in the face of an absolute necessity one may not follow the rules of war.

The renewal and reformulation of just war theory which Walzer has carried out has enjoyed a wide success over the past several decades. A cursory glance at the titles of essays and books published in the last few years enable us to see how well-established this approach is in the Anglo-Saxon world and elsewhere.[20] We take as instances the issues published over the last few years by two important and internationally reputable journals: *Ethics* and *Philosophy and Public Affairs*.[21] Further-

---

Rempublicam Nulla Iustitia?" *Philosophy and Public Affairs* 34 (2006): 147-175; Thomas Pogge and Darrel Moellendorf, ed., *Global Justice: Seminal Essays* (St. Paul: Paragon House, 2008).

17   M. Walzer, *Just and Unjust Wars: A Moral Argument with Historical Illustrations* (New York: Basic Books, 1977). On Walzer's just war theory, see, for example, Brian Orend, *Michael Walzer on War and Justice* (Montreal, Ithaca: McGill-Queen's University Press, 2000); Kimberly A. Hudson, *Justice, Intervention and Force in International Relations: Reassessing Just War Theory in the 21ˢᵗ Century* (London: Routledge, 2009).

18   M. Walzer, *Arguing about War* (New Haven: Yale University Press, 2004).

19   M. Walzer, *Just and Unjust Wars*, xiii and xv, for the following quotation.

20   Among recent French studies which follow an approach similar to Walzer's, see Monique Canto-Sperber, *Le bien, la guerre & la terreur. Pour une morale internationale* (Paris: Plon, 2005) especially part III "La morale et la guerre," 249-346; Christian Nadeau and Julie Saada, *Guerre juste, guerre injuste. Histoire, théories et critiques* (Paris: PUF, 2009).

21   Jeff McMahan, "The Ethics of Killing in War," *Ethics* 114 (2004): 693-733; Daniel Statman,

more, we have to recognize that books centered on these themes published over the past five years are countless. One could only mention the volumes written and edited by Larry May,[22] an American-based scholar interested in the philosophical foundations of international penal law, and a couple of important collections of studies, such as *Intervention, Terrorism and Torture: Contemporary Challenges to Just War Theory* (2007)[23] and *The Price of Peace: Just War in the Twenty-First Century* (2007).[24]

Why reformulate the main assumptions of this important tradition of western political philosophy? Why this tradition rather than others? I would reply in the following way: because this tradition offered precise standards for judging war. Moreover, because this tradition offered the possibility to think in a more articulate way about the relation among morals, law and politics, besides and beyond the tradition of political realism, which does not thematize the relation between morals and politics. One should also not forget that in the decades following World War II political realism, in its various—systemic and non-systemic—formulations, was the common denominator of the different approaches to the relations between states, to international politics.

At this stage, we should look at some of the main characters of the just war tradition and on its conceptualisations, in order to better investigate the way in which these conceptualisations have been retrieved and reformulated during the last decades. This would allow us to single out and to bring the distortions and reductions of such reformulations into full focus.

"Supreme Emergencies Revisited," *Ethics* 117 (2006): 58-79; Allen Buchanan, "Institutionalizing the Just War," *Philosophy and Public Affairs* 34 (2006): 2-38. Jeff McMahan's recent publications include *The Ethics of Killing: Problems at the Margins of Life* (Oxford: Oxford University Press, 2002); Allen Buchanan's include *Justice, Legitimacy and Self-Determination: Moral Foundations for International Law* (Oxford: Oxford University Press, 2004), and *Human Rights, Legitimacy and the Use of Force* (Oxford: Oxford University Press, 2010).

22 Larry May, *War Crimes and Just War* (New York: Cambridge University Press, 2007); Larry May, *Aggression and Crimes against Peace* (Cambridge: Cambridge University Press, 2008); Larry May, ed., *War: Essays in Political Philosophy* (New York: Cambridge University Press, 2008).

23 Steven P. Lee, ed., *Intervention, Terrorism and Torture: Contemporary Challenges to Just War Theory* (Dordrecht: Springer, 2007). This collection of essays includes Rex Martin, "Walzer and Rawls on Just Wars and Humanitarian Interventions," 75-88.

24 Charles Reed and David Ryall, ed., *The Price of Peace: Just War in the Twenty-First Century* (Cambridge: Cambridge University Press, 2007). See also, for example, Mark Evans, ed., *Just War Theory: A Reappraisal* (Edinburgh: Edinburgh University Press, 2005); Michael W. Brough, John W. Lango, Harry van der Linden, ed., *Rethinking the Just War Tradition* (Albany: SUNY Press, 2007); David Rodin and Henry Shue, ed., *Just and Unjust Warriors: The Moral and Legal Status of Soldiers* (Oxford: Oxford University Press 2008).

The tradition of just war has a complex conceptual architecture. As it is well known, first of all it distinguished and tackled the questions of the legitimacy of war, which fell within the category of the *jus ad bellum*: in this way it focused on the just causes of war, the right authority and right intent of the subjects which wage war. It then conceptualised the problems of the legality of war, which fell within the category of the *jus in bello*, formulating, in particular, the criteria of discrimination and proportionality. Finally, it examined the close relation between legitimacy and legality, setting down the thesis according to which a legitimate war, that could only be fought illegally, was to be considered unlawful, thus the war was not to be fought.[25] Therefore, by putting legitimacy and legality in relation, and individuating a sort of retroactivity of legality on legitimacy, the tradition of just war set precise standards or criteria to determine the overall lawfulness of war.

Let me add a remark: I think that the complex conceptual structure of the just war tradition, from Aquinas to Vitoria, Suárez and the other authors of the second Scholasticism, should be taken seriously. That is to say, it deserves, in my view, that we move beyond those representations, which, following Carl Schmitt's interpretation in *Nomos der Erde*, conceive it as an exclusively medieval or pre-modern tradition.[26]

It is barely necessary to remind ourselves that just war theory has a long history in the Christian world.[27] The concept of "bellum iustum"

---

25 Francisco de Vitoria, for example, argued that this kind of war was a "bellum [...] iustum per se et illicitum et iniustum per accidens." See Francisco de Vitoria, *Relectio de iure belli o paz dinamica*, ed. L. Pereña et al. (Madrid: Consejo Superior de Investigaciones Científicas, 1981), 160; eng. trans. in Francisco de Vitoria, *Political Writings*, ed. A. Pagden and J. Lawrence (Cambridge: Cambridge University Press, 1991), 314.

26 For a reconsideration and critique of Schmitt's interpretation, see for example Enrico Berti, "Francisco de Vitoria nell'interpretazione di Carl Schmitt," in *L'universalità dei diritti umani e il pensiero cristiano del '500*, ed. S. Biolo (Turin: Rosenberg & Sellier, 1995), 139-147; Nestor Capdevila, "L'impérialisme entre inclusion exclusive and exclusion inclusive: Schmitt lecteur de Vitoria," in *Reconnaissance, identité et intégration sociale*, ed. Christian Lazzeri and Soraya Nour (Paris: Presses Universitaires de Paris Ouest, 2009), 339-359. See also Martti Koskenniemi, "International Law as Political Theology: How to Read *Nomos der Erde*?" *Constellations* 11 (2004): 492-511; Louiza Odysseos and Fabio Petito, ed., *The International Political Thought of Carl Schmitt* (London: Routledge, 2007).

27 The standard history of the just war tradition in the Christian world is presented by Robert H.W. Regout, *La doctrine de la guerre juste de Saint Augustin à nos jours d'apres les théologiens et les canonistes catholiques* (Paris: Pedone 1934). For more recent studies, see for example James T. Johnson, *Ideology, Reason, and the Limitations of War: Religious and Secular Concepts. 1200-1740* (Princeton: Princeton University Press, 1975); James T. Johnson, *Just War Tradition and the Restraint of War: A Moral and Historical Inquiry* (Princeton: Princeton University Press, 1981); Guillaume Bacot, *La doctrine de la guerre juste* (Paris: Economica, 1989); G. M. Reichberg, "Jus ad

was formulated by Roman jurists,[28] and it was put forward again by Cicero both in Book III of *De Re Publica*—where the "bellum iustum" was defined as that which was fought "pro fide aut pro salute"[29]—and in Book I of *De Officiis*.[30] Augustine of Hippo introduced the term and the concept to the Christian world in *De Civitate Dei* by recapitulating Cicero's remarks and arguing for the possibility that Christians could fight just wars. Augustine had already argued that Christians could fight wars *quae ulciscuntur iniurias*, wars in vengeance and punishment of injustices which had been perpetrated against them, in *Contra Faustum* and in the *Quaestiones in Heptateuchum*, and he was going to repeat these arguments elsewhere.[31] He was therefore shedding the radical pacifist and non-violent approach of the early Church Fathers, from Tertullian to Origen, to Lactantius. Following Augustine, many canonists and many theologians put forward and elaborated the concept of "bellum justum." We can mention the canonist Gratian, who in his *Decretum*—also known as *Concordia Discordantium Canonum*—addressed the issue of "quid sit bellum iustum." He had argued that war needed to be declared by a legitimate authority, that it must have its "causae" or reasons—to be indentified in the repelling an enemy aggression ("propulsandorum hostium causa") or in the recover of stolen goods ("de rebus repetendis")— and lastly that it must not involve clerics and that it must exclude all uncontrolled violence, since it must be carried out as "bellum pacatum ex animo".[32] The most authoritative theological systematization of the

---

Bellum," in *War: Essays in Political Philosophy*, ed. L. May, 11-29; N. Rengger, "The Jus in Bello in Historical and Philosophical Perspective," in *War: Essays in Political Philosophy*, ed. L. May, 30-48.

28 Among recent studies, see Antonello Calore, ed., *"Guerra giusta?" Le metamorfosi di un concetto antico* (Milan: Giuffrè, 2003); in particular Francesco Sini, "*Ut iustum conciperetur bellum*: guerra 'giusta' e sistema giuridico-religioso romano," 31-76; Alfredo Valvo, "Il *bellum iustum* e i generali romani nel III e II secolo a.C.," 77-100; Aldo A. Cassi, "Dalla santità alla criminalità della guerra. Morfologie storico-giuridiche del *bellum iustum*," 101-158.

29 Marcus Tullius Cicero, *De Republica*, III, 23, 34; see also II, 17, 31 and III, 23, 35.

30 See Marcus Tullius Cicero, *De Officiis*, I, 11, 34 and I, 13, 41.

31 See Regout, *La doctrine de la guerre juste*, 39-44; Anna Morisi, *La guerra nel pensiero cristiano dalle origini alle crociate* (Florence: Sansoni, 1963), 95-120; Frederick H. Russell, *The Just War in the Middle Ages* (Cambridge: Cambridge University Press, 1975), 16-39. For recent discussions, see Robert L. Holmes, "St. Augustine and the Just War Theory," in *The Augustinian Tradition*, ed. Gareth B. Matthews (Berkeley: University of California Press, 1999), 323-344; John M. Mattox, *Saint Augustine and the Theory of Just War* (New York: Continuum, 2006).

32 See *Decretum Magistri Gratiani*, p. II, c. XXIII, q. 2, c. 1-2, in *Corpus Juris Canonici*, ed. E.L. Richter and E. Friedberg, (Leipzig: B. Tauchnitz, 1879), vol. 1, coll. 889-895. On Gratian's contribution, see R.H.W. Regout, *La doctrine de la guerre juste*, 61-66; F.H. Russell, *The Just War in the Middle Ages*, 55-85.

concept was undoubtedly the one proposed by Thomas Aquinas, in the fortieth *quaestio* of the *"Secunda Secundae"* of the *Summa Theologiae*, therefore in the context of the discussion of the sins which are opposed to the theological virtue of charity.[33] In the first article of that *quaestio*, in asking himself "utrum bellum semper sit peccatum," Aquinas had defined the conditions of legitimacy of any possible war fought by Christians. He had argued that one could speak of a just war when three conditions were simultaneously present: (i) that the war was declared by public authority, and not by private persons; (ii) that it was undertaken for *iustae causae*, first and foremost for self-defence, and (iii) that war was fought with *recta intentio*, with the objective of peace and not for more contingent material benefits—e.g., the enlargement of territories or of the domains of the political community.

The modern formulation of just war theory is usually traced back to Francisco de Vitoria and to his *relectiones* of 1539: *De Indis* and *De Iure Belli*.[34] In these solemn lectures, held in the presence of the entire academic body of the University of Salamanca, Vitoria reinterpreted the key concepts of the tradition of the just war and proposed a philosophical and juridical legitimation of war basically in terms of the notion of natural Law, understanding natural law as the expression of natural justice.[35] The two *relectiones* enjoyed an extraordinary success in European culture, both Roman Catholic and Protestant. These lectures offered intellectuals of the second half of the sixteenth century and of the first half of the seventeenth century an overall picture of the problems which needed to be covered when one was dealing with the topic *de iure belli*, together with a series of categorizations which oriented and structured discourse. The model was somehow defined and the tradition could now be developed.

---

33 See Thomas Aquinas, *Summa theologiae*, IIa, IIae, quaest. 40. Among recent studies, see John Finnis, *Aquinas. Moral, Political, and Legal Theory* (Oxford: Oxford University Press 1998), in particular 275-293; Giuseppe Pirola, "La teologia della guerra di Tommaso d'Aquino," in *Figure della guerra. La riflessione su pace, conflitto e giustizia tra Medioevo e prima età moderna*, ed. Merio Scattola (Milan: Franco Angeli, 2003), 43-62.

34 See Francisco de Vitoria, *Relectio de Indis o Libertad de los Indios*, edicion critica bilingüe por L. Pereña y J.M. Pérez Prendes (Madrid: Consejo Superior de Investigaciones Cientificas, 1967); Francisco de Vitoria, *Relectio de iure belli o paz dinamica*; eng. trans. in Francisco de Vitoria, *Political Writings*.

35 See for example Daniel Deckers, *Gerechtigkeit und Recht: Eine historish-kritische Untersuchung des Gerechtigkeitslehre des Francisco de Vitoria* (Fribourg: Universitätsverlag, 1991); Giuseppe Tosi, "La teoria della guerra giusta in Francisco de Vitoria," in *Figure della guerra*, ed. Merio Scattola (Milan: Franco Angeli, 2003), 63-87.

In Roman Catholic culture, the *relectiones* were decisive for a succession of thinkers, first Dominicans and then Jesuits: from Domingo de Soto and Melchior Cano, from Luis de Molina to Francisco Suárez. In sixteenth and seventeenth century Protestant culture, Vitoria's *relectiones* were destined to have an equally significant impact. It is sufficient to recall two names: Alberico Gentili and Hugo Grotius.

We cannot pursue any further the topic of Vitoria's presence, and more generally the theme of just war, in modern culture, up to the French Revolution. I will simply mention that even after Grotius, between the end of the seventeenth century and the first half of the eighteenth century—at the heart of what many scholars consider the season of the *jus publicum europeum*, during which the category of "just war" was supposedly superseded by that of "regular war"—we can still find thinkers, such as John Locke and Christian Wolff, who refer to many of the categorizations of the just war tradition.[36]

Two approaches to the tradition of just war and its contemporary reformulations are possible, which lead to two different kinds of criticism: (i) On the one hand, there is a radical criticism, which I would define as an *external* criticism. This form of criticism rejects this tradition as a whole, by arguing that between the sixteenth and seventeenth centuries it was an instrument of legitimisation of European wars, especially against the Turks and the inhabitants of the New World. It argues that its contemporary reformulations are sheer rhetorical instruments in order to legitimize the unilateral interventions of the United States and the Western countries.[37] (ii) On the other hand, an *internal* criticism argues that the conceptual structures of the just war tradition deserve to be taken into serious examination, for they aimed not only at allowing, but at strictly limiting war as well. Thus, its elaborations cannot be reduced to the sheer rhetoric of legitimisation. Modern assumptions of just war should be taken seriously in order to evaluate whether their contemporary reformulations are faithful and persuasive or distort and reduce their significance.

---

36 For an interesting critique of the historiographical interpretations based on Carl Schmitt's periodization, see Gabriella Silvestrini, "Diritti naturali e diritto di uccidere: Teorie moderne della guerra fra modelli teorici e tradizioni di pensiero," *Filosofia politica* 21 (2007): 425-452; Gabriella Silvestrini, "Justice, War and Inequality: The Unjust Aggressor and the Enemy of the Human Race in Vattel's Theory of the Law of Nations," *Grotiana* 31 (2010): 44-68.

37 See for example, Danilo Zolo, *Cosmopolis. La prospettiva del governo mondiale* (Milan: Feltrinelli, 1995) in particular 82-116; eng. trans. *Cosmopolis: Prospects for World Government* (Cambridge: Polity Press, 1997).

In this paper, I intend to develop this second approach. Thus, I will examine the contemporary reformulations on the backdrop of the classical conceptual architectures of the just war tradition. To begin with, it is important to point out that, in contemporary discussions, the questions of legitimacy and legality often are separate. The emphasis is put entirely on the conditions of the legitimacy of war, that is to say, whether the *iustae causae* exist or not, as if their existence allowed a nation to fight a war without asking further moral questions. The problems of the legality of war and of the retroactivity of legality over legitimacy have been superseded, or even disappeared in many elaborations. In short, the overall lawfulness of war too often is reduced to its legitimacy, to the existence of the *iustae causae*.

Such reduction and simplification of the tradition's demanding conceptual framework is apparent in several thinkers, who invoke the "logical priority" of legitimacy over legality, of the *jus ad bellum* over the *jus in bello*. These authors maintain that "the question whether to use force takes logical priority over the question of what force to use and conditions of it," thus transforming such logical priority into a moral priority: "the justice of the cause was allowed to override the justice of the particular means used to serve the cause."[38]

By focusing their attention exclusively on legitimacy, on the *jus ad bellum*, some thinkers have forced, or even twisted, the strict criteria of legitimacy set by the tradition. In the whole tradition, and in the most different formulations of the just war theory, a just war has always and exclusively been a war responding to a previous offence or a previous wrong. Recently, thinkers such as Jeff McMahan have drawn this strict principle into question in order to provide a moral justification of unilateral policies. They asked themselves whether an aggressive war may be permissible: diverging from the standards of the just war tradition, McMahan argued that aggressive and punitive wars can be just.[39]

---

38   James T. Johnson, *Can Modern War Be Just?* (New Haven: Yale University Press, 1984), 30. Johnson was arguing against Michael Walzer and the argument of supreme emergency. Among more recent studies, see for example Brian Orend, "Is There a Supreme Emergency Exemption," in *Just War Theory: A Reappraisal*, ed. Mark Evans, 134-153; David Duquette, "From Rights to Realism: Incoherence in Walzer's Conception of *Jus in bello*," in *Intervention, Terrorism and Torture: Contemporary Challenges to Just War Theory*, ed. Steven P. Lee, 41-57.

39   See J. McMahan, "Aggression and Punishment," in *War: Essays in Political Philosophy*, ed. L. May, 67-84, in particular 74-84. McMahan has the legitimization of unilateral humanitarian interventions in mind: see 78.

The fact of focusing the attention on the legitimacy of war, and not at the same time on its legality, on the way in which the war may be carried on as well, has allowed, almost without problems, to judge a series of wars, waged by the US and their European allies, as just wars.

Now, let us consider the *jus in bello*. The *jus in bello* set the criteria of discrimination and proportionality, which were to be respected under conditions of warfare. First of all, the principle of discrimination, distinguishing between *innocentes* and *nocentes,* the innocent and the guilty persons, essentially between civilians and soldiers. Then, the principle of proportionality of the military intervention compared with the offence, or wrong, which originated the just war. It is important to point out that in their reformulations of just war theories, contemporary thinkers have not dwelled on these criteria as deeply as their early modern predecessors, for instance Vitoria. A series of questions have not been sufficiently investigated, and too many answers have been taken for granted. For instance: in contemporary conventional wars, who are the innocents? Should the soldiers of the armies of authoritarian or totalitarian countries be considered innocent or guilty? Referring to a recent historical case, were the tens of thousands of Iraqi soldiers, killed around Basra in 1991 during the retreat from Kuwait, to be considered guilty or innocent? Were they to be deemed responsible for the application and the execution of Saddam's orders? Were they morally responsible for the war? Too many thinkers who have re-proposed a theory of just war over the last few years have failed to elaborate a theory of collective responsibility, most likely taking it for granted.[40]

Moreover, I am convinced that many contemporary philosophers have not investigated the distinctive characters, the peculiarities of the new wars in depth: first of all, the fact that they are fundamentally asymmetric wars. This asymmetry—the fact that these wars rely upon a massive use of technological information; that they are predominantly air wars, in which the western countries that wage them do not want to suffer losses—has not been dwelled upon enough. In the light of these remarks, in my view, the slaughters of civilians, the so-called "collateral damage" of air bombings, cannot not be conceived as unintentional and

---

40   On the problem of collective responsibility, see the recent interesting essay by Philip Pettit, "Responsibility Incorporated," *Ethics* 117 (2007): 171-201.

cannot be justifiable through some version of the "double effect"[41] doctrine any longer.[42]

Many scholars failed to ask themselves the radical question of whether contemporary wars—the new or asymmetric wars—may actually be limited, or whether they should be included in the twentieth century war trend, in which civilians are the increasingly larger and most significant part of the victims.[43]

In short, it is possible to point out two elements in many of the contemporary reformulations of the just war theory. (i) A significant reduction of the restrictive claim of the traditional just war theory. Such theory was elaborated, on the one hand, to provide, in certain cases, moral justification for the recourse to war; on the other, to strictly limit it as well. In more recent formulations, these limits have been significantly weakened, or made less restrictive. (ii) A significant lack of investigation into the structural characters of the new wars. Philosophers have kept reading philosophers, and have not paid sufficient attention to other social sciences, nor read enough works (if any) in the fields of strategy, international relations, history and sociology. The question of whether the theory of just war is adequate to address the challenges issued by the new scenario of unilateral interventions, ethnic cleansing and international terrorism, the scenario of the new wars, seldom has been raised.[44]

---

41   For a first introduction to the principle of double effect, see P.E. Devine, "Principle of Double Effect," in *The Cambridge Dictionary of Philosophy*, ed. R. Audi (Cambridge: Cambridge University Press, 1995), 644-645 and Alison McIntyre, *Doctrine of Double Effect*, 2009, http://plato.stanford. edu/entries/double-effect/. For a justification of the killing of non-combatants in war through the principle of double effect, see Walzer, *Just and Unjust Wars*, 151-159. Among recent discussions, see Alex Bellamy, "Supreme Emergencies and the Protection of Noncombatants in War," *International Affairs* 80 (2004): 829-850; David Lefkowitz, "Collateral Damage," in *War: Essays in Political Philosophy*, ed. Larry May, 145-164, in particular 147-154.

42   For a critique of the justifications of the killing of innocent civilians that have recourse to the principle of double effect, see for example Giuliano Pontara, "Il 'vicolo cieco' della guerra e le difficili vie della pace," in *Lezioni Bobbio: Sette interventi su etica e politica*, with a preface by Marco Revelli (Torino: Einaudi, 2006), 121-144, in particular 127-134; Uwe Steinhoff, *On the Ethics of War and Terrorism* (Oxford: Oxford University Press, 2007), 33-60.

43   Some contemporary philosophers, starting from different theoretical premises, have argued that contemporary wars—the new wars included—could not be limited and therefore could not find a moral justification. See for example, Peter Sloterdijk, *Luftbeben. An den Quellen des Terrors* (Frankfurt a.M.: Suhrkamp 2002), eng. trans. *Terror from the Air* (Cambridge, MA: MIT Press, 2009); Luigi Ferrajoli, *Principia iuris. Teoria del diritto e della democrazia. 2. Teoria della democrazia* 2nd ed. (Rome, Bari: Laterza, 2009), 501-503.

44   But now see the remarkable exception: Steven P. Lee, ed., *Intervention, Terrorism and Torture: Contemporary Challenges to Just War Theory*.

4. Humanitarian Wars to Promote Human Rights

In modern just war tradition, pre-emptive strikes and pre-emptive wars were altogether excluded from the definition of a lawful war. Only a war, which answered to a wrong previously committed by others, could be a just war. It aimed at re-establishing the law of nature (*lex naturae*) or the international law (*jus gentium*) which had been violated.

In the last decade, starting with the Nato intervention in Kosovo, as I have already pointed out, the United States and other Western countries have presented their armed interventions in other countries as "humanitarian interventions," as armed interventions directed at the protection and the promotion of human rights. These states have argued that current international law, with its precise restrictions on the use of force, must be superseded by appealing to the principles of international ethics and centered on the protection of human rights.[45]

Over the same years, and in relation to these international events, there has been a wide-ranging debate among jurists on the possibility and desirability to substitute the current positive international law—which refers to the United Nations Charter, and which was centered on the idea that the only exception to the prohibition of the use of force was represented by legitimate defence[46]—with new international humanitarian law, which would allow the use of force, even in the absence of authorization or a mandate from the Security Council. The vast number of contributions to this debate ranged from open support of the new humanitarian law, as expressed by the U.S.-based jurist Michael Glennon and by the Italian Antonio Cassese,[47] to a firm criticism of uni-

---

45 The 1991 Gulf War was legitimated in terms of law—as a sanction and as a redress of the invasion of a sovereign state by Iraq—with the authorization of the Security Council of the United Nations. In the case of NATO intervention in the Kosovo conflict in 1999, NATO governments involved were well aware of the impossibility of arguing the legitimacy of their intervention in terms of international law. They therefore appealed to an immediately moral justification for the intervention, which could avoid the questionable legality of the intervention.

46 See for example Olivier Corten, *Le droit contre la force: L'interdiction du recours à la force en droit international contemporain* (Paris: Pedone, 2008).

47 See Michael J. Glennon, "The New Interventionism: The Search for a Just International Law," *Foreign Affairs* 78, no. 2 (1999): 7-21; Michael J. Glennon, *Limits of Law, Prerogatives of Power: Interventionism after Kosovo* (New York: Palgrave 2001); Antonio Cassese, "'Ex iniuria ius oritur': Are We Moving towards International Legitimation of Forcible Humanitarian Countermeasures in the World Community?" *European Journal of International Law* 10 (1999): 23-30. See also the collections of essays: J. Gardam, ed., *Humanitarian Law* (Brookfield: Ashgate 1999); J.L. Holzgrefe and Robert O. Keohane, ed., *Humanitarian Intervention: Ethical, Legal and Political Dilemmas* (Cambridge: Cambridge University Press, 2003); Gilles Andréani and Pierre Hassner, ed., *Justifier*

lateral interventions, as expressed by the German Bruno Simma and the Italian Luigi Ferrajoli.[48]

Philosophers, and Anglo-Saxon scholars in particular, have provided arguments in favour of this new approach, to this new legitimation of war. Thus, a large number of theories of humanitarian intervention have been developed, from extremely different metaphysical and epistemological premises. One finds a justification of humanitarian military interventions even in the subtle and abstract pages of John Rawls, especially in those of *The Law of Peoples*.[49] Moreover, it is not difficult for philosophers of Kantian inspiration to found human rights deontologically, hence proceeding to the justification of humanitarian interventions. For instance, Carla Bagnoli argued that a humanitarian intervention must be thought as a perfect duty: it has to be conceived "as a duty rather than permission, and as a perfect duty than an imperfect one—a duty that proceeds from the respect of humanity rather than from charity."[50] Philosophers far more sceptical about the possibility of founding the universality of human rights from a transcendental viewpoint, philosophers who took the lesson of Isaiah Berlin over, such as Michael Ignatieff, come, in a similar way, although from different paths, to the point of defending the use of force. Both in the pages of *Human Rights as Politics and Idolatry* and in those of *The Lesser Evil. Political Ethics in an Age of Terror*, Ignatieff argues in favour of humanitarian military interventions and considers the military interventions of the United States and their European allies in Iraq and Kosovo perfectly legitimate.[51] Some scholars, such as Fernando Teson, proceed to justify

la guerre? De l'umanitarisme au contre-terrorisme (Paris: Les Presses de Science Po, 2005); Herfried Münkler and Karsten Malowitz, ed., *Humanitäre Intervention. Ein Instrument außenpolitischer Konfliktbearbeitung: Grundlagen und Diskussion* (Wiesbaden: VS Verlag, 2008).

48 B. Simma, "Nato, the UN and the Use of Force: Legal Aspects," *European Journal of International Law*" 10 (1999): 1-22; L. Ferrajoli, "Guerra, 'etica' e diritto," *Ragion pratica* 7, no. 13 (1999): 117-128.

49 See John Rawls, *The Law of Peoples*, 94, footnote 6: "Is there ever a time when forceful intervention might be called for? If the offenses against human rights are egregious and the society does not respond to the imposition of sanctions, such intervention in the defense of human rights would be acceptable and would be called for."

50 C. Bagnoli, "Humanitarian Intervention as a Perfect Duty: a Kantian Approach," in *Humanitarian Intervention. Nomos XLVII*, ed. Terry Nardin and Melissa S. Williams (New York: New York University Press, 2005), 117-141.

51 See Michael Ignatieff, *Human Rights as Politics and Idolatry* (Princeton: Princeton University Press, 2001) and idem, *The Lesser Evil: Political Ethics in the Age of Terror* (Princeton: Princeton University Press, 2004). For a philosophical critique of the intervention in Kosovo, see Danilo Zolo, *Chi dice*

humanitarian interventions by showing that the rights of the individuals have priority over the rights of the states, and by arguing "that sovereignty is contingent because the rights of a state are derivative of the rights of the individuals who constitute them."[52] Others, such as Mona Fixdal or Joseph Boyle, are convinced that it is possible to justify humanitarian armed interventions on the grounds of a radical reformulation of some of the key-notions of the just war tradition. Others resort to more controversial notions: Nancy Sherman, for instance, grounds our duties to ensure the protection of human rights for those outside our borders in our supposed common membership in a "global moral commonwealth."[53]

It is not possible to examine here the various attempts to justify the so-called "humanitarian" armed interventions on the grounds of the different theories of human rights, and of different philosophical principles. I would rather mention the fact that two types of criticism can be, and have been, addressed to this kind of theories. The first type is an *external* criticism, which questions the actual universal character of human rights. It argues that the theory of human rights lacks both analytical rigour and philosophical foundation. In particular, it argues that the human rights enumerated in the various Bills of Rights, and discussed in the works of the philosophers, have an extremely heterogeneous nature and are characterised by deontic antinomies, which frustrate any attempt to provide them with a coherent and unitary foundation. The thesis of the normative universality of human rights appears to these critics as the dogmatic postulate of ethic rationalism and of old and new forms of the doctrine of natural law. In their view, such a thesis is not confirmed theoretically, and is denied with convincing arguments both by western philosophies of historicist and realist orientation, and by various expressions of non-western cultures. It is often pointed out that members of these cultures reproach western theories of human rights for their claim to universality and, particularly, their strictly individualistic character; and that they oppose to them other ideals and

---

umanità. Guerra, diritto e ordine globale (Torino: Einaudi, 2000), eng. trans. Invoking Humanity. War, Law and Global Order (New York: Continuum, 2002).

52 See Fernando Tesón, Humanitarian Intervention: An Inquiry into Law and Morality, 3rd ed. (Ardsley: Transnational Publishers, 2005).

53 See Nancy Sherman, "Empathy, Respect, and Humanitarian Intervention," Ethics and International Affairs 12 (1998): 103-119.

values—which include, recently, the so-called "Asian values." According to these arguments, the so-called "humanitarian interventions" are conceived to be devoid of real justification, and simply the expression of the unilateral and imperial policies of the only superpower left on the international scene.

Another type of criticism, an *internal* one, may be addressed to those theories which justify military interventions in the name of a humanitarian ideology. For the sake of discussion, one can accept the claim of the universality of human rights, and investigate the way in which these human rights are promoted or implemented instead. Thus, it is possible to draw the attention to the end-means relationship. That is to say, it is possible to ask the question of whether an asymmetric war is an adequate means for achieving the end of human rights. It is awkward to observe how most reflections concerning the so-called "humanitarian interventions" are reflections on their possible legitimacy. Seldom are they reflections on the effective course of action or on the methods of their realisation, and on the problems inevitably raised by such methods.

Against these simplifications, and the disquieting blindness of an important part of the Anglo-Saxon moral philosophy, a serious ethical reflection, up to the present situation, should at least: (i) take the critical contributions of the pacifist tradition into account, even though without choosing to adopt its assumptions. And, especially, two of its contributions: the constant problematization of the end-means relation, and a deep analysis of the unintended consequences implicit in the recourse to violence.[54] (ii) It should also take Weber's lesson into account, according to whom, when thematizing the relation between ethics and politics, ethics should not be understood exclusively in terms of an ethics of conviction, but should incorporate some form of ethics of responsibility.

Due to space limits, these remarks are inevitably schematic. But I don't want to give the impression of discrediting the entire Anglo-Saxon moral reflection. I would like to remind the admirers of Anglo-Saxon philosophy that one of its most important representatives, and one of

---

54 For interesting discussions of these issues, from a pacifist point of view, see for example, Giuliano Pontara, *Se il fine giustifichi i mezzi* (Bologna: Il Mulino, 1974), Giuliano Pontara, *L'antibarbarie: La concezione etico-politica di Gandhi e il XXI secolo* (Turin: EGA, 2006).

the most subtle interpreters of the contemporary ethical debate, Bernard Williams, in his posthumous book *At the Beginning was the Deed* denounced and distanced himself from what he called "moralism in political theory." Without suggesting a relation of direct subordination, he proposed a more problematic relationship between ethics and politics, raising more than one doubt on the so-called "humanitarian interventions," on their justifications and possibilities of realisation.[55]

5. Some Concluding Remarks

In this essay I attempted to show how widely two late medieval and early modern concepts—the concept of just war and the concept of human rights—have been reconsidered and reformulated over the last decades. I also tried to criticise some of these philosophical and political positions from within, taking the arguments of those who reformulated the fundamental notions of the just war tradition and of the theorists of humanitarian interventions seriously.

Nonetheless, I do not want to suggest that it is impossible to think in a fruitful philosophical way about violence and war. In these concluding lines, I would like to draw attention to a way of philosophizing over the problems of contemporary war, which has emerged over the last ten years, and which I consider more congenial. It does not aim at justifying military interventions, but to investigate terrorism and state-sponsored violence, its ultimate roots and ways of reacting against it. Taking over some of Lévinas's suggestions, it has its starting point in an anthropology developed around the notion of vulnerability. In short, I have two works in mind, which are, in my view, exemplary: the first one is Judith Butler's *Precarious Life. The Power of Mourning and Violence* (2004).[56] The second is Adriana Cavarero's 2007 book, *Horrorism: Naming Contemporary Violence*.[57] Unfortunately, it is not possible

---

55 See the two papers written in the last years of his life: "Realism and Moralism in Political Theory" and "Humanitarianism and the Right to Intervene," published in Bernard Williams, *In the Beginning Was the Deed: Realism and Moralism in Political Argument*, ed. Geoffrey Hawthorn (Princeton: Princeton University Press, 2005), 1-17, and 145-153.

56 Judith Butler, *Precarious Life: The Powers of Mourning and Violence* (London: Verso, 2004). See also Judith Butler, *Frames of War: When is Life Grievable?* (London: Verso 2010).

57 A. Cavarero, *Orrorismo, ovvero della violenza sull'inerme* (Milan: Feltrinelli, 2007), eng. trans. *Horrorism: Naming Contemporary Violence* (New York: Columbia University Press 2009). See also L. Bernini and O. Guaraldo, ed., *Differenza e relazione. L'ontologia dell'umano nel pensiero di Judith*

for me to develop these thoughts here.

Let me add one remark. In this paper I attempted to highlight some of the conceptual inconsistencies and the risks of those philosophical perspectives which reformulate the theory of just war or thematize the legitimacy of humanitarian interventions on the grounds of the normative theories of human rights. I tried to show how, through elaborate conceptual architectures of a normative type, these perspectives often ended up legitimizing western military interventions, rather than providing elements of criticism. In the first pages of this essay, I mentioned the fact that many philosophers saw in the fall of the Berlin Wall the possibility of—and had hope for—of the creation of a just cosmopolitan order. And I pointed out how many of them have often been self-referential, failing to examine the more critical contributions of other social sciences. As a result, they brought arguments in favour of the powers that are legitimising their unilateral choices, instead of bringing their dark side into full light. Let me say, to conclude, that I feel the need for, and that I would recommend a philosophical work that focuses on criticism, rather than foundation, on deconstruction and demystification, rather than legitimisation. "To understand the world through suffering: that is the tragic," it's often recalled on the paths of Nietzsche.[58] I would prefer a philosophy, or an intellectual work, which keeps alive, in its conceptual structures and in its practice of writing as well, the sense of the endless tragedies around us.

Butler e Adriana Cavarero. Con un dialogo tra le due filosofe (Verona: Ombre corte, 2009).

58   See for example Reiner Schürmann, *Des hégémonies brisées* (Mauvezin: Trans-Europ-Repress, 1996), 7.

Justice Over Charity:
Some Dangers in Faith-Based Poverty Initiatives

SAM FLEISCHACKER

1.

Religious groups that reject modern science and liberal rights theories have notoriously been on the rise in recent years. No particular religion has a monopoly on such groups: they include traditional Jews, Christians, Muslims, and Hindus. I do not of course mean to suggest that all traditional religious people belong to groups of this sort: religious views do not align neatly with political ones, and there are many devoutly religious people with liberal political beliefs. However, certain religious views are held by their adherents to entail an expressly anti-liberal politics, and groups representing such views have, since the demise of communism, become perhaps the greatest threat worldwide to liberalism. As a religious person myself, I sympathize with the marginalization that these groups feel in the modern, secular world; as a liberal, I am appalled by much that they stand for. The dilemma, for a liberal, is that, while they threaten liberalism itself, they cannot be suppressed without violating the rights of conscience, perhaps the most basic liberal principle.

The question of how to accommodate illiberal groups within a liberal democracy is a deep and vexed one that divides political theorists. It is not my topic here, however. I am concerned instead with a way in which liberals may unwittingly *foster* the growth of illiberal religious groups. I have in mind the idea, endorsed by many liberal theorists and activists, that religious groups can constructively partner with the state in the struggle against poverty. Christian Democrats in Europe have maintained such a view for decades, and over the past 15 years a bipartisan agreement has emerged, even in the United States, that it could be a good idea for the government to work together with "faith-based" anti-poverty programs.[1] President Bush picked a long-time Democrat, John

---

1   See Lew Daly, *God's Economy: Faith-Based Initiatives and the Caring State* (Chicago: University of

— 154 —

DiIulio, as the first head of his office for faith-based initiatives, and President Obama, while reversing many Bush policies, has retained that office. There are differences between Republicans and Democrats over the degree to which anti-poverty programming should be in the hands of religious groups, and over the conditions religious groups should meet if they are to get Federal assistance, but there is considerable agreement that governments can work together with religious groups in fighting poverty. The idea seems to be that religious groups will bring greater compassion to their work than government bureaucrats, and provide moral and spiritual inspiration, along with material aid, to their clients.[2]

There is a grain of truth to these claims, and I do not want to deny that it is a good thing for religious groups to run soup kitchens and other projects that help the poor. I do not even want to deny that a carefully designed government effort to help religious groups engage in such efforts—focusing, let us say, on small groups based in local communities, as part of a wider effort to encourage small-scale, community-based welfare programs, whether religious or secular—might have some value.[3] But each of the claims I listed above is also problematic, and the rosy picture of religious participation in the public realm that they add up to is highly misleading. The problems I have in mind have not been much addressed. There has been a lot of controversy over whether programs that involve proselytizing can receive government aid, whether cults, and other potentially dangerous religious groups, need to be given government aid if they run programs similar to those of more mainstream religions, and whether religious groups that accept government

---

Chicago Press, 2009) on the theological and political underpinnings of Christian Democratic thought in Europe, and the ways in which they may also support the new U.S. support for faith-based initiatives. Daly seems to welcome the fact that such efforts, in both Europe and the US, may amount to tacit support by the government for Christianity; I think this is something to worry about.

2   The evidence that faith-based groups are effective in dealing with poverty is, thus far, quite mixed. A Rockefeller Institute report on faith-based programs, called "Taking Stock," released in 2009, found no clear evidence that they are more effective than secular programs; it also found that most faith-based groups lacked the means to apply for government grants to help them. Daly, who strongly supports such efforts, also reports doubts about the evidence for their effectiveness: see Daly, *God's Economy*, 3 and note 2 to that page.

3   To some extent, Bush's original initiative was aimed in this direction, although in practice it did not reach out to secular groups alongside religious ones, nor did it distinguish, as I think it should have done, between large and small religious groups, or local and national ones. As we shall see, the political dangers of religious groups are far greater when those groups are large and national, than when they are small and local.

aid must be bound by general American anti-discrimination policies in their hiring (whether they can refuse to hire gay people, for instance, or people outside their faith community). But these issues are not my main concern. I think that putting social programming in the hands of religious groups poses significant practical and symbolic threats to a liberal democracy, even if those programs do not proselytize, are run by mainstream communities, and do not discriminate in their hiring. I will try to bring this out with the help of some early modern texts. Early modern thinkers were clearer than we are today about the importance of drawing sharp lines between religious institutions and the state, per-haps because they were closer to a theocratic age. In any case, we can often illuminate contemporary issues by looking back a few centuries and seeing how analogous issues were treated then. Here I will consider first some passages in Adam Smith's *Wealth of Nations*, and then a debate from shortly after Smith's time over whether the poor had a right to aid from the state. After that, I will return to our contemporary situation and argue that liberal governments need to be very careful about how, if at all, they encourage religious efforts to help the poor.

2.

Let us start with Smith's critique of the aid given to the poor by the medieval Catholic Church. Towards the end of the *Wealth of Nations*, Smith wrote a wonderful chapter on state support for religion. The argument of the chapter as a whole is complex, and, like much of the *Wealth of Nations*, directed to a series of ironies: in this case the irony a) that an enlightened, liberal attitude towards religion is most likely to come about if the state does not directly encourage that attitude, and b) that fanatical, anti-liberal religious groups can make a positive contribution to liberal societies, and c) that the dangerous power of the medieval Catholic church came in large part from its charitable works, and that it became tamer and less dangerous when the selfish vices of its clergy brought down those efforts. The last of these points is the most important for our purposes, but before focusing on it, let me summarize the overall argument.

Smith's overall question is whether states should support religious institutions at all, and he begins by summarizing the dry, delightfully perverse claim of his friend David Hume that established churches are a good thing because they weaken religion, since a state-supported cleric will have no incentive to defend his church's dogmas with any enthusiasm. The state can "bribe [the] indolence" of the clergy, says Hume: "assigning stated salaries to their profession" will lower the temperature of their religious commitment, and therefore of their disputes.[4] Smith responds that complete disestablishment can achieve the same effect, since religions that have no government to support them will eventually dwindle into small sects, whose teachers, "finding themselves almost alone," will have to respect the teachings of all the other sects in order to survive. In this way, says Smith, the doctrine of most religions may eventually be reduced "to that pure and rational religion, free from every mixture of absurdity, imposture, or fanaticism, such as wise men have in all ages of the world wished to see established."[5] Smith then adds that even quite fanatical religious groups, when small, can be beneficial to a liberal society: they provide, above all, a moral community for laborers who move to a large city, who might otherwise be lost in anonymity.[6]

Having said all this on behalf of disestablishment, Smith goes on to acknowledge that practically no nation in his day was following or likely to follow any such policy, and to allow for certain judicious uses of government power to manage the dominant church of a country. This is a compromise for Smith and an example of his pragmatism, but he winds up arguing that governments should aim for their established churches to resemble the Presbyterian one in his native Scotland: where the benefices of pastoral positions were very modest, and distributed equally to all the clergy. It is this argument that he supports with a historical account of the rise and decline of the Catholic Church, the point of which is to show the grave dangers that a wealthy church can pose to peace and freedom.

And one central piece of this account involves the way that the Catholic Church had used charity to gain "influence over the common people."[7] What Smith says here is remarkably astute, both psychologi-

---

4   David Hume, *The History of England*, vol. 3, 30-1, quoted in Adam Smith, *An Inquiry Into the Nature and Causes of the Wealth of Nations*, ed. R.H. Campbell, A.S. Skinner, and W.B. Todd (Oxford: Oxford University Press, 1976), 791. Henceforth I will refer to this edition as *Wealth of Nations*.

5   Smith, *Wealth of Nations*, 793.

6   Ibid., 794-6.

7   Ibid., 800-1.

cally and politically. The medieval clergy used its "immense surplus" of revenue, says Smith, to "maintain . . . almost the whole poor of every kingdom,"[8] and by this it gained tremendous power. The poor came both to depend materially on the church and to admire it; in explaining the power of the church, Smith indeed stresses its reputation for virtue among the poor over its material hold on them. For their charitable efforts, Catholic clerics were rewarded with "the highest respect and veneration among all the inferior ranks of people."[9] "Every thing belonging or related to so popular an order, its possessions, its privileges, its doctrines, necessarily appeared sacred in the eyes of the common people, and every violation of them, whether real or pretended, the highest act of sacrilegious wickedness and profaneness." As a result, sovereigns found it almost impossible to resist the church's demands. Smith explains the long struggle between civil and ecclesiastical power in this light, saying that, from the tenth through at least the thirteenth century, "the church of Rome may be considered as the most formidable combination that ever was formed against the authority and security of civil government."[10] In that capacity, he adds, the church was also an implacable threat to "the liberty, reason, and happiness of mankind, which can flourish only where civil government is able to protect them." The stake that the common people had in the well-being of the church, together with the veneration they had for it, made them cling passionately to the "superstition" (Smith's word) it propounded; "all the wisdom and virtue of man" was unable to shake the hold of that superstition.[11]

Smith has an economic story to tell about how the clergy eventually lost its power, which again centers on the fact that it diminished its works of charity. Much like the story Smith tells earlier in *Wealth of Nations* about the decline of feudal lords,[12] this is a tale in which the private venality of powerful people turns out to have good public consequences. (Although Smith criticizes Mandeville's moral philosophy sharply, he very much agrees with Mandeville that the private vices of

8   Ibid., 801
9   Ibid., 801-2.
10   Ibid., 802.
11   Ibid., 803.
12   Ibid., Part III, chapter iv, to which Smith repeatedly alludes in the chapter from which I have been quoting.

some people—powerful ones—can have public benefits.) As members of the clergy found outlets for their revenue other than charity and hospitality,[13]

> [T]he inferior ranks of people no longer looked upon [them] . . . as the comforters of their distress, and the relievers of their indigence. On the contrary, they were provoked and disgusted by the vanity, luxury, and expence of the richer clergy, who appeared to spend upon their own pleasures, what had always before been regarded as the patrimony of the poor.[14]

The way now lay open for kings to gain greater control over the church, as well as for reformers to win people away from Rome. And among the reformers, says Smith, the most poorly paid clergy—the Presbyterian clergy of Holland, Switzerland, and Scotland—tended to have the most lasting and effective spiritual authority over the common people. Their modest salaries encouraged in them the development of virtue—"Nothing but the most exemplary morals can give dignity to a man of small fortune"—and the common people "look[ed] upon [them] with that kindness with which we naturally regard one who approaches somewhat to our own condition, but who, we think, ought to be in a higher."[15] The kindness of the parishioners in turn evoked a like kindness in the clergy: a Presbyterian pastor "becomes careful to instruct [his congregation], and attentive to assist and relieve them. He does not even despise [their] prejudices . . . and never treats them with those contemptuous and arrogant airs which we so often meet with in the proud dignitaries of opulent and well-endowed churches." So a lack of great wealth conduces to a healthy sort of religious influence.[16] In Smith's ideal religious regime, as we have seen, each sect would be so small, and have such minimal means, that "[its] teachers] . . . would be obliged to respect those of almost every other sect," and eventually

---

13   Adam Smith, *Theory of Moral Sentiments*, 184, ed. D.D. Raphael and A.L. Macfie (Oxford: Oxford University Press, 1976); compare with *Wealth of Nations*, 418-419. These outlets for revenue were basically manufactured goods, which Smith likes to call "baubles and trinkets."
14   Smith, *Wealth of Nations*, 804.
15   Ibid., 810.
16   Wealth "destroys almost entirely that sanctity of character which can alone enable [a clergyman] to perform [his] duties with proper weight and authority." Smith, *Wealth of Nations*, 41.

reduce its doctrines to "pure and rational religion."[17] But even if that ideal is impossible, or unlikely to arrive for a long time, he thinks we can approximate it by having poorly paid clergy. The riches that enabled the Catholic Church to maintain the poor were a source of great and dangerous power, a temptation to vices that corrupted the real good that a clergy can accomplish. According to Smith, poorly-endowed small churches that focus on teaching their parishioners and doing small acts of kindness are far more likely to achieve ends for which believers and non-believers alike can respect them.

What can we learn from this account? First, Smith gives us a thoughtful, non-reductive account of the hold that a clergy can gain over the people by charitable institutions. It is not just that the poor come to be materially dependent on a church that dominates its society's welfare practices, but that their gratitude for this overwhelms their ability to judge the church impartially. This two-sided mode of explanation, appealing to moral approval as well as self-interest, runs through Smith's account.[18] The people initially admire their clerical benefactors as well as depending on them; later, they are not only frustrated by the reduction in charity, but contemptuous of clerics who spend so much on themselves. And finally, they feel respect and affection for the Presbyterian clergy who have hardly anything to spend. Poor clerics may thus achieve their religious mission better than rich ones. That churches might do the greatest good even in their own terms, if they are not well-enough endowed to run large charitable programs, is an interesting idea that still has something to teach us today.

Second, as a historical matter, Smith is quite right to say that the consolidation of civil power in sixteenth-century Europe went together with an attempt by kings to wrest poor relief from the church. Charles V tried to regularize relief throughout the Netherlands in 1531.[19] Hamburg mandated employment and easy loans for the able-bodied poor and aid to the disabled in 1529, and Sweden set up a system of poor relief in

---

17   Ibid., 793.

18   This is one example of why it is a mistake to read *Wealth of Nations* as premised on the idea that self-interest alone governs human nature. For more on that misreading, see Sam Fleischacker, *On Adam Smith's Wealth of Nations: A Philosophical Companion* (Princeton: Princeton University Press, 2004), ch. 5.

19   His decree met "with the determined . . . resistance of the Church." Jan de Vries and Ad van der Woude, *The First Modern Economy: Success, Failure, and Perseverance of the Dutch Economy, 1500-1815* (Cambridge: Cambridge University Press, 1997), 655.

1571.[20] The English Poor Law of 1601 formalized a similar requirement, initially legislated under Henry VIII.[21] All these laws were attempts to gain control over the church, whatever other aims they may have had, and it is no coincidence that they were implemented at the height of the struggles over the Reformation.[22]

Smith responds to these historical developments by noting the political and moral advantages of a world in which relief of the poor is treated as a civil rather than a religious right. Putting this relief in the hands of the state, rather than churches, transforms it from a matter of charity into a matter of justice. At the same time, it takes from churches a great source of temporal power. In calling the medieval Roman church a formidable combination against civil government, and thereby against "liberty, reason and happiness," Smith expresses neatly the distinct roles of religious and mundane power. Governments, not churches, have the responsibility and the right kinds of power to protect our ability to pursue our earthly happiness, and the liberty and reason we need to figure out which religious doctrines we should hold. Smith indicates clearly that the liberty he so fervently promotes leads him to oppose the material and spiritual power that a clergy can gain by dispensing aid to the poor. Aid to the poor, for Smith, should be something that enhances their ability to make their own choices, not a gift from a moral superior, to which they should respond with humility and veneration. Of course, Smith was not arguing for or against government-church partnerships in the administration of welfare programs. The very idea of state "welfare programs" was virtually unheard of in his day. I've argued elsewhere that it is a mistake to see Smith as opposed to the idea that states should run such programs—the idea we

---

20 T. W. Fowle, *The Poor Law* (Littleton, CO: Fred B. Rothman & Co, 1980, [originally published: London: Macmillan, 1893]), 23.

21 In 1531, England imposed a requirement to look out for the poor on "mayors, justices of the peace, and other local officials." At the same time, it restricted the movements of the poor in various ways, and provided for punishment of able-bodied beggars. Both the constructive and the punitive aspects of this measure have antecedents that go back as far as 1349. Walter Trattner, *From Poor Law to Welfare State*, 5th ed. (New York: The Free Press, 1994), 8-12.

22 Gareth Stedman Jones notes that, outside of England, these policies did not last: "Tax-based local relief had been practised in other parts of Europe in the sixteenth century, but only in England did it survive in an elaborated form through to the eighteenth century." He also points out that revolutionary France instituted policies of state assistance programs in good part "to secure the loyalty of the poor to the new order by removing welfare from the control of the church," thereby repeating what the reformers had done in the sixteenth century. Stedman Jones, *An End to Poverty?* (London: Profile Books, 2004), 75-6, 61.

today we call "social" or "distributive" justice.[23] It is worth noting that Smith's critique of church-based welfare supports this reading of his views.

3.

If aid to the poor counts as part of the government's charge to protect our "liberty, reason, and happiness," it would seem to be bound up with the rights of the poor. This brings us to a debate that began to rage just after Smith died, over whether the poor should receive help as charity, or instead have a right to relief or maintenance. In my *Short History of Distributive Justice*, I argued that the idea that aid to the poor should come under the heading of justice rather than charity is quite new, dating back no further than the end of the eighteenth century.[24] Since that time, I have come to think that this point is best put in terms of "rights" rather than "justice." The phrases "social justice" and "economic justice" do not really come into circulation until the twentieth century, while already in the eighteenth century there are explicit debates over

---

23   See my *On Adam Smith's Wealth of Nations*, chapter ten, and *Short History of Distributive Justice* (Cambridge, MA: Harvard University Press, 2004).

24   Roughly, that argument ran as follows: Aristotle used "distributive justice" to designate the virtue of giving goods to people in accord with merit, not a distribution of "fair starting points," let alone an equal share of all resources, to all. Moreover, his distributive justice was primarily concerned with political, not material, goods—the distribution of a role in government is his main example of it. The early Christian emphasis on helping the poor, on the other hand, was largely part of a commitment to humbling oneself before God, not an attempt to eradicate poverty. Jesus and his apostles tried to live with the poor, not to end poverty. And the paradigm Christian mode of giving to the poor, until the end of the eighteenth century, was one in which giver and recipient alike saw the gifts as undeserved, as a reflection of God's grace to man in Christ. The poor deserve nothing from the wealthy, but receive something anyway out of the wealthy person's grace. The main criticisms I have received about this thesis have come from religious people who want to say that the Torah or the books of Amos and Isaiah, or the Gospels, or the Quran, already clearly express the idea of social justice. For reasons I cannot go into here, I think this is incorrect, but I would certainly acknowledge that there are passages in all the Abrahamic sacred scriptures—and quite possibly in the scriptures of other religious traditions— that can be read as anticipating the idea of social justice. Nobody in fact did read them that way, I think, until after the Enlightenment, but it seems to me that a modern believer can see these texts as nevertheless always latently containing the idea of social justice: that it was God's intention, in producing these texts, that they would eventually be read to convey the idea that people have a right not to be poor. It just took the Enlightenment to "unlock" that meaning of the texts. One happy consequence of this suggestion is that it might help religious believers see how they can learn something useful from the secular world: it could enable those of us who are religious to regard the secular Enlightenment as having helped us understand our sacred texts better, and not simply as an attack on our faith.

the notion of a right to relief or subsistence. In his wonderful book *An End to Poverty?*, Gareth Stedman Jones quotes a passage from a 1792 summary of the work of the Comité de Mendicité in France according to which "every man has a right to subsistence through work, if he is able-bodied; and to free assistance if he is unable to work." He quotes a 1793 writing of Thomas Ruggles to much the same effect.[25] He also notes that Pitt, in his proposed Poor Law Bill of 1796, called for England to "make relief, in cases where there are a number of children, a matter of right, and an honour." In the same year, Babeuf made the right to "an equal enjoyment of all wealth" the center-piece of his abortive attempt to renew and radicalize the French Revolution.[26] And a year or so after that, probably under Babeuf's influence, both Thomas Paine and J.G. Fichte wrote works declaring that there was a right to subsistence—Fichte indeed offered a derivation of such a right from the right to property:

> To be able to live is the absolute, inalienable property of all human beings. We have seen that a certain sphere of objects is granted to the individual solely for a certain use. But the final end of this use is to be able to live. . . . [Hence a] principle of all rational state constitutions is that everyone ought to be able to live from his labor, . . . and the state must make arrangements to insure this.[27]

At the same time we see a backlash against the idea of subsistence rights. In 1797, Arthur Young noted ominously that "that relief which formerly was and still ought to be petitioned for as a favor, is now fre-

---

25 Jones, *End to Poverty?*, 61, 74-5.
26 David Thomson, *The Babeuf Plot* (London: K. Paul, Trench, Trubner, 1947), 33.
27 J.G. Fichte, *Foundations of Natural Right*, trans. M. Baur, ed. Frederick Neuhouser (Cambridge: Cambridge University Press, 2000), 185. The passage continues: "[A]ll property rights are grounded in the contract of all with all, which states: 'We are all entitled to keep this, on the condition that we let you have what is yours.' Therefore, if someone is unable to make a living from his labor, he has not been given what is absolutely his, and . . . the contract is completely canceled with respect to him." In *The Closed Commercial State*, Fichte says that every "rational state" should institute a distribution of goods, ensuring that all its citizens have an agreeable life, and that the share each citizen would have in this distribution "is his own by right"; quoted in H.S. Reiss, ed., *The Political Thought of the German Romantics* (New York: Macmillan, 1955), 90. Both of these writings appeared shortly after Babeuf's abortive uprising, and Fichte is said to have been influenced by Babeuf; Reiss, 16.

quently demanded as a right."[28] Frederick Eden, in his contemporaneous *State of the Poor*, wrote, "It is one, and not the least, of the mistaken principles on which [laws for the relief of the poor are based] that every individual . . . has not only a claim, but a right . . . [to be supplied with] employment when able to work, and with a maintenance when incapacitated from labor."[29] Pitt, in the passage Stedman Jones cites, called for England to "make relief . . . a matter of right"—believing, presumably, that it was not already such. [30] Thomas Paine was very restrained about grounding any sort of welfare on rights in his 1792 *Rights of Man*, moving in that direction only in his later, more radical work *Agrarian Justice*.[31] Thomas Malthus, in 1803, understood English law as having granted people "a right to subsistence," but insisted that there should be no such right: "There is one right which man has generally been thought to possess," says Malthus,

> which I am confident he neither does, nor can possess—
> a right to subsistence when his labour will not fairly
> purchase it. Our laws indeed say that he has this right,
> and bind the society to furnish employment and food to
> those who cannot get them in the regular market, but in
> so doing, they attempt to reverse the laws of nature.[32]

In sum, a heated debate broke out in the late eighteenth century over whether the poor have a right to relief or subsistence, or should instead

---

28 Arthur Young, General View of the Agriculture of the County of Suffolk, as quoted in A. J. Peacock, *Bread or Blood: A Study of the Agrarian Riots in East Anglia in 1816* (London: Victor Gollancz, 1965), 35. See also Lynn Lees, *The Solidarities of Strangers: The English Poor Laws and the People, 1700-1948* (Cambridge: Cambridge University Press, 1998), 77.

29 Eden, *State of the Poor* (Frank Cass & Co, 1966: facsimile of 1797 edition), 447. Eden goes on to doubt the existence of any right that cannot practicably be gratified, and quote Burke's Reflections in support of a more libertarian conception of economic rights.

30 Jones, *End of Poverty?*, 77, my emphasis.

31 I argued in my *Short History* that the fact that Paine defended his proposal in the *Rights of Man* for a retirement benefit on the peculiar grounds that the elderly deserve a rebate on past taxes suggests that even radicals did not feel they could make a convincing case for the idea that all people have a right to maintenance in 1792. The fact that Paine appeals to a more comprehensive right to maintenance in his 1797 *Agrarian Justice* reinforces this interpretation of the *Rights of Man*. Paine wrote *Agrarian Justice* after the abortive uprising of Babeuf, and apparently somewhat under Babeuf's influence; see Jack Fruchtman Jr., *Thomas Paine: Apostle of Freedom* (New York: Four Walls Eight Windows, 1994), 355-6.

32 Jones, *End of Poverty?*, 104-5.

be "petitioning for [it] as a favour." Those on the latter side of the debate appealed both to nature and to morality. Malthus, as we just saw, argued against a right to subsistence on the grounds that it tries "to reverse the laws of nature." Joseph Townsend had suggested earlier that making poor relief a matter of right rather than a gift was harmful to the virtues of both the receivers and the would-be givers:

> Nothing in nature can be more disgusting than a parish pay-table, attendant upon which ... are too often found combined, snuff, gin, rags, vermin, insolence, and abusive language; nor in nature can any thing be more beautiful than the mild complacency of benevolence, hastening to the humble cottage to relieve the wants of industry and virtue, to feed the hungry, to cloath the naked, and to sooth the sorrows of the widow with her tender orphans; nothing can be more pleasing, unless it be their sparkling eyes, their bursting tears, and their uplifted hands, the artless expressions of unfeigned gratitude for unexpected favours. [33]

The other side of this debate can be represented by Immanuel Kant, who railed throughout his moral writings against helping the poor merely out of benevolence. In his *Lectures on Ethics*, he argued that giving alms "flatters the giver's pride," while "degrad[ing]" those to whom the alms are given. The money we give the poor should be seen, not as alms, but as something to which the poor have a right.[34] Every human being "has an equal right to the good things which nature has provided,"[35] Kant says, so anything we give the poor should be seen "as a debt of honour rather than as an exhibition of kindness and generosity."[36] Kant also worries that the pleasures of flattery with which charity is rewarded may lead people to perform acts of charity in place of other, less pleasurable, moral

---

33 Joseph Townsend, *A Dissertation on the Poor Laws* (Berkeley: University of California Press, 1971 [originally published in 1786]), 69. We see here the language of Christian grace: the rich benefactor is Christ, dispensing "unexpected favours" to his or her unworthy, but suitably grateful, recipients.

34 Kant considers a respect for the rights of others, rather than their needs, to form the core of proper beneficence: see Immanuel Kant, *Lectures on Ethics*, trans. L. Infield (Indianapolis: Hackett, 1963), 193-194. (Compare also *Groundwork of the Metaphysics of Morals*, Ak, 423.)

35 Kant, *Lectures on Ethics*, 192.

36 Ibid., 236.

acts, or to expect similar flattery for moral acts that are not normally re-warded in such a way: "A man should not be flattered for performing acts of kindness," he says, "for then his heart inflames with generosity and he wants all his actions to be of that kind." A sentimental understanding of charity may thus corrupt the entire moral realm. Accordingly, Kant indicates that the state ought to find ways of helping the poor that clearly mark the fact that poor aid is a right: "It would be better," he says, "to see whether the poor man could not be helped in some other way which would not entail his being degraded by accepting alms."[37]

Kant greatly influenced Fichte, and the views he lays out may also fairly be taken, I think, to express the ideas of many of the British advo-cates of making poor relief a matter of rights. There is a clear argument for this position from within the liberal view, which Kant represents, that governments are primarily designed to protect individual freedom. The idea that such freedom requires only negative rights seems to me a mistake.[38] Rights are necessary conditions for freedom, but freedom has both negative and positive necessary conditions, so there must be both negative and positive rights. Free agency is a process that needs to be developed, to be nurtured in a number of ways, not simply left alone.[39] It is not something human beings have at birth, or develop without ad-equate nurture; it requires, rather, a variety of mental skills and must be fostered by institutions allowing people to maintain basic levels of physi-cal and mental health, and to understand the options among which they can choose.[40] Most of us take it to be intuitively obvious that a person desperate for food or shelter is not properly free, and that an illiterate person in a literate society has very limited freedom, and I know of no good argument showing this intuition to be incorrect.

So there is a straightforward liberal argument, along the lines of the

---

37 Ibid., 236.
38 The idea that positive rights are impossible to enforce, or indeed foreign to the American Constitution, is also, surely, a mistake: both the right to vote and the right to a jury trial are positive rights, requiring governments actively to provide certain facilities and not merely to stand back and let citizens do as they will.
39 This conception of freedom is shared by many moral and political philosophers today. I attempted to lay out a version of it in my *Third Concept of Liberty*, (Princeton: Princeton University Press, 1999).
40 In this I agree very much with the position nicely laid out in Lesley Jacobs' *Rights and Deprivations*, (Oxford: Clarendon Press, 1993), chapter 7. Frank Michelman offers what we might call a "citizenship" rather than a "justice" basis for welfare rights: see below, note 42. But these two approaches converge in many ways: see § 4 below.

one Fichte proposes, for welfare rights being as much a condition for freedom as property rights. There is also a different line of argument for such rights, drawn from the conditions for shared citizenship rather than the conditions for individual freedom—drawn from a more civic republican view of government. One of the most important representatives of the civic republican tradition in the eighteenth century was of course Rousseau, and a Rousseauvian line of argument for welfare rights seems to have run alongside the Kantian one. It maintained that nations will never achieve true equality and fraternity among their citizens without an end to poverty. Poor relief—or, indeed, a full-blown basket of welfare policies that prevent poverty from arising—thus becomes a condition for a properly educated and independent democratic citizenry. Stedman Jones brings excerpts from Thomas Paine, Condorcet, and other English and French writers in the wake of the French revolution, to suggest that a concern for the poor as fellow citizens rather than (just) fellow human beings is the main consideration behind their welfare proposals.[41] And it is also a thought of that kind that, two centuries later, some have proposed as a basis for seeing welfare rights in the American Constitution. Education, especially, and perhaps also food and shelter, may be a precondition for our being able to vote meaningfully, and to participate in the political process. In that case, the right to vote may entail a correlative right to a certain level of welfare. This line of argument was taken very seriously in the U.S. Supreme Court of the late 1960s and early 1970s, and some prominent Constitutional scholars continue to defend it to this day. [42]

---

41 Jones, *End of Poverty?*, 50-63, 224, 235.
42 See especially *San Antonio v. Rodriguez*. The majority argued, in the course of rejecting a constitutional right to education, "How . . . is education to be distinguished from the significant personal interests in the basics of decent food and shelter? Empirical examination might well buttress an assumption that the ill-fed, ill-clothed and ill-housed are among the most ineffective participants in the political process, and that they derive the least enjoyment from the benefits of the First Amendment." (1299). Justice Marshall in dissent, trying to defend a constitutional right to education without granting a constitutional right to food and shelter, responded, "Whatever the severity of the impact of insufficient food or inadequate housing on a person's life, they have never been considered to bear the same direct and immediate relationship to constitutional concerns for free speech and for our political processes as education. . . . Education, in terms of constitutional values, is much more analogous in my judgment, to the right to vote in state elections than to public welfare or public housing." id., fn 74 to 1339; see also 1337-1339, passim. So neither the majority nor the dissent actually recognized a broad constitutional right to welfare, but they both clearly saw an argument from the prerequisites of citizenship that could lead one in that direction. Cass Sunstein has

4.

How much difference does it make whether we defend welfare rights as a matter of justice or a precondition for citizenship? At first glance, it may seem to make a great deal of difference. If the state's duties to the poor are rooted in the demands of citizenship, they will go out exclusively to those who are our fellow citizens, not to immigrants, or those who live transiently among us (what the Germans call *Gastarbeiter*), let alone strangers far across the globe. Moreover, the point of such duties will in that case have more to do with building a harmonious and mutually respectful society than with rights individuals hold independently of their social relationships. The right to aid might also then be linked to a duty to contribute in some way to one's society, and might even be made contingent on the poor person's willingness to contribute. A right to aid rooted in justice, on the other hand, would seem to entail no such reciprocal obligation; its point would have to do with each individual's ability to act freely, not his or her membership in a society; and it would go out, at least in principle, to human beings everywhere.

But it is difficult to separate issues of citizenship from issues of justice. The kind of society we want to build with our fellow citizens is a just society: without justice, it will hardly consist of people who respect one another. Nor can we expect our fellow citizens to contribute to building such a society unless we treat them justly. On the other side of the coin, all duties of justice are to some extent limited by fellow citizenship, and to some extent entail reciprocal obligations on the part of those who benefit from them. We do not normally go out to protect people against rape or murder in countries other than our own, nor can they appeal to our courts to restore their rights against an oppressive government. And while we do not make the protection of our fellow citizens against violence contingent on their doing anything to safeguard or enhance our country, we tend to expect the protection of those rights to instill in them some sense of obligation to pay taxes, serve on juries, and oth-

---

suggested that the Court had been moving towards endorsing this argument in the late 1960s, and only the fact that Richard Nixon was able to appoint a large number of new Justices in his first term blocked that movement; see Sunstein, *The Second Bill of Rights* (New York: Basic Books, 2004). Frank Michelman has argued since the 1970s for the correctness of the argument; see his "In Pursuit of Constitutional Welfare Rights: One View of Rawls' Theory of Justice," *University of Pennsylvania Law Review* 121, 5 (1973): 962-1019, and "Welfare Rights in a Constitutional Democracy," *Washington University Law Quarterly*, 3 (1979): 659-693. Sunstein endorses this theory in *Second Bill of Rights*, 152, 170.

erwise support the institutions that grant them freedom and security.

So citizenship and justice are interwoven, at least if the basis of citizenship in one's country is a shared commitment to certain principles. As long as a state is grounded in a civic nationalism—as long its nationhood rests primarily or solely on a sense that its members are committed to building a civic whole together—the duties owed to fellow citizens should more or less coincide with the duties of justice. We will then owe certain duties to our fellow citizens because they are fellow human beings, although we may not owe such duties to fellow human beings who happen not to be fellow citizens.

Where a sharp difference between rights owed to fellow citizens and rights owed simply to fellow human beings can arise—where it will, consequently, make a considerable difference whether welfare rights are based on citizenship or on justice—is where citizenship is understood as based in significant part on shared ethnicity or culture. Theorists of nationalism today distinguish between ethnocultural and civic nationalism, reserving the former term for states that see themselves as representing a particular linguistic, religious, or cultural group.[43] Israel, Malaysia, and Singapore are paradigm examples of ethnocultural nationalist states; Germany, Italy, and Denmark are states that, we might say, are at one stage or another in the process of recovering from ethnocultural nationalism, and trying to reconstitute themselves as civic nationalist states; the US is perhaps the paradigm example of a civic nationalist state, a state in which citizenship is almost entirely based on shared principles.[44]

---

43 For an excellent discussion of this distinction, see Chaim Gans, *The Limits of Nationalism* (Cambridge: Cambridge University Press, 2003), 8-15.

44 As this sentence indicates, I think the difference between ethnic and civic nationalism is almost everywhere a matter of degree. (Gans suggests something similar: ibid., 11-13.) It would be a gross historical inaccuracy to ignore the role that having Anglo-Saxon roots, and being white, for a long time played, and to some extent still plays, in the way citizenship has been understood in the US, and it would be a similar distortion to portray all the institutions in countries like Israel and Malaysia as upholding ethnic nationalism. The recent Malaysian court decision striking down the government's attempt to limit the use of the word "Allah" to Muslims is a striking example of how the dominant ethnic group can lose its pet causes even in that quite undemocratic country, and Yoram Hazony's long list of complaints about Israel's educational and judicial system, in the opening chapters of a polemic in favor of Jewish ethnic nationalism, demonstrates the degree to which Israel has quietly been moving from an ethnic to a civic nationalism, even as it officially remains an ethnic-nationalist state. See Yoram Hazony, *A Jewish State* (New York: Basic Books, 2001).

5.

And those principles are the principles of liberal democracy. This brings us back to our question about whether it is consistent with liberal democracy to allow welfare programs to be seen as within the purview of churches, and appropriately motivated by charity, or whether they should instead be kept strictly under the control of the state, because they are properly entailed by the rights of justice or citizenship. We may sum up the lines of argument for and against seeing aid to the poor as a matter of justice rather than charity, as follows:

For: Welfare construed as a right expresses respect for the recipient, and avoids inappropriately flattering the pride of those who give. It also conveys a sense that the recipient is a fully equal fellow citizen. And it reduces the power of religious groups, keeping the poor from becoming dependent on them, and developing excessive veneration for them.

Against: Welfare construed as charity expresses true love or compassion on the part of the giver; the opportunity for developing and displaying such feelings will be greatly reduced if aid is disbursed by anonymous state bureaucrats. Receiving charity also discourages complacency on the part of the recipient, who might otherwise feel he does not have to work to earn a living. In addition, state welfare gives too much power to the state, diminishing the healthy countervailing influence that voluntary associations, including churches, can have. (This is a point that does not appear in eighteenth-century debates, but it parallels the argument about private welfare giving too much power to churches.)

Which of these views should we accept today? I have tried to be fair to both sides of the argument—I think there is validity to each—but there are strong reasons for any believer in liberal democracy to favor the case for. In the first place, anyone who regards human beings as essentially equal in dignity should favor aid to the poor being the responsibility of the state. Only thereby do we declare that all human beings, just by virtue of their humanity, deserve the same chance at achieving basic happiness, and realizing their freedom.

In the second place, if our state is democratic, putting welfare programs in its hands amounts to a declaration that they ought to be accountable to the citizenry, rather than to the whims or dogmas of religious leaders: we express our belief that such programs need to live up to certain norms of fairness and that it is our duty to ensure that all our fellow citizens have enough means that they can participate in the democratic process.[45]

Finally, having religious groups carry out any substantial welfare programs will inevitably bring them great power, which will ultimately threaten the liberty of secular people, and members of minority religions. Where the state is democratic, no friend of freedom should want to undermine its organs in favor of religious organizations.[46]

All of which is not to deny that critics of state-run welfare programs have a point when they say that welfare bureaucracies tend to be anonymous, cold, and inefficient. They are also right to worry about the centralization of power that comes about when the state carries out a large number of social functions. But these reasonable points have in recent decades obscured the dangers of religiously run welfare programs. The harm it does to a sense of equal citizenship to have welfare distributed as a "gift" from the rich to the poor, the morally corrupting effect of charity on both giver and recipient, and the danger that religious groups will gain excessive power by way of their aid to the poor, were all clearer to eighteenth century thinkers than they are to writers on welfare today.

---

45 Both of these points are compatible with the possibility that faith-based initiatives, in practice, do more to help the poor than any state bureaucracy. I doubt that is true, as a matter of fact, but if it were, one could square the theoretical points I have made with this practical one by making the state the official guarantor of welfare, while "sub-contracting" the actual programs that carry out this charge, as it were, to religious organizations.

46 Perhaps, if voluntary organizations are better than state bureaucracies in running welfare programs, one might want to advocate on behalf of voluntary secular organizations (nonprofits), like the ones Bill Gates has been setting up in recent years. But even then there is a danger that the individuals running such organizations, who are not accountable to the democratic process, will direct their efforts according to their personal whims or dogmatic convictions rather than the demands of the truly needy. Religious groups are, however, more dangerous: people are unlikely to flock to a private secular individual, and worship him, especially if he acts in whimsical or dogmatic ways. Religious groups, by contrast, already draw such followers, normally by way of a not wholly rational faith. Empowering them is therefore encouraging a mode of belief that is dangerous to a political realm based on reason. (I am assuming here that liberal politics must be as rational as possible: we will not long remain free if our laws are not rationally grounded.) I do not mean to say that all ethical commitments need be rational: it seems possible to me, and indeed desirable, to maintain a non-rational religious faith alongside rationalist political commitments. Robert Audi and Paul Weithman have been prominent among those defending such a position in recent years; I offer my own defense in *Divine Teaching and the Way of the World* (Oxford: Oxford University Press, 2011), Part V.

6.

With these thoughts in mind, let us come back to the effort to promote faith-based initiatives established under Bush and maintained by Obama. I see the argument of this paper as warning of the considerable dangers in such an effort, but not entirely ruling it out. It seems hard to deny that in some places a church may deliver social services more effectively than any other agency would—think of a poor small town, or inner-city neighborhood, where practically everybody attends the local church but no other institution, including the school, is respected. I do not want to deny the value of having a soup kitchen, or homeless shelter, or educational program run out of the church, in these circumstances, or of having the government underwrite such a program if it could not survive on its own. Even better, if this is possible, would be to have the government support an interfaith program to help the poor, thereby signaling clearly that it is not setting out to help any particular religious group.[47]

What lines might we draw between appropriate and inappropriate partnerships between liberal governments and religious groups? Suppose we draw the following two broad lessons from the early modern debates we have considered: first, aid to the poor can be used as a way of gaining great material and spiritual influence over an especially vulnerable segment of the population—liberal governments have an interest in taking care that that does not happen; and second, poor people have a right to aid that enables them to rise out of poverty (out of pressing and oppressive need) and can best achieve respect and self-respect if they receive such aid as the fulfillment of a right, not out of charity. Then we have a *prima facie*, but not an insurmountable, case against governmental support for welfare programs to be run by religious groups. Any particular proposal that such a program be supported would have to show that it does not run afoul of the two considerations militating against such support. As long as a religious group involved is very small, hence unlikely to exercise much political power, or to control the lives of the people it serves, as long as it does not use its poverty programs to spread its religious message, and as long as it represents its programs as a contribution to justice rather than something for which the poor

---

47   One person on Obama's new Advisory Council to the office of faith-based initiatives (see note 48 below), is Eboo Patel, whose Interfaith Youth Core promotes programs of this kind.

should be grateful, it can make an acceptable partner for a liberal government.

Surely, there are groups that meet these conditions. Religious institutions today often represent what they do to help the poor under the rubric of "social justice" rather than the rubric of "charity." This may reflect the influence of Enlightenment thought, but that hardly matters. The point is that now, unlike in earlier centuries, a church may itself see the poor as entitled to aid, rather than having to petition for it as a favor. And where a church is the only respected institution for miles around, where it knows the population better than any outside agency and is trusted by the population more than any outside agency, it may well carry out the work of social justice better than the government could do directly. Here the argument that church officials can provide smarter and better-motivated help to the community than government officials has real weight, while at the same time there may be little realistic reason to fear that the church will gain excessive influence by its efforts. Accordingly, it could be unnecessary, and foolish, for the government to refuse to work with the church.

What liberal governments need to avoid is any partnership with any large churches or religiously-affiliated organization and with even small churches that mix their aid to the poor with indoctrination, or oppose the idea that welfare is a right. The size consideration may rule out working even with such well-meaning, non-proselytizing organizations as Habitat for Humanity and Catholic Charities: their very success runs too much of a danger of serving as advertising for their religious message. Every individual citizen has of course a moral as well as a legal right to support such groups, and religious people may well want to donate to them rather than to secular groups: there is good reason for Christians to support Christian social justice groups, Muslims to support Muslim ones, etc. But governments do their citizens as a whole a disservice, according to both liberal and civic republican principles, if they partner with such groups.[48]

---

48 The problem is that it can be hard to differentiate between innocuous and dangerous modes of government-church partnerships. Part of Bush's original hope for his Office of Faith-based Initiatives was that it would fund *"small* faith-based groups" (my emphasis)—the sort of local institutions that I've indicated might make appropriate partners for government; see David Kuo, *Tempting Faith* (New York: Free Press, 2006), 136. But Bush also explicitly saw the Office as out to "save souls," and members of a peer-review panel that selected faith-based groups for federal funding under his administration later admitted that they eliminated non-Christian groups from

This paper was written for a conference on how early modern liberal and civic republican ideas might illuminate contemporary politics in Europe and Israel, so I'd like to conclude with a few words on how the issues I have explored apply to Israel. If we look at both Israel and Palestine, the most obvious example of a religious group that has gained dangerous political power by way of its poverty programs is Hamas. Hamas is often described as having two very different sides, one by which it carries out charitable activities, and does great things for Palestinian civil society, and other by which it represents political Islam and carries out terrorist activities in the name of that program. I think it is a mistake to separate these two things. Hamas's charitable activity has been central to its acquisition of political power, and is surely seen that way by the party as a whole.[49]

Within Israel proper, we might point to Shas as an illiberal religious party that has used charitable work as a means to power. But on the whole, Israel has not had much space for religious groups to gain power in this way, precisely because it was founded as a social democratic rather than a libertarian state: as a state in which freedom from poverty, along with the freedom to speak and to vote, was treated as basic to citizenship. I applaud this social democratic orientation, of course, and my argument here has been meant to indicate that something like the welfare state, something indeed like a right to welfare, has deep roots in the so-called "classically liberal" political thought of the late eighteenth century—that it is not a betrayal but an extension of the principles of classical liberalism. One need not give up on the stress on individual rights characteristic of liberals to support state-based aid to the poor: such aid can be considered itself a right, a part of or condition for our individual freedom, and was so considered by some of the founding figures in the history of liberalism. In that light, social democracy has as much reason to trace itself back to eighteenth-century liberal thought as libertarianism does. Israel has been moving further and further from

---

consideration; Kuo, 257, 215-216. Obama has been more careful to keep the Office from turning into a federal effort to promote Christianity; he set up a new Advisory Council to the office that includes two Jews, a Muslim, and a representative of a secular organization. But he too has yet to draw any distinction between small local churches and the sorts of large organizations that could use the honor they gain from running charitable programs to promote wide religious and political change.

49   This can be true whether or not individual Hamas officials and activists are carrying out charity work out of a sincere personal religious commitment or compassion for those they help.

its social democratic roots in recent years, however, and the characteristically American understanding of classical liberalism—which I regard
as a misunderstanding—by which it is incompatible with welfare programs, has been taking hold there. If this is so, and if poverty programming is allowed in consequence to fall increasingly into the hands of
religious groups, the danger of such a transformation, I fear, will be yet
greater than it is in the U.S.

In Israel, there is already a great deal of tension between the attempt
to preserve democracy and the attempt to preserve a specifically Jewish
public space; Israel is, as noted earlier, an ethnocultural nationalist state,
and that commitment can sit uneasily alongside liberal democracy. In
this context, keeping aid to the poor firmly in government hands is an
especially important way to maintain the liberal democratic side of the
balance. Welfare programs that go out to Jews and non-Jews alike help
bridge the gap between the two groups and help promote a common
sense of citizenship. If programs to lift people out of poverty become detached from citizenship, and become attached instead to one's religious
identity, there will be one less reason for non-Jews to see themselves
as Israeli. In addition, if the distribution of welfare comes to depend on
religious institutions, it will create envy and anger among those who
feel they get a smaller amount of aid because they are of the "wrong"
religious group. Finally, the religious institutions that help the poor
will be able to parlay the influence they thereby acquire into a basis for
an increasing share of political power. So Adam Smith's dire history of
how the Catholic church used charity to squelch freedom, and the late
eighteenth-century advocates of a right to welfare who wanted to wrest
political power, thereby, from all churches, offer cautions that Israelis
have reason to heed even more than Americans do.

Distinguishing the valuable alliances between government and religious groups from the dangerous ones is so difficult that it is tempting
to say that liberal governments should simply not work with religious
groups at all. That seems impractical, in many cases, so we are left with
the problem of drawing the right sort of line. I do not have any clear idea
of how to do that; philosophers are rarely much good at resolving practical problems. Philosophers can remind us of the larger values at stake in
our practical deliberations, however, and I hope that the considerations
I have laid out will at least remind any believer in liberal democracy—
including libertarians—to worry less about state welfare programs and

more about a society in which aid to the poor is in the hands of churches and synagogues and mosques. The criticisms of that practice that we find in early modern theorists are ones we need very much still to bear in mind. Their experience made it crystal clear to them, as it needs to be for us, that to put the welfare of the weakest among us into the hands of religious groups is to make it a matter of charity instead of justice. That is something that religious and secular people alike should be able to see as wrong.[50]

---

50   I am grateful to audiences at Loyola Marymount University, and at the 2010 University of Haifa conference on liberalism and civic republicanism, for input on this paper. I would particularly like to thank Urte Weeber, Fania Oz-Salzberger, Thomas Maissen, and Fonna Forman-Barzilai for challenging questions that very much helped me rework the paper.

Has the Wheel Come Full Circle?
Civic Service Debates in Israel

RAEF ZREIK

1. Introduction

In recent years, two seemingly conflicting trends can be discerned in the discourse of citizenship in Israel, leading to an apparent inconsistency in the measures taken by the Israeli state organizations towards its Palestinian citizens. On the one hand, there is a distinct increase in demographic discourse that views the very existence of a Palestinian population in Israel as a problem, even as an imminent threat to the state of Israel, and proposals advocating a population swap have become legitimate in public discourse. As a result, we are currently witnessing a conspicuous increase in bills aiming to put a serious question mark over the status of the Palestinians in Israel as full-fledged citizens. On the other hand, the state is simultaneously promoting a new law designed to establish and institutionalize civic service. As it stands now this platform offers Palestinian citizens (but not only them) the chance to perform a two-year term of civic service in a designated public institution in place of the mandatory military service usually required by law. Those who choose this course are entitled, upon completion of the service, to the same rights and benefits granted to those who serve in the army. In order to advance this option, the government has established a special body titled "The Administration of National and Civic Service" for the coordination and supervision of this project. This council explains the aims of the new civic service project in civic terms, as a means for allowing the Palestinian citizens to serve their community, and apparently offers a new path of inclusion for the Palestinian citizens of Israel.

At first glance it seems that this move stands in stark opposition to the first tendency described above: while the state is trying to get rid of its Palestinian citizens, or at least to put substantial limitations on their civic rights, it is simultaneously offering them an alternative path towards citizenship. How are we to understand this duality? Is there a true contradiction here, or is something else happening?

One way to resolve this apparent tension would be to argue that the state has not formulated any clear, consistent policy regarding the Palestinians in Israel, and as a result it is following two adverse strategies without being aware of the contradiction involved. This claim presumes that there is no such coherent entity named "Israel" or "the Jewish Majority"; rather, there are various sites of power with distinct agendas that are at times consistent with each other, at times contradictory. This paper does not aim to exclude this option completely, but only to suggest an alternative analysis that views these two moves, despite the apparent tension between them, as complementary moves heading in the same direction.

While focusing on civic service in particular, this paper uses this debate as an occasion to discuss the development of the Israeli discourse of citizenship in general. After decades in which the Israeli discourse of citizenship was almost completely devoid of meaning, during the nineties a civic discourse started to emerge that culminated in the slogan promoting Israel as "a state of all its citizens"—a formulation that challenged the state's self-definition as a Jewish state. The logic and rhetoric of this discourse was universalistic and liberal, shifting the focus onto citizenship and away from national or religious affiliations. As is often the case with minorities, it was the Palestinians themselves who launched this debate in order to gain equal footing in state and society. The Palestinians deployed the rhetoric of civic discourse in order to bring to light the inherent tension between the Jewish nature of the state and its universalistic, liberal aspirations. This discourse simply asked the state to normalize its relation to the Palestinian citizens and stop treating them as enemies.

This paper argues that in the past decade, the Israeli state (if one can discuss it as a coherent entity at all) has appropriated the civic discourse originally launched by the Palestinian minority, and is currently turning it against the Palestinians themselves. Realizing the Palestinian demand that the state normalize its relations with its Palestinian citizens could be twisted around and used in the opposite direction: the state is now demanding that the Palestinians normalize *their* relations with their state, and not treat the state as *their* enemy. This demand entails an elimination of the psychological barriers between the Palestinians and their state, requiring them to treat the state as their own. Furthermore, the state is deploying the same civic rhetoric to transfer the contradiction between the Jewish discourse and the civic liberal one over to the Palestinian sphere by pointing out the discrepancy between their own civic demands and their national identity as Palestinians. In this way, while the discourse of citizenship was initiated and developed by Palestinians in order to bring to light the state of Israel's inherent contradiction, the very same discourse has backfired, and is now being used by the state to launch a counterattack.

In this reading there is no contradiction between the two approaches outlined above. The state's recourse to civic discourse represents the continuation of the ethnic-national "war" through the deployment of civic language. This claim amounts to arguing that the state is not offering the civic service in good faith, and is not truly committed to the civic language it is deploying. To this, the state might respond that the Palestinians, when they promoted the idea of "a state of all its citizens," never really meant to commit to it either, but only to confuse and embarrass the Jewish state; that their original evocation of the civic discourse was deployed in bad faith in the first place.

The first part of this paper deals with the genesis of the Israeli concept of citizenship, from the establishment of the state until the mid seventies, and argues that during these years citizenship was practically a hollow category, lost in a zero-sum dynamic between conqueror and defeated. The second part traces the major turning points that created a certain sense of commonality from the eighties onwards. It goes on to elaborate on the developments in the eighties and nineties that allowed the discourse of citizenship to emerge, culminating in the slogan "a state of all its citizens," which shifted the discourse from an ethnic-national sphere over to a civic sphere. The third part focuses on civic service and its history in Israel. It begins by following the developments in the Israeli legal and political system that led up to the recent platform, and goes on to trace the internal dynamics and the way in which the idea of an alternative civil service developed through the encounter with the problem of Orthodox Jews and exemptions from military service for observant women. This section also outlines the basic arrangements of the proposed law of civic service and its main clauses as they currently stand. In the fourth part, I juxtapose the optimistic reading of the first two chapters with a more structural reading that stresses the antagonistic relation of the state towards its Palestinian population. I base this interpretation on a perception of the nature of the Israeli project as an ethnocracy, caught in a perpetual attempt to dispossess the Palestinians and treat the issue of their citizenship as a mere technical, formal matter that does not touch on the basis of the Israeli regime. According to this reading, the purpose of the civic service project is not to achieve any deep structural changes; it strives, rather, to exert more pressure on the Palestinians by transferring the internal contradictions of the Jewish state over to them.

The argument upheld in this paper does not exclude the possibility that the civic service project might also lead to unintended consequences: to the development of a true civic discourse regardless of the will of those who designed it. The exploration of this possibility, which depends on a variety of factors, is beyond the scope of this paper.

2. The Birth of Israeli Citizenship

In the beginning there was the *Ethnos*. It is He who declared the state, and He who provides the reason for the state.[1] The concept of Israeli citizenship was born crippled and hallow, and in many ways almost meaningless. In those first years, Israeli citizenship meant only limited things to those who held it; it was, rather, one's national-ethnic affiliation that played the major role in determining the well-being of individuals, their shares in the public good, and their position in the social and economic web of power and influence.[2] What really mattered during the years after the establishment of the state was not whether you were an Israeli citizen or not, but whether you were a Jew or a Palestinian: that was the

---

1   The Declaration of Establishment of the State of Israel, reprinted in Official Gazette: Number 1; Tel Aviv, 5 Iyar 5708, May 14, 1948, available at http://www.knesset.gov.il/docs/eng/un_dec_eng.htm.

2   I purposely avoid using the terminology of "rights" and any other legalistic approach. Being a Jew or a Palestinian did, at times, mean having different set of rights, but the core of the problem did not lie in this legal distinction—as I am trying to show in this paper. It was, rather, the fundamental setup of the situation that created two distinct systems. An additional caveat is necessary here. To say that citizenship was meaningless does not mean that for those Jews who were holocaust survivors or war refugees, the foundation of the state of Israel was meaningless, or that holding an Israeli passport was an empty category for them. This is far from the truth. The argument claims, instead, that even if they were not (yet) formal citizens, the state of Israel was significant for them by virtue of the mere fact that they were Jews. Thanks to the Law of Return, they could always change their status from potential citizens to actual ones. The combination of Israel's Law of Return with the Israeli Law of Citizenship thus renders citizenship a redundant category compared to the category of the Jew. See the Law of Return, 4 LSI 114 (1950). See also The Law of Citizenship, 6 LSI 50 (1952).

crucial fact that would determine your life and destiny. You could be a Palestinian citizen of Israel, but that status provided no guarantee that the state would care for you, or work to promote your interests. On the other hand, if you were a Jew, Israeli citizen or not, the state would undoubtedly provide assistance to promote your interests and well being. This general state of inclusion/exclusion can be explored in more detail through several characteristics that distinguished the new Israeli state.

2.1 Over-Inclusiveness of the Jewish State

In the first place, the over-inclusive nature of the newly born state as a state for all the Jews, all over the world, had several consequences that rendered the category of citizenship almost vacant regardless of the existence of the Palestinians. According to the Israeli Law of Return,[3] any Jew can immigrate to the state; upon her arrival she can, by virtue of the Law of Citizenship,[4] apply for citizenship immediately. This combination means that all Jews, all over the world, are potential citizens of the state and can turn this potentiality into actuality whenever they choose to do so. Being inside or outside the state, a citizen or not, is not of crucial importance; as long as you are a Jew you can materialize your civic right at any time. This setup, in which the state is preceded by the ethnic nation and is conceived as serving it, is modeled after the concept of Eastern European primordial citizenship.[5]

The second point is an extension of the first: since the Jewish state aimed at solving the problems of Jews all over the world, and since the state belongs to all of them, then those who happened to be present in Israel when the state was established and received citizenship as a result of these contingent circumstances are in fact only trustees of the state's assets and land. The true owner and beneficiary is the Jewish people, wherever they may be.[6] In this sense Israel's over-inclusive policy puts limits on the power of the state's Jewish citizens as well as that of the Palestinians.

The third point, related to but also distinct from the first two, is the

---

3   The Law of Return, 4 LSI 114 (1950), Art. 1.
4   The Law of Citizenship, 6 LSI 50 (1952), Art. 2.
5   Roger Brubaker, *Citizenship and Nationhood in France and in Germany* (Cambridge, MA: Harvard University Press, 1992).
6   This fact is manifested in the existence and by-laws of the Jewish National Fund, the organization that owns the lands in trusteeship in the name of the whole Jewish nation.

fact that Israeli citizenship has always been a dynamic condition. The establishment of the state was not the end of the Zionist revolution, though it was an important stage in that revolution. Zionism's ultimate goal was to gather together all Jews from all over the world, to transform their lives, and finally, to create the New Jew. Keeping this in mind, the state is understood as a mere tool in this process, subjected to a higher mission; accordingly the logic of citizenship was derived from the teleological logic of the Jewish Zionist revolution.

2.2. Over-Exclusion of the Jewish State

This over-inclusiveness of the Jews is complemented by the specific exclusion of Israel's Palestinian citizens. The State of Israel was undoubtedly established at the expense of the Palestinians and a certain level of negation of the Palestinian national project was implied between the lines of the Zionist project. In fact, without the radical demographic change of 1948 that culminated in hundreds of thousands of refugees, the establishment of the state of Israel as a Jewish state would not have been possible in the first place.[7]

The Palestinians who remained within Israeli borders after 1948 did not treat the state as their own. They experienced the state as an imposition, a defeat of their own national project. The state, on its part, never treated the Palestinians fully as its citizens.[8] The newly-established state considered it a happy miracle that of over 700,000 Palestinians who had resided within its borders (according to the partition plan) prior to the 1948 war, only about 150,000 remained, while the rest ended up beyond its borders. For the remaining Palestinians, the fact that they were able to remain in their homeland was in itself reason to rejoice in their good luck. In this sense, the Israeli citizenship granted to the Palestinians that remained in Israel was imposed on both parties—on the state as well as on the Palestinians.

The Zionist mission of gathering the Jews together into the new state, the negation of exile which lies at the heart of Zionism[9] and in-

---

7 Benny Morris, *The Birth of the Palestinian Refugee Problem, 1947-1949* (Cambridge: Cambridge University Press, 1987); Ilan Pappé, *The Ethnic Cleansing of Palestine* (Oxford: Oneworld, 2006).

8 This is clearly a generalization and needs qualification. These citizens were granted the right to vote and received many other formal political rights, but in countless other aspects they were completely marginalized in the newly born state.

9 On the negation of exile in Zionism see Amnon Raz-Karkotzkin, "Sovereign Exile: a Critique of 'Exile Negation' in Israeli Culture, Part 1," *Theory and Critique* 4 [in Hebrew] (1993): 23; Amnon

evitably entails the maintenance of a Jewish majority in Israel, had a dark side: the negation of the existence of a Palestinian nation. Since the mission of absorbing the Jews is a continuous, ongoing effort, the negation of the Palestinians is also not a mere passing event, but rather one that needs to reproduce itself on a daily basis. Thus the zero-sum game that usually characterizes the violent moment of the birth of a new state was, in the Israeli case, extended over time.

Another factor that contributed to the emptiness of the concept of citizenship was the fact that the borders themselves were not agreed upon and Israel was never officially recognized by its neighbors. To this ongoing state of war one must add the fact that when the state was established, the Jews owned only about seven percent of the land even within Israeli territory. The state was not satisfied with having territorial jurisdiction over the land; it worked hard towards transferring ownership of property from Palestinian hands to Jewish hands,[10] and in the process had to "capture" or appropriate much of the land from its Palestinian owners.[11] In this sense being "inside" the borders did not eliminate the feeling and the practice that this is a contested land. Hence the process of taking over Palestine did not end with the establishment of the state of Israel; in certain ways, 1948 was just the beginning of this process, and Israel is in a state of war, or revolution, to this day.[12]

3. The Jews and the Palestinians in Israel: The Evolvement of Civic Discourse and Citizenship

3.1 From Zero-Sum Game to Two Parallel Lines

The relations between the Palestinians in Israel and the state in the first two decades after Israel's foundation moved gradually from a state of

---

Raz-Karkotzkin, "Sovereign Exile: a Critique of 'Exile Negation' in Israeli Culture, Part 2," *Theory and Critique* 5 [in Hebrew] (1994): 113; Eliezer Don-Yehiya, "The Negation of Galut in Religious Zionism," *Modern Judaism* 12 (1992): 129.

10 Alexander Kedar, *"The Israeli Law and the Redemption of Arab Land, 1948-1969"* (PhD diss., Harvard University, 1996).

11 Raef Zreik, "Notes on the Value of Theory: Readings in the Law of Return—A Polemic," *Law & Ethics of Human Rights* 2 (2008): 10.

12 An example of this state of perpetual revolution can be found in Israel's initiation of several projects in the fifties that aimed to create irreversible "facts on the grounds" by establishing Jewish settlements (within its own borders) with the explicit purpose of dispersing the Jewish population across the country and, in several occasions, using these settlements as shields preventing the return of Palestinian refugees.

total conflict in 1948 to one of negative toleration. Although their existence was not desired, the Palestinians did not constitute a threat to the state and were not perceived as posing any real challenge to the state's identity. While they were not expelled, the remaining Palestinians in Israel were never incorporated into the Israeli polity and society. They were, instead, pushed to the margins of the state and society and the two groups, Jews and Palestinians, came to conduct themselves as two parallel societies, with distinct geographies, economies, histories and languages. In those early years, there was hardly any contact whatsoever between the two communities.

There were several factors that contributed to this separation. The first was the military rule imposed on the Palestinians of Israel until 1966, which meant that despite the fact that they were Israeli citizens, they were nevertheless subject to separate laws. During these years, two different regimes prevailed within Israel proper: one for Israeli Jews and one for Israeli Palestinians.[13]

Apart from the distinctions made in official policy, the state of Israel was in many ways a direct continuation of the Jewish *Yishuv*, the pre-state Jewish society of Palestine during the years of the British Mandate. The *Yishuv*, based purely on exclusive ethnic Jewish affiliation, had been responsible for all aspects of civic life: economy, health, banking system, labor unions, construction and food concerns, insurance companies etc.[14] The state of Israel inherited this ethnic structure, a type of "state within a state" that had developed during the years of the mandate. The Palestinian citizens played no part in the young state's agenda, which revolved around the absorption of hundreds of thousands of Jewish immigrants and their settlement, stabilization of the economic crisis, defining the state's relations with Germany, and issues of borders and security.[15]

The two groups constituted such separate and distinct entities to the point that it is difficult to see what they had in common. The Jews

---

13   For the years of military rule see Yosi Amitai, "The Arab Minority in Israel: Years of the Military Government 1948-1966," *The Independence, the First Fifty Years, Collected Essays*, ed. Anita Shapira [in Hebrew] (Jerusalem: Zalman Shazar Center, 1998), 129; Sabri Jiryis, *The Arabs in Israel*, trans. Inea Bushnaq, (New York: Monthly Review Press, 1976).

14   On the move from the *Yishuv* to statehood see Dan Horowitz and Moshe Lissak, *Origins of the Israeli Polity*, trans. Charles Hoffman (Chicago: University of Chicago Press, 1978).

15   For the agenda of the new state see Shmuel N. Eisenstadt, *Israeli Society* (London: Weidenfeld And Nicolas, 1967).

were establishing a state and a homeland while the Palestinians were losing one; the Jews were gathering together and uniting, while the Palestinians were splitting up, fragmenting and becoming refugees; the Jews were ending their time of exile, while the Palestinians were thrown into a state of exile; the Jews were for the most part urban Europeans, while those Palestinians who remained were mostly peasants living in the countryside. The Jews were winners, the Palestinians were losers... What kind of equality could possibly be achieved, even imagined, under such circumstances? Does not equality presuppose some kind of common denominator, one that could at least render a comparison possible? But how can we compare two such different groups? This could almost be conceived as a *Differend* situation, in which it is practically impossible to draw a comparison between the needs of the two groups.[16]

At this stage, the state did not need to "discriminate" explicitly. The two groups were so distinct, with such different needs, that any discrimination could be articulated as simply responding to the specific needs of the two groups. For the language of discrimination to make sense, one needs a certain level of sameness and commonality against which one can notice the differential treatment. This common ground was lacking.

This explains, in my view, why the debate regarding the tension between the Jewish and the democratic definitions of the state did not arise in the first two decades after the establishment of the state: because there was no common ground on which this tension could reveal itself. Since such a high level of separation already existed, there was no real need for discriminating legislation. The laws were instead formu-

---

16   Jean-François Lyotard, *The Differend: Phrases in Dispute*, trans. George Van Den Abeele (Minneapolis: University of Minnesota Press, 1988); for the problems facing equality discourse see Peter Westen, *Speaking of Equality: An Analysis of the Rhetorical Force of 'Equality' in Moral and Legal Discourse* (Princeton, NJ: Princeton University Press, 1990). An example can illuminate the picture. During the first years of the state, there were waves of mass immigration of Jews from Arab countries to Israel that created an urgent need for the establishment of new settlements. These new settlements were purposely located at border areas and other "strategic" areas unpopulated by Jews in order to manufacture a *de facto* situation in which the whole country was populated by Jews, while simultaneously "strengthening" the border line in order to prevent Palestinian refugees from attempting to return "illegally" to their land. The Palestinians, for their part, were already settled; in the establishment of new settlements, the state was apparently just meeting the needs of the new immigrants. Under these circumstances, what meaning could a demand for equality have? Should the Palestinians also ask to establish new "Palestinian" settlements? But they need no such new settlements: they already live in their houses. It would be even more absurd if they would ask to have settlements on the border in order to share in the Jewish effort to prevent Palestinians from attempting to return to their homes.

lated to address specific needs of certain groups, such as laws that grant benefits of adjustment for new Jewish immigrants, or laws providing for those who fought in the 1948 war. The Jewish nature of the state was conceived of almost as an analytical, *a priori* truth that need not declare itself. To say "the State" and to say "the Jewish State" was synonymous; the state could not imagine itself as anything other than a Jewish state. The need for the state to assert itself as a Jewish state came only later on—in 1980—when the potential for the state to be otherwise was first acknowledged.

The state never recognized itself fully as a state *per se*, as something separate from both Jewish *and* Palestinian society. The "Jewish" aspect of the Jewish and democratic formula went unfettered from the restriction imposed on it by the state's declared commitment to democracy. For the democratic aspect to emerge, and for citizenship to crystallize and to be able to "bite," the state had to move forward from its condition of ongoing revolution to a condition governed by the logic of statehood and civic institutions, which could manufacture a certain level of commonality. Another two decades were to pass before this was to occur, and to that I will turn in the next section.

3.2 From Parallel Lines to Intersecting Lines: The Beginning of the Evolvement of Citizenship

Due to both the national-ethnic structure and the socialist attitudes of the state's founders in the early years, many commentators have argued that the state and civic society were hardly distinguishable.[17] Many have also argued that law and politics were at this time inextricably intertwined, in the sense that law was very much in the service of politics and the Supreme Court did not take enough distance from the executive branch.[18] I take this insight a step further and argue that state and *Jew-*

---

17 This is what Baruch Kimmerling claims in his article, "The Relations of the State and Society in Israel," *The Israel Society, A Critical View*, ed. Uri Ram [in Hebrew] (Tel Aviv: Brerot, 1993), 328. See also Baruch Kimmerling, *The Invention and Decline of Israeliness: State, Society and the Military* (California: University of California Press, 2001).

18 This follows the argument of some legal scholars in Israeli academia, such as Menachem Mawtner, Pnina Lahav, and Ronnen Shamir. Shamir writes that in the early years of the state, state and society were hardly distinguishable and Israelis could not allow themselves the "luxury" of individual rights; this had to wait several decades to emerge. See Ronnen Shamir, "Society, Judaism and Democratic Fundamentalism: On the Social Roots of Judicial Review," *Iyuney Mishpat* 19 (1995): 703-706 [in Hebrew]. For the dynamic of the Supreme Court in the formative years see Pnina Lahav, "Foundations of Rights: Jurisprudence in Israel," *Israel Law Review* 24 (1990): 211; Pnina

ish society were hardly distinguishable. The gradual distinction between the Jewish society and the state allowed the latter to appear—albeit very slowly and mildly—as an abstract entity above both the Jewish and the Palestinian societies, and this relative abstraction of the state *qua* state allowed the beginning of a civic discourse to emerge.

In the following section, I will mention some of the political, eco- nomical and legal changes that allowed for the development of civic discourse. On the political level I will, for the most part, address two main events: the 1967 war and the elections of 1977.

The war of 1967 led to the Israeli occupation of the Palestinian lands that were not previously included in Israeli territory: the West Bank and the Gaza Strip. Through this acquisition, Palestine was reunited as a single, geo-political unit. The 1967 war expanded Israel's *military* borders, which had been established after the 1948 cease-fire, and simultaneously gave new meaning to its *political* ones. Until the 1967 war, Israel's borders had been accepted as arbitrarily traced cease-fire borders and nothing more. Both Israelis and Arabs understood them as "temporary" borders. In contrast, after the occupation of the rest of the Palestinian land in 1967, the 1948 borders (the "Green Line") gained a political meaning, becoming the internationally acknowledged political borders of a recognized state (U.N. Resolution 242).[19]

In this new state of affairs, Nazareth (1948) and Al-Khalil–Hebron (1967) became part of the same physical unity, as both of them were subjected to Israeli control. It was precisely this unity, however, that al- lowed the difference between the "here" and "there" to appear: between the citizenship of the Palestinians in Israel (though incomplete) and the absence of such citizenship among the Palestinians living in the oc- cupied territories. Here (in Israel) there are citizens, both Palestinians and Jews, and there (in the occupied territories) there are non-citizens only. This distinction between the Palestinians made the concept of Israeli citizenship visible, and in this sense, the meaning of citizenship

----

Lahav, *Judgment in Jerusalem: Chief Justice Simon Agranat and the Zionist Century* (California: University of California Press, 1997).

19   S.C. Res. 242, U.N. Doc. S/RES/242 (November 22, 1967), available at http://www.mfa.gov.il/ MFA/Peace+Process/Guide+to+the+Peace+Process/UN+Security+Council+Resolution+242.htm. See also Security Council Resolution 338, S.C. Res. 338, U.N. Doc. S/RES/338 (October 22, 1973), available at http://www.mfa.gov.il/MFA/Peace+Process/Guide+to+the+Peace+Process/UN+Secur ity+Council+Resolution+338.htm.

in Israel was constructed from without.[20]

The other major turning point in the discourse of citizenship was the 1977 elections and the victory of the Likud Party, which ended the monopoly of the Labor Party dating back to the pre-state years of the *Yishuv*. This event in and of itself marked a crucial change in the way the state perceived itself and the stability of its own institutions. The smooth and stable transfer of power from one party to another meant that Israel was not the mere continuity of the *Yishuv*; it had truly become a state in the full sense of the word. The identification between the Labor Party and the state was finally brought to an end. The elections induced the state to be thought, imagined and reproduced as a practice of government, distinct from the Labor Party, standing on its own as an autonomous and abstracted entity released from the historical powers, bodies and ideas that brought about its birth. This is even truer when considering the fact that the Israeli *Demos* of 1977—those who elected the new government—were not the same ones as those who had established the state in 1948: the majority was now composed of new immigrants from the Arab countries. In this sense the elections comprised the victory of the present over the past and of the state over the *Yishuv*.[21]

The regime changeover was swiftly followed by economic change: the liberalization of the economy manifested in the privatization of many government-run companies that had run considerable sections of the national economy and industry. Markets were opened for competition and foreign investments were allowed into the country. These changes were not only a result of the Likud economic program; they were also dictated from without, imposed on Israel by the international community during the eighties as a condition for receiving an inflow of funds aimed at rescuing Israel from the financial crisis that raged during the eighties.[22] All these factors put together brought about a substantive

---

20 On this dialectics of 1967 war, see Azmi Bishara, "On the Question of Palestinians in Israel," *Theory and Critique* 3 [in Hebrew] (1993): 7.

21 For a comprehensive review of the 1977 election, the *Herut* rising power, and the emergence of the Mizrachi Jews in Israeli politics, see Yonathan Shapiro, *The Road to Power* (New York: State University of New York Press, 1991). For a general analysis of the 1977 elections, see Asher Arian, ed., *The Elections in Israel* (Tel Aviv: Ramot, 1977).

22 For the relation between privatization in Israeli economy and the global economy see Yoav Peled, "From Zionism to Capitalism: the Political Economy of Israel's Decolonization of the Occupied Territories," *Middle East Report*, 194/5 (1995): 13-17; Adam Hanieh, "From State-Led Growth to

growth in the private sector, and decentralized the state and its agencies as the main employer and the main player in the market.[23]

On the legal level, the seventies and eighties witnessed some major changes that culminated in the Constitutional Revolution of the nineties. Here I will focus on three main developments that left their impact on politics and society in Israel.[24] The first is the slow but steady erosion of the requirement of "standing" in petitions submitted to the Supreme Court.[25] During these decades, this requirement was relaxed and eroded to the point that nowadays any petitioner can approach the court and ask for remedies. As a result, the court is accessible to each and every citizen, allowing everyone to take an active role in defending the rule of law, and maintains an open-door policy towards public petitions.[26]

In addition to removing the limits on the identity of the petitioner, the court has also gradually eliminated another barrier erected before petitions: the precondition of "justiciability."[27] Today, in principle every-

---

Globalization: the Evolution of Israeli Capitalism," *Journal of Palestine Studies* 32 (2009): 5.

23 For a review of the relation between the Likud and the liberalization of economy see in general Oren Sussman, "Financial Liberalization: the Israeli Experience," *Oxford Economic Papers* 44 (1992): 387. There are some who oppose this analysis completely and offer an alternative analysis that distinguishes between the process of economic liberalization and that of democratization of Israeli society. See Lev Greenberg, "The Mapai Party between Democratic and Liberal Change: on the Truth of Contradicted Duality of State/Civil Society," *Studies in the Israeli Society* [in Arabic] (Bet Berl: Center of Studies of the Israeli Society, Bet Berl Publishing, 1995), 97.

24 In this analysis "the legal" is not understood as the passive shadow of politics or economics; rather it is in itself an important factor in shaping the other fields. As such this view does not accept the classic Marxist view or other comprehensive theories that treat law as a mere instrument of power. See Duncan Kennedy, "The Stakes of the Law, or Hale and Foucault!," *Sexy Dressing Etc.* (Cambridge, MA.: Harvard University Press, 1993), 87.

25 The requirement of "standing" obliged anyone wishing to petition the Supreme Court of Justice to show that she has a stake in the case and that her own particular interest might be encroached, as a precondition for the readiness of the court to hear the case. The idea behind this requirement is that the court should not be asked to review "theoretical" cases, limiting access to the court to those who might be personally hurt by a decision taken by the administrative branch. For a general review of the concept of standing see Amnon Rubinstein and Barak Medina, *The Constitutional Law in the State of Israel*, vol. 1, [in Hebrew] (Jerusalem: Shoken, 2001), 174-180.

26 The following cases invalidated this requirement: HCJ 217/80 Segal v. the Minister of Interior, PD 34 (4) 429; HCJ 1/81 Shiran v. the Broadcasting Authority, PD 35 (3) 365; HCJ 243/82 Zichroni v. the Broadcasting Authority, PD 37 (1) 757; HCJ 428/86 Barzilay v. Israel's Government, PD 40 (3) 505; HCJ 852/86 Aloni v. the Minister of Justice, PD 41 (2) 1; HCJ 910/86 Resler v. the Minister of Defense, PD 42 (2) 441; HCJ 2148/94 Gelbart v. the Supreme Court's President, PD 48 (3) 573.

27 On justiciability in general see Amnon Rubinstein and Barak Medina, *The Constitutional Law in the State of Israel*, vol. 1, [in Hebrew] (Jerusalem: Shoken, 2001), 182-190. The basic idea here is that certain subjects, due to their inherent nature, can be subjected to legal discourse and as such can be brought to court; others by definition can not (such as deciding who should win a beauty contest.) In the past, the court employed this barrier often to close its doors to cases in which it

thing is deserving of the court's attention, and justiciability is no longer a threshold or precondition for hearing cases. As a result, the number of issues and conflicts brought to court has multiplied profusely.

The third important change was much more substantive and relates to the conditions under which the Supreme Court may intervene and review the decisions made by the administrative organ. During the seventies and eighties, the court took on a more active role in reviewing the administrative branch whenever it deemed that it used "unreasonable discretion."[28] This activism limited the free discretion previously enjoyed by the administrative branch.

These three shifts meant that law in general, and the Supreme Court in particular, became the main site where disputes were resolved. The court came to be much more powerful than in the past at the expense of other branches of government, and rendered almost every conflict potentially subject to legal resolution. As a result, the whole of political culture went through a process of legalization.

The new tendency towards legal discourse was another factor that brought forth the discourse of citizenship. The courts speak the language of rights, which is the language of citizenship: the citizen is defined, first and foremost, as a bearer of rights abstracted from religious or ethnic affiliations. This process reached its climax in the early nineties, in the establishment of two fundamental laws that amounted to what became known as the Constitutional Revolution.[29] The rise of constitutionalism in Israel signaled a shift from simple majoritarian politics dominated by the Jewish majority to the more liberal politics that subject the judgment of the majority to certain restrictions.[30]

The final event that gave impetus to the civic discourse was the signing of the Oslo Accords between Israel and the PLO.[31] The Accords, at

---

preferred not to interfere with the administrative decision.

28 See the leading two cases on this by Justice Barak: HCJ 840/79 the Contractors and Constructors' Center of Israel v. Israel's Government, PD 34 (3) 729; HCJ 389/80 the Yellow Pages v. the Broadcasting Authority, PD 35 (1) 421.

29 Basic Law: Human Dignity and Liberty, 1391 LSI 60 (1992); Basic Law: Freedom of Occupation, 1454 LSI 289 (1994).

30 Of course in this perspective, there is a certain tension between liberalism—and here constitutionalism is a manifestation of the liberal approach—and democracy which could, in the case of Israel, be associated with the rule of the majority, i.e. with national ethnic politics. For the tension between constitutionalism and democracy see Amnon Rubinstein and Barak Medina, *The Constitutional Law in the State of Israel*, vol. 1, [in Hebrew] (Jerusalem: Shoken, 2001), 55-57.

31 For the text of the Oslo Accords see Declaration of Principles on Interim Self-Government

least at first glance, seemed to create the image of two entities (or two states); an image which entailed, among other things, the establishment of agreed and permanent political borders for the state of Israel. This new state of affairs promised to bring the process of the state's establishment to an end, releasing it from its condition of ongoing revolution and transferring it over to the logic of statehood and institutions.

3.3 The 1990s and "A State of All Its Citizens"

The above developments prepared the ground for the rise of the civic discourse during the nineties, especially after the so-called Constitutional Revolution and the signing of the Oslo Accords. Civic discourse was originally introduced by the margins of society: the Palestinian party *Balad* adopted the slogan "a state of all its citizens" as its main platform in the 1996 elections and left its impact on the whole of Israeli discourse for years to come.[32]

The rhetoric that proposed redefining Israel as "a state of all its citizens" can be understood in a variety of ways. It can be interpreted as a slogan that aimed to end the over-inclusiveness of Israel as a Jewish state whose goal is to serve all Jews throughout the world, by abolishing (or at least modifying) the Law of Return which favors Jews over other ethnic-religious groups. In addition, the slogan also strived to end the exclusion of the Palestinians in Israel from being equal partners in the Israeli *Demos*, abolishing all structural and institutional discrimination against them and turning them into full and equal citizens.[33] The slogan demanded that Israel de-familiarize and de-normalize its rela-

---

Arrangements, September 13, 1993, Israel-P.L.O., 32 I.L.M. 1525 (1993); Interim Agreement on the West Bank and the Gaza Strip, September 28, 1995, Israel-P.L.O., 36 I.L.M. 551 (1997). For a critique of the Oslo from a Palestinian perspective see Edward W. Said *The End of the Peace Process: Oslo and After* (New York: Pantheon Books, 2000).

32 This does not imply that civic discourse was an invention of Palestinians in Israel. In fact, it was the political party *RATZ*, led by Knesset member Shulamit Aloni, that probably fore-grounded the civic discourse and put the citizen at the center of her political program. Only in the nineties, however, this discourse gained momentum, for many reasons, some of which are mentioned above. One could add to these the claim that the discourse gained power because it was reformulated by a Palestinian party. For *Balad* and the discourse of "a state of all its citizens" see Raef Zreik, "The Palestinian Question: Themes of Justice and Power Part II: The Palestinians in Israel," *Journal of Palestine Studies* 33 (2003): 42.

33 For structural discrimination against Palestinians see David Kretzmer, *The Legal Status of the Arabs in Israel* (Boulder: Westview Press, 1990). See also *Adalah*'s NGO Report, "Additional Information to the UN CERD Committee in Response to the List of Issues Presented to Israel," *available at* http://www.old-adalah.org/eng/intl07/adalah-cerd-feb07.pdf.

tions with the Jewish Diaspora, while simultaneously normalizing and familiarizing itself with its own Palestinian citizens. In order for this to happen, the state needed to abstract itself—*qua* state—from its prior attachments, and to privatize religious and national affiliation. In this imagined situation, the state would approach the Palestinians in Israel as its citizens and normalize its relation to them, instead of treating them as its potential enemies.[34]

Analytically, the rhetoric propagating "a state of all its citizens" can also be read in a different manner: as a demand that takes issue with the Palestinian rhetoric regarding the right of return of Palestinian refugees into Israel proper. This interpretation aims at cutting the Gordian knot connecting between the Palestinians living outside Israeli borders to the state of Israel, while also cutting this knot with the Jewish Diaspora. According to this logic, the state must close its door to *both* groups existing outside its borders: the Jewish Diaspora and the Palestinian refugees. The "deal" could be viewed in the following manner: the Jews give up on their potential immigrants and the Palestinians give up on their refugees; the state belongs solely to those who are its citizens here and now. This rhetoric could thus be used not just to put restraints on the state. It could also be harnessed to put restrains on the Palestinians themselves, and not only to support the demand for full rights, but also to generate civic duties and to put limitations on the Palestinian narrative, history and identity. The demand to abstract the state from any identity might reproduce the counter demand by the state itself from its citizens to become "abstract citizens"—i.e., stripped from their particularity, identity and history.

My argument is that this is precisely the rhetoric strategy that the state has adopted as its response to the Palestinian demand for equality. It is also the logic that stands behind its current promotion of civic service. But before that, let us take a closer look at the issue of civic service and its history.

---

34 In fact, on the symbolic level one can discern several steps taken in this direction during the nineties, although these achievements did not change much in reality. Among these achievements, one can mention the Supreme Court case of Ka'adan that struck down the state policy that discriminates against Palestinians in issues of land allocations. See HCJ 6698/95 Ka'adan v. Israel Land Administration (1995) 44 (1) PD 264.

4. Military Service and Civic Service: A Short History

In this section I will tell the story of the rise of civic service discourse
and its internal dynamic throughout the years, as well as its relation
to military service as a distinct, yet related, path to Israeli citizenship.
From this vantage point, the civic service option for the Palestinians
in Israel can be understood not as a concrete policy designed for and
geared toward the Palestinians, but rather as part of an overall approach
that the Israeli state and society have reformulated over the past two
decades, after the collapse of the "melting pot" ideal and other founding
myths that accompanied the country in its early years. Following this
approach, the pressure to deal with the issue of civic service for Palestinians did not only originate in the bi-polar relations between the state
and its Palestinian minority, but rather arose from a complex problematic through which the state is trying to reformulate itself and its ethos,
and to give new meaning to the concepts of belonging, community and
citizenship in light of the changes undergone by Israeli society.

The history of civic service in Israel is closely connected to the history
of military service. In the newly-born state, mandatory military service
functioned as the melting pot of society. The army was considered to be
a "people's army," a fundamental pillar in the project of nation-building.
Its duties went far beyond the mere defense of Israeli borders and other
security issues; the army took on a central social and educative role in
the crystallization of Israeli society.[35] In the army, all social differences
were (supposedly) bracketed: poor and rich, Ashkenazi and Sephardi,
new immigrants and old ones. In addition, the military paradigm cast
the New Israeli in stark opposition to the image of the helpless, weak,
parasitic Jew in exile. As a new state and society, born in war and living
in a state of war for so many decades, the ethos of the soldier, the rhetoric of sacrifice, and the representations of heroism were constitutive in
evoking the image of the New Citizen. Military service also opened the
road for integration into society at large with the business, administrative and political opportunities to which it allowed access.

Even at the beginning, however, there was a certain level of mismatch
between the Jewish citizen and the Jewish soldier (leaving the question

---

35 For the central role of the army see Gal Levy and Orna Sasson-Levy, "Militarized Socialization,
Military Service, and Class Reproduction: the Experience of Israeli Soldiers," *Sociological
Perspectives* 51 (2008): 349.

of the Palestinians aside for the moment) and it was clear that a "supplement" was needed to complement the path towards full citizenship for those Jews who were not, for a variety of reasons, full soldiers. The image of the citizen-soldier could not be the only organizing principle responsible for regulating, explaining and maintaining Israeli citizenship even for the Jews themselves.

From the start, there were two main sectors within the Jewish community that were released from mandatory military service: Orthodox men (and women) and non-Orthodox observant women. In 1949, the Knesset passed the Defense Service Law[36] which authorized the minister of defense to call upon any Israeli citizen to perform military service.[37] A clause within this law excluded observant religious women from this duty.[38] Palestinians, on the other hand, were not legally exempted. They were nevertheless not called upon to serve in the army as a matter of policy (excluding the Druze, who were in fact recruited) by virtue of the clause that subjected military duty to the discretion of the Defense Minister.[39] As for the Jewish Orthodox population, the arrangement was different: their service was deferred for a year, and the postponement was almost automatically renewed every year until they reached the age of exemption (thus the deferment arrangement meant a *de facto* exemption from military service).

In the following section, I will briefly sketch the development of each group's relation to military service, and where the matter stands today.

4.1 Orthodox Jews[40]

During the 1948 war, Prime Minister Ben Gurion reached an agreement with the leaders of the *Yeshivas* (Orthodox Talmudic colleges) that allowed them to defer the enrollment of their students into the army. The agreement stipulated that those who are to benefit from the deferment

---

36 Defense Service Law, 3 LSI 112 (1949).
37 Ibid., Art. 6.
38 Ibid., Art. 11d.
39 Ibid., Art. 12.
40 For a general survey see Tzvi Tal, *The Committee to Determine the Proper Arrangement on the Draft of Yeshiva Students (The Tal Committee) Report*, Vol. 1 [in Hebrew] (Jerusalem: Government Printing Press, 2000); Naomi Mi-Ami, "The Drafting of *Yeshiva* Students to the IDF and the Law for Deferral of Military Service for *Yeshiva* Students," available at http://www.knesset.gov.il/mmm/data/pdf/m01759.pdf. See a more general take on the attitude of Orthodox Jews to the army in Ezekiel Cohen, *Drafting the Orthodox Jews: on the Exemption of Yeshiva Students from the IDF* [in Hebrew] (Jerusalem: Religious Kibbutz, 1993).

must declare their dedication to the study of *Torah* and must not practice any other profession, be it for money or voluntarily; their religious studies must be their sole and only "profession." When this arrangement was first reached in 1948, the number of Orthodox Jews that benefited from it stood at some 400; in 2006 the number was estimated to reach about 44,854.[41]

A myriad of arguments was called on to support this arrangement. It is not my aim in this paper to evaluate them, but only to illuminate the most salient. The head Rabbi of Israel at the time wrote to Ben Gurion in 1949, justifying the request for deferrals by referring to the fact that during the Holocaust many *Yeshiva* students died, putting the entire intellectual community in grave risk of annihilation. He went on to state that the *Yeshiva* played a major role in the preservation of the Jewish people throughout the centuries and as such, the students should be acknowledged as contributing to the national effort through their religious studies. Another argument evoked for the justification of deferrals was that the Orthodox Jews maintained a distinct and segregated lifestyle that would be endangered if they were to mingle with secular Jews, and the contact with a secular way of life would threaten the very existence of the group.[42]

This arrangement was not grounded in clear-cut legislation. In fact, the Defense Service Law formulated in 1949, and the Defense Service Law (Consolidated Version) of 1959, were replaced by alternative legislation in 1986. Both laws included an article that gave discretion to the minister of defense to grant exemption or deferments.[43]

During the late sixties and early seventies, people began having second thoughts about the *de facto* exemptions administered to the Orthodox population. A petition was brought to the Supreme Court questioning the legality of the arrangement; the court dismissed the petition without even going into its details.[44] During the eighties, more petitions were submitted to the Supreme Court, all of them challenging the legality of the arrangement. In most of these cases, the court dismissed the

---

41   Naomi Mi-Ami, "The Drafting of *Yeshiva* Students to the IDF and the Law for Deferral of Military Service for *Yeshiva* Students," 3.

42   For a list of the arguments see Tzvi Tal, *The Committee to Determine the Proper Arrangement on the Draft of* Yeshiva *Students (The Tal Committee) Report*, vol. 1 [Hebrew] (Jerusalem: Government Printing Press, 2000).

43   Defense Service Law (Consolidated Version), 1170 LSI 107 (1986), Art. 36.

44   HCJ 40/70 Becker v. Minister of Defense, PD 24 (1) 238.

petitions offhandedly as they had done before.[45] Gradually, however, the court began to show some tolerance toward the petitioners, and a significant shift can be discerned in the court's response to a petition that was filed in the late nineties.[46] This petition argued that the arrangement contradicts the principle of equality, as it discriminates *de facto* against those who perform mandatory military service. This time the court accepted the petitioners' arguments and ruled that such an arrangement could not be left to the discretion of the defense minister but should be the subject of primary legislation by the Knesset (Israeli Parliament) itself.

Following this decision, the Tal Committee was established in order to evaluate all aspects of the matter. The committee, headed by Justice Tzvi Tal, submitted its report and conclusions on March 23, 2000. While the report concluded that there was no urgent military need for drafting Orthodox Jews, it also stated that the arrangement had destructive effects on the cohesion of the Israeli state and society and on the readiness and motivation of other segments of society to serve in the army.[47] Ultimately, however, the commission's conclusions did not propose a revolutionary reconstruction that would shatter the original *status quo* arrangement, but only mild reform through alternative paths of service and new combinations of religious studies with military service. The Knesset approved the conclusions and in 2002 passed a law known as Tal's Law, which anchored the practice of deferral for full-time *Yeshiva* students in legislation.[48]

This new law launched another round of petitions which all revolved around the claim that the Tal Law contradicted the principle of equality.[49] While the Supreme Court accepted the petitioners' basic arguments once again, it was nevertheless aware of the high political stakes involved, and eventually decided to give the law a chance, and to see how it worked in practice. The issue is still on the agenda.

---

45 These petitions are the following: HCJ 448/81 Ressler v. Defense Minister, PD 36 (1) 81; FA 2/82 Ressler v. Defense Minister, PD 36 (1) 708; HCJ 179/82 Ressler v. Defense Minister, PD 36 (4) 421; HCJ 910/86 Ressler v. Defense Minister, PD 42 (2) 441.

46 HCJ 3267/97 Rubinstein v. Minister of Defense, PD 52 (5) 481.

47 Tzvi Tal, *The Committee to Determine the Proper Arrangement on the Draft of* Yeshiva *Students (The Tal Committee) Report*, vol. 1 [in Hebrew] (Jerusalem: Government Printing Press, 2000), 34.

48 Deferral of Service for Full Time Yeshiva Students Law, 1862 LSI 521 (2002).

49 HCJ 6427/02 The Movement for the Quality Government in Israel v. The Knesset, Tak-SC 2006 (2) 1559.

4.2 Observant Religious Women

Since observant women had been legally exempt from service from the start, a law was passed in 1953[50] that made it compulsory for observant Jewish women who are exempted from military service to serve a two-year term in an alternative path of "national service." This law was never enforced, and no by-laws were promulgated that could ensure its implementation. Nevertheless, throughout the sixties and seventies, a voluntary practice of national service for religious women developed. In 1977 this practice gained legal recognition in the form of an amendment in the National Insurance Law (1968). The amendment granted the volunteering women the same benefits usually imparted to soldiers serving in the army, and thus equalized the women's legal status to that held by soldiers.[51] Through this amendment, the state linked between national/military service and certain benefits, a link that would lead, later on, to a myriad of other amendments that confirmed this formula.[52]

In 1997 there was suddenly a conspicuous increase in the demand to expand the groups entitled to perform national service. A petition was submitted to the Supreme Court by two Palestinian women and one Jewish man (exempted from military service due to his own personal circumstances). All three demanded to be allowed to perform national service and thus enjoy the same status as those who serve in the army.[53] The petition was dismissed based on the state's commitment to reconsider the issue. For that purpose, another commission was established—the Ben Shalom Commission—whose purpose was to study the various aspects of civic service as an alternative to military service.[54] The commission's recommendations included the expansion of national service, opening it up to anyone who does not perform military service for whatever reasons.[55] The report went on to propose the establishment of

---

50   National Service Law, 134 LSI 163 (1953).

51   National Security Law (Consolidated Text), 530 LSI 108 (1968). The amendment was made in February 1977.

52   Discharged Soldiers Law, 1461 LSI 132 (1994); National Security Law (Consolidated Version), 1522 LSI 207 (1995).

53   HCJ 9173/96 Daniel v. the Head of the National Insurance, (unpublished).

54   The Ben Shalom Commission was headed by Yigal Ben Shalom, the general director of the Labor and Welfare Ministry. The commission was established by the government in 1997, and it submitted its conclusions in the same year.

55   See Rachel Verzberger, *National Service for Minorities: a Report for Knesset Member Ehud Yatom* [in Hebrew] (Jerusalem: Knesset Research Center Press, 2003), 5.

a new committee whose goal would be to settle the whole issue of civic service once and for all. In 1997, the Ivry Commission, headed by David Ivry, was set up for this purpose. The commission submitted its findings in 2005.

4.3 The Ivry Commission Report

One of the main recommendations of the commission's report was the expansion of civic and national service to include every citizen that does not perform military service (Recommendation No. 1). The commission suggested that the overall concept must take into account "the particular needs of the different populations within Israeli society" (Recommendation No. 2). Nevertheless, the commission distinguished between civic service and national service (see Recommendation No. 23 and on), stipulating that civic service should operate on a voluntary basis only, and should aim primarily at two sectors: the Orthodox Jews and the Arab-Palestinians. National service, in contrast, was defined as mandatory (for the most part), and addressed a variety of groups, mainly those who in principle should have served in the army, but could not do so for particular reasons. In addition, the commission stressed the "priority and seniority" of military service as the main path of service to the state (see list of principles in Recommendation No. 2). Thus the commission created a three-tier system of service: military at the top, national below, and civic at the very bottom. While the first two are generally mandatory, the third is voluntary.

The commission adds the following regarding the Palestinian citizens:

> The commission believes that such a step will constitute a compromise between the principle of equality and the civic duties attached to this principle on the one hand, and the objective national problem that hinders their [the Palestinians'] military recruitment to the IDF [Israel Defense Forces] on the other. Such a move is expected to have positive social consequences on the status of the Israeli Arabs and on the web of Jewish-Arab relations in Israel.[56]

---

56   Recommendation No. 25.

The Ivry Commission's report was adopted by the government in February 2007 and is now the official policy of the Israeli government.

In light of this narrative, one might be tempted to argue that the demand to enact new arrangements and laws regulating the issue of civic service was conceived by the internal Israeli debate. The old structures and models could no longer hold water in the evolving Israeli society, and this led to the emergence of a need to rearticulate the role of the army in society and to establish new paths of citizenship. This line of argument fits very well with the story that was told in the first section regarding the development of civic discourse in particular and the rise of citizenship in general. This is undoubtedly part of the story, but it's not the whole story.

5. The Counter Story: Persistence of the Ethnos

Alongside the developments in civic discourse during the eighties and nineties, one can clearly discern the parallel development of an ethno-religious discourse in Israel. Here the story I want to tell is one that insists on the confrontational nature of the relation between Jews and Palestinians within the state itself, casting the citizenship discourse as a thin and superficial layer of veneer.

The Israel occupation of the West Bank in 1967 and the subsequent unification of the Jews with their holy sites fostered powerful religious forces within Israeli society and thrust them into the heart of the political discourse. Many of the political questions that had always existed were reformulated as theological dilemmas, and the question of the future of the West Bank and Gaza Strip was reconceived as a religious question. The religious base underpinning Zionist discourse gradually gained power and confidence. The 1967 war and the occupation of the rest of the land (of Israel/Palestine) opened up a conceptual gap between the "land of Israel" and the "state of Israel" on the one hand, and between the "citizens of Israel" and the "people of Israel" on the other. Now that we possess the religious sites, do we have the right to relinquish them? Who is to decide on these matters?[57] One way or another, the 1967 occupation gave rise to an ethno-religious discourse. Thus, at

---

57   Menachem Freidman, "The State of Israel as a Theological Dilemma," *The Israeli State and Society Boundaries and Frontiers*, ed. Baruch Kimmerling (New York: New York Press, 1989), 165.

the same time that the citizenship discourse was establishing itself, a parallel ethno-religious discourse was developing.

It was precisely these developments—the emergence of civic discourse on the one hand, and the occupation of the 1967 territories on the other—that forced Israel to declare its identity. When Rabbi Kahane[58] decided to run for Knesset, voices were heard calling for his banishment from elections in light of his blatantly racist agenda. Following the debate awakened by Kahane, an amendment to the *Basic Law: The Knesset* was introduced that prevented parties that openly deny Israel as both a Jewish and a democratic state from participating in elections.[59] The amendment, however, was merely a reaction to the fundamental dilemmas that the Rabbi Kahane episode brought to light: the post-1967 state, confronted with the civic developments described above, simply had to formulate its identity.

The counter story I propose here insists, in contrast to the previous narrative, on the ongoing priority and primacy of the *Ethnos*—the Jewish *Ethnos*—and views the state of Israel as a primarily ethnic colonial project which aims at perpetual expansion in order to maintain Jewish ethnic dominance over the native Palestinian population. Oren Yiftachael coined the term "ethnocracy" to describe such regimes as Israel, Estonia, Sri Lanka and several other countries.[60] In these regimes the *Ethnos* takes priority over the *Demos*, and the system acts in a structural manner to promote the interests of a single ethnic group that holds almost exclusive power over the majority of resources and capital flow in the country. This type of regime is neither democratic nor authoritarian: while on the one hand it incorporates some features of a democratic polity at the level of basic rights and free elections, these symptoms of democracy are, for the most part, purely superficial. On a

---

58 Rabbi Martin David Kahane (1932-1990) was a Knesset member and a radical right-wing political leader. He established KACH party and was banned by the Central Elections Committee from being a candidate on the grounds that KACH was a racist party.
59 Basic Law: The Knesset (Amendment No. 9) 1155 LSI 196 (1985).
60 See Oren Yiftachel, *Ethnocracy: Land and Identity Politics in Israel/Palestine* (Pennsylvania: University of Pennsylvania Press, 2006). But for a classical formulation of Israel mainly as a settler state see Maxime Rodinson, *Israel: a Colonial-Settler State?*, trans. David Thorstad (New York: Monad Press, 1973); Gershon Shafir, *Land, Labor, and the Origins of the Israeli-Palestinian Conflict, 1882-1914* (Cambridge: Cambridge University Press, 1989); Baruch Kimmerling, *Zionism and Territory: The Socio-Territorial Dimensions of Zionist Politics* (Berkeley: Institute of International Studies, University of California, 1983); Elia T. Zureik, *The Palestinians in Israel: A Study in Internal Colonialism* (London: Routledge & Kegan Paul, 1979).

deeper level, the structure of power relations clearly aims at promoting the collective good of one group only. The democratic surface is thus unable to launch any deep structural change whatsoever; unable even to put substantial restraints on the power of the dominant ethnic group. This group is the one who has the final say in the most crucial decisions, and the democratic body as a whole—the civic body—is marginalized. Ethnocracy manifests itself in policies of immigration and citizenship, land allocation, settlement planning, and flow of capital, as well as in the roles played in society by the military, legal system, and popular culture.[61]

This analysis views the processes underway inside Israel proper and the developments in the occupied territories as a coherent continuity rather than stressing the differences between the two.[62] In this paradigm the Zionist project is an ethnic settler project and is therefore in a state of constant expansion, attempting to grab as much land as it possibly can. This vision makes clear the fact that a zero-sum dynamic is still underway between the Palestinian natives and the expansionist Israeli policies that strive to ethnicize the space and territory, and that in this situation, the rhetoric of citizenship cannot be taken at face value. The difference between Palestinians in the occupied territories and those inside Israel, though it bears some importance, is at the end of the day only marginal since in both cases the Palestinian is considered to be an enemy standing in the way of the Zionist settler project.

According to this approach, the civic discourse of the nineties never managed to initiate any real structural impact, remaining only on the surface level of discussion. The regression to demographic discourse and to zero-sum game politics, in which the shared citizenship discourse is in constant retreat, is blatantly obvious in an array of developments that have taken place since the outbreak of the second Intifada in 2000, posing serious question marks over the citizenship status of the Palestinians in Israel.[63]

---

61 See Oren Yiftachael and Asad Ghanem, "Understanding Ethnocratic Regimes: The Politics of Seizing Contested Territories," *Political Geography* 23 (2004): 647.

62 For a recent articulation of this vision that aims to see the continuities between the 1948 war and the 1967 war, or between the settlers project before 1948 and the one after 1948 see Yehouda Shenhav, *The Time of the Green Line: A Jewish Political Essay* [in Hebrew] (Tel Aviv: Am Oved, 2010). See also Ariella Azoulay and Adi Ophir, *This Regime Which Is Not One: Occupation and Democracy Between the Sea and the River (1967)* [in Hebrew] (Tel Aviv: Resling, 2008).

63 See for example a survey of Israel policies after the second Intifada by Nadim Rouhana and Nimer

1. The events of October 2000 and their aftermath. The killing of thirteen Israeli Palestinians by policemen in October 2000 during demonstrations that took place in Nazareth and other Palestinian localities highlighted the fact that the Israeli police treat the Palestinian Israelis as enemies, not as full citizens. This conclusion was explicitly stated in the report submitted by the Or Commission, established to investigate the events and issue recommendations.[64] The report, submitted on September 1, 2003, also demanded a further investigation within the police forces to decide whether or not to bring to justice those police officers who killed innocent citizens. Despite the recommendations, and notwithstanding evidence presented to the attorney general by *Adalah*,[65] the case was closed without further investigation.[66]

2. The rise of demographic discourse and its social legitimization as part of the mainstream discourse in Israeli society. This trend is manifested most explicitly in the sweeping victory in the 2008 elections of Avigdor Lieberman (currently serving as Israel's minister of foreign affairs), who explicitly advocates the demographic discourse.[67] This discourse, which treats the Palestinians in Israel as a threat to the state, is not limited to the margins of society; it pervades many respectable and reputed figures and institutions. Conferences are held and working papers are written to deal with this issue.[68]

Sultany, "Redrawing the Boundaries of Citizenship: Israel's New Hegemony," *Journal of Palestine Studies* 33 (2003): 5.

64   Theodor Or, *Report of the State Commission of Inquiry to Investigate the Clashes between the Security Forces and Israeli Citizens in October 2000* [in Hebrew] (Jerusalem: Government Printing Press, 2003).

65   *Adalah*: the Legal Center for Arab Minority Rights in Israel.

66   See attorney general letter to *Adalah* on this regard (April 15, 2004), available at http://adalah. org/features/commission/mazoz_response_150404.pdf. See also Marwan Dalal, *October 2000: Law and Politics before the Or Commission of Inquiry*, (*Adalah*: the Legal Center for Arab Minority Rights in Israel, 2003), available at http://adalah.org/eng/features/commission/oct2000_eng. pdf.

67   See *Israel Beitenu* election platform, available at http://www.knesset.gov.il/elections/knesset15/ beiteinu_m.htm. According to the platform, *Israel Beitenu* aims at turning Israel into "a state of all its citizens."

68   See for example Arnon Sofer, "The Role of Demography and Territory in Jewish-Arab Relations in Israel," *Contemporary Israeli Geography* 60-61 (2004): 333; Elia Zureik, "Demography and Transfer: Israel's Road to Nowhere," *Third World Quarterly* 24 (2003): 619. On April 4, 2005, a conference on the issue was held in the Interdisciplinary Center of Herzeliya, titled "National-Civic Service in Israel: Discussing the Ivry Commission's Recommendations" [in Hebrew]. A protocol of the conference is *available at* http://www.herzliyaconference.org/_Uploads/2612Ivry.pdf.

3. The amendment to the Law of Citizenship—The Citizenship and Entry into Israel Law (Temporary Provision). This amendment *de facto* forbids Palestinians from Israel who choose to marry Palestinians from the occupied territories to live in Israel, thus preventing family unification. After the law was passed, it was immediately brought before the Supreme Court and there, too, it received the stamp of legitimacy (albeit by a slim majority).[69]

4. A variety of other changes made to the Law of Citizenship. These amendments grant the minister of interior affairs the right of revocation for any citizen under certain circumstances;[70] hinting to all Palestinian citizens of Israel that they should not take their citizenship for granted and reminding them that their status can be negotiated at any time according to the will of the government.

5. The newly formulated Law of Students. In this legislation, there is an article designed to bypass the decision delivered by Haifa District Court which banned the use of military service as a factor in deciding whether to grant students the right to subsidized housing. In stark opposition to the court's decision, the law states that the university is allowed to take that consideration into account.

6. The statement delivered by the *Shin Beit* (Israeli Security Services) that they plan to tape activists who advocate the redefinition of Israel as a democratic "state of all its citizens," in contrast to the Jewish nature of the state, and the endorsement and backing of this plan by the attorney general.[71]

7. The recent bill forbidding public institutions that receive state funding (directly or indirectly) to participate in the commemoration of the Palestinian *Nakba*.[72]

8. New policies of house demolitions, especially in the Negev area.[73] Statistics point to a palpable rise in the number of demolished houses

---

69 The Citizenship and Entry into Israel Law (Temporary Provision), 1901 LSI 544 (2003); HCJ 7052/03: Adalah v. The Minister of the Interior (2006) (awaiting publication).
70 The Law of Citizenship, 6 LSI 50 (1952), Art. 11.
71 See *Adalah*—The Legal Center for Arab Minority Rights in Israel, "Israel Attorney General Supports Shabak Mandate to Act Against Legal and Democratic Political Work," *The Alternative Information Center*, May 28, 2007, http://www.alternativenews.org/english/index.php/topics/news/884-israel-attorney-general-supports-shabak-mandate-to-act-against-legal-and-democratic-political-work.
72 Clause 3b(a)(1) of the Budget Law (Amendment—Illegal Expenditure), 2009, Bill No. 1403/18.
73 See Negev Coexistence Forum, http://www.dukium.org/modules.php?name=Content&pa=showpage&pid=23.

owned by Palestinian citizens.

9. The bill recently approved that relates to the selection committees in community settlements. This proposal is commonly viewed as a law designed to bypass the Supreme Court decision in the Ka'adan case.[74]

10. In general, the victory of the right wing in the Israeli elections of 2008 and the anticipation that the right wing would win even more votes if new elections were to be held now. The lenience practiced by police officers towards the killing of Palestinians. According to reports, since the events of October 2000, some thirty Palestinians have been killed by police officers on various occasions and under obscure circumstances (during routine arrests, car chasing, etc.) that call for investigation, at the very least. So far, none of the officers responsible for these deaths have been put on trial.[75]

This is not a full list of the recent manifestations of Israel's growing ethnocratic inclinations; for that one may review *Adalah*'s report on the matter.[76] But even these few examples of bills and policies are enough to show that the status of the Palestinians in Israel is in a state of regression, and even the continuation of their status as citizens is no longer taken for granted. These developments do not go hand in hand with the purported image of the civic service bill as a reflection of Israeli state policy aiming at the promotion of civic discourse and the enhancement of the status of Palestinian citizens.

6. Has the Wheel Come Full Circle?

In this paper, I have proposed an interpretation of the civic service proposals as another aspect of the recent ethnocratic developments, instead of an act that conflicts with them. In this reading, the civic discourse introduced by the state does not aim at evoking the inherent contradictions between the Jewish nature of the state and its definition

---

74 Bill for the Amendment of the Communal Settlements Order (Amendment No. 8), 2010, Bill No. 1740/18.

75 See the Coalition against Racism in Israel, "Racism Report 2010," chapter 4 [in Hebrew], available at http://www.fightracism.org/index.php?option=com_content&view=article&id=22:2010-04-18-18-26-18&catid=5:-2010&Itemid=6.

76 See *Adalah*, "New Discriminatory Laws and Bills in Israel," *available at* http://australiansforpalestine.com/33722.

as a democracy, and does not aim at replacing Jewish ethnic discourse with a liberal, civic one. There is no hidden plan to transform Israel into a civic republic lying behind the civic service proposals. Instead, they reveal the dynamic in which civic discourse has been appropriated by the state itself, following the discourse of "a state of all its citizens" and exporting the contradictions that this challenge brought to light over to the Palestinian sphere.

This reading views the apparent civic discourse as a mere continuation of the old national conflict through other means. The Palestinians first discovered that they could rearticulate most of their historic demands and national aspirations by submitting to the civic discourse, and they employed it in order to confront the Jewish state with its own liberal and universal aspirations. The discourse of "a state of all its citizens" succeeded in putting the Israeli state in a position of self-defense. The Israeli state was quick to defend itself against this confrontation by launching a counter-attack: it discovered the potential of using the very same discursive language against the Palestinians, and employed this rhetoric to redirect demands away from the state and towards the Palestinian population. The demand that the state treat its Palestinian citizens as true citizens, to normalize its relation to them and to end its enmity toward them, could be countered by a reciprocal demand on the part of the state towards its Palestinian citizens: it is now they who are required to normalize their relation to the state and to treat it as their state, not their enemy.[77] However, the very nature of the discourse of citizenship focuses on the citizen while assuming the existence of the state, since there can be no citizenship as long as there is no state. The discourse of citizenship thus has two poles: the citizen on one side, and the state on the other. On the other hand, the rhetoric of rights may, by its very nature, lead to the discourse of duties, since there is a certain relationship between the discourse of rights and that of duties.

In certain ways one might view the setback in civic discourse and the rise of demographic claims as proof that we are back to square one, back to a perception of relations in terms of a zero-sum game, and that the concept of citizenship has again been eviscerated of its substance,

---

77   For this double nature of the discourse of "a state of all its citizens" see Raef Zreik, "The Palestinian Question: Themes of Justice and Power Part II: The Palestinians in Israel," *Journal of Palestine Studies* 33 (2003): 42.

regressing from the relative progress that had been achieved over the last two decades. Yet I would like to end with a picture that is a bit more complex, adding three reservations to what might be considered the structuralist-determinist approach I have presented in this paper. These remarks do not change the overall picture; nevertheless, the picture will not be comprehensive without bearing them in mind.

First, even if there is a fall back to an ethno-national zero-sum game, the participants—including those acting on behalf of the state—feel more obligated to formulate their policy in civic terms than they felt in the past. This shows that the civic language of discourse, although it is for the most part used superficially, still holds some appeal. In deploying its rhetoric, the meaning of the terms is not altogether lost.

Second, those who support civic service within the Jewish majority are not a monolithic and united block and they support it for many different, sometimes even opposing, reasons. There are more than a few on the left who advocate civic service as a step that could potentially strengthen the civic nature of the state, and even pose a challenge to its hegemonic Jewish nature by pushing the state toward a more civic, republican discourse.

My third and last reservation is that at times, bad intentions might lead to good results. Even if some agents within the state are acting in bad faith, this does not mean that the project itself cannot lead to unexpected positive results.

Something happened in the last two decades that seems to have put some restraints on the means and language used by the State of Israel, if not on its ultimate goals: nowadays even right-wing parties feel a minimal obligation to formulate their demands in the language of civic discourse; in this sense, this rhetoric has gained some prominence. Is this, however, enough to bring about any deep structural change? This does not seem to be the case. That question, however, remains to be answered.

Universal Jurisdiction, Really Serious Crimes, and the Liberal-Republican Debate

1. Introduction

One fine morning in February of 2003, the people of Israel were informed by the Belgian Court of Appeals that Prime Minister Ariel Sharon and distinguished retired Generals may be tried in Belgium for crimes they allegedly committed in relation to the Sabra and Shatila massacre in 1982, while Mr. Sharon was the Israeli Defense Minister and the Generals were commanding the Israeli forces. The suit in Belgium was commenced some year and a half earlier, in the summer of 2001, by victims—private individuals—allowed under Belgian law[1] to file a criminal complaint against an alleged offender. Under the Belgian law as it then stood the private complaint had to be reviewed by a prosecutorial judge, and if found to have merit, it was to proceed to trial. Israel appealed the affirmative conclusion of the first instance, and lost.[2] The stage was set for a rather remarkable development: one nation-state (the peculiar bi-national makeup of Belgium notwithstanding), moved by individuals, was to exercise jurisdiction against citizens (and previously office-holders) of another nation-state for grave crimes they allegedly committed against the foundations of the international order itself. Has the concept of sovereignty, closely associated with the Westphalian Order, been so thoroughly eroded in the 21st century as to usher in a new era of political thought? And if indeed a new era is upon us, what can we make of it in terms of the liberal-republican debate?

In order to address these questions, this chapter will advance three

---

*   Faculty of Law, University of Haifa. I wish to thank the participants of the conference for their useful insights and Fania Oz-Salzberger for the constructive comments. Any and all errors are mine.

1   Act Concerning the Punishment of Grave Breaches of International Humanitarian Law, translated and reprinted in 38 I.L.M 918, 921(1999).

2   Abbas Hijazy v. Sharon et al. Belgium Court of Cassation, ruling no. P.02.1139. F/1, Judgment of 12 February 2003; http://www.indictsharon.net/cmptENen.pdf.

themes: It will first examine the debate concerning universal jurisdiction and its relation to sovereignty and self-determination in its historical context, and highlight the historical irony surrounding the Israeli shift on point. After all, it was Israel, established in part as a consequence of World War II, that convincingly claimed that the lessons learnt from the Holocaust require such jurisdiction. The chapter will then examine the justification of universal jurisdiction and its relation to the liberal and republican justifications of sovereignty, and suggest that contrary to our initial reservations, if some conditions are met, universal jurisdiction is actually justified under a modern, i.e., post World War II, understanding of the Westphalian Order. Sovereignty, therefore, should not be discredited, only better understood (and therefore slightly reconfigured). Lastly, this chapter will take a closer look at the implications of the emergence of universal jurisdiction vested in national courts on the liberal-republican debate. Here the chapter will suggest that while, at first glance, it appears that the emergence of such jurisdiction embodies liberal principles of universal human rights, it may, in fact, indicate a republican approach, according to which a supra-national polity is emerging.

2. Universal Jurisdiction: Some Historical Ironies

The official reaction in Israel to the exercise of universal jurisdiction by Belgium ranged from outrage to disgust. The President spoke harshly against this development and Shimon Peres, the Nobel Peace laureate and a leading figure in the Labor Party (then at the opposition to Sharon's government), chided the Belgians for their uncivil behavior.[3] Legal teams were dispatched to Belgium, and all efforts were made to debase the legitimacy of universal jurisdiction *per se*.

The irony is evident: it was Israel that played a crucial role in modern time in developing the concept of universal jurisdiction. In the *Eichmann* case (1961), Israel asserted its jurisdiction over Adolf Eichmann at least in part because he committed crimes against humanity itself.[4] Israel's plea was convincing. Some crimes are so severe that no state may turn

---

3   A. Ben, E. Bareket and U. Barzilai, "The Israeli Ambassador in Belgium was Called for 'Consultations' in Jerusalem," *Ha'aretz* February 13, 2003.

4   See 40/61 (Crim. Jerusalem) Attorney General v. Eichmann (Dist. Ct. 45 (1965) 3, and Crim. App. 336/61 Eichmann v. Attorney General PD 16 2033.

away and close its courts on the grounds that it has no jurisdiction because the crimes are not "linked" to it. Some crimes are the concerns of the family of nations as such, and thus the concern of each member in this family. A similar position was echoed by Lord Nicholls and Lord Hoffmann in the *Pinochet* decision (1998),[5] in concluding that Senator Augusto Pinochet cannot enjoy the immunity granted to heads of state. Under that reasoning, some means fall so far beyond the purview of those which a head of state may legitimately deploy that exercising them cannot be under the color of an official position. Therefore, in exercising such means one cannot be taken as acting as a head of state, and thus cannot claim the immunity enjoyed by heads of states.[6] The rationale of the decision follows the *Eichmann* rationale in that it recognized fundamental principles upon which the world order rests, and which all national courts must respect.[7]

The position of the state of Israel in the *Eichmann* case can be traced to the work of a prominent European thinker, Hugo Grotius, who in 1625 published his seminal work, titled *On the Rights of War and Peace*, in which he developed the idea of natural law as the law of nations, resting not necessarily on divine law, but being an expression of universal reason.[8] It is the work of Grotius that later provided the foundation for the international community in legally tackling the crimes committed by the Nazis. Similarly, one cannot understand the position of Lords Nicholls and Hoffmann (and later Lord Millet) of the

---

5   R v. Bartle and the Commissioner of Police for the Metropolis and Others, Ex Parte Pinochet, [1998] UKHL 41; [1998] 4 All ER 897 (November 25, 1998). Lord Millet was of the same opinion when the matter reached the House of Lords again (R. v. Bow Street Metropolitan Stipendiary Magistrate and Others, Ex parte Pinochet Urgate (No. 3),[1999] 2 All E.R 97(H.L) (March 24, 1999) but this time the case was decided on different grounds, elaborated in footnote 33 and accompanying text.

6   "And it hardly needs saying that torture of his own subjects, or of aliens, would not be regarded by international law as a function of a head of state. All states disavow the use of torture as abhorrent, although from time to time some still resort to it. ... International law recognises, of course, that the functions of a head of state may include activities which are wrongful, even illegal, by the law of his own state or by the laws of other states. But international law has made plain that certain types of conduct, including torture and hostage-taking, are not acceptable conduct on the part of anyone. This applies as much to heads of state, or even more so, as it does to everyone else; the contrary conclusion would make a mockery of international law." Lord Nichoff in Pinochet (1998), *supra* note 5.

7   Lord Slynn in Pinochet (1998) indeed cites the Israeli court in the Eichmann case for the proposition that national courts may exercise universal jurisdiction when confronted with (some) international crimes.

8   H. Grotius, *The Rights of War and Peace*, trans. A.C. Campbell (New York, 1901), 258-259.

House of Lords in the *Pinochet* saga without understanding the structure developed by Grotius. But was Grotius right? Is universal jurisdiction justified, in our positivistic—or post-positivistic—age? After all, Grotius relied on reasoned-based natural law, and today we tend to view such an approach as antiquated and/or romanticized. Surely, law is not "natural," but is rather enacted by humans as an expression of their will (as positivists believe). Critics may take a step further, and suggest that law is the expression of the power of the elites, and clocking it in natural terminology only serves the powerful to dominate the masses (as some post-positivists belief). As mentioned above, the Israeli official reaction to the indictment of Sharon, based on universal jurisdiction, rejected the idea that the exercise of such jurisdiction is required by natural law. Rather, the reaction was as close to collective fury as one can imagine: the Israeli position was that such an indictment was totally *un*reasonable (and may amount to political manipulation of the Belgian legal system).[9]

3. Universal Jurisdiction: An End to Westphalian Sovereignty?

The Sharon case was indeed peculiar: Mr. Sharon was an acting Prime Minister and none of the defendants were present in Belgium during any stage of the proceedings. These two facts alone should have led to its dismissal under accepted principles of procedural immunity and due process (and indeed, the case against Sharon was ultimately dropped, in part pursuant to a decision by the International Court of Justice in The Hague regarding the scope of immunity serving officials enjoy).[10] Yet the real challenge the case poses stems from a different root—the offence had no links to Belgium: the victims were not Belgian, nor were the alleged offenders; the crimes were not committed on Belgian soil, nor was Belgian soil traversed by the offenders or victims before or after

---

9   Conol Urquhart, "Israel Scorns 'Anti-Semitic Little Belgium'; Furious Backlash after Court Rules against Sharon," *The Guardian*, Feb. 14, 2003; James Bennet, "Israel Rejects Belgian Court Ruling on Sharon," *The New York Times*, Feb. 14, 2003.

10   Case Concerning the Arrest Warrant of 11 April 2000 (The Democratic Republic of Congo v. Belgium) (Int'l Ct. Justice, Feb. 14, 2002) 41 I.L.M. 536. The Court in Belgium decided that the case against Sharon could not proceed as long as he was in office. However, the case could have proceeded once his term ended, and in any event could have proceeded against the retired generals. The reason it did not relates to the amendment of the Belgian statute on point, as will be discussed below.

the crime; Belgian state interests were not implicated by the crime. In short, under a traditional understanding of jurisdiction, Belgium had no jurisdiction to try the case.[11]

The Belgian system relied on its universal jurisdiction statute. That statute was enacted in Belgium and in other European countries pursuant to the call made in several international conventions, that states harness their courts to adjudicate very serious crimes even if those crimes bear no traditional connection to the forum state. For example, in the International Convention against Torture (1985), such a call was part of the obligations that states undertake upon entering the convention.[12] Pursuant to this obligation, Britain enacted its universal jurisdiction section in the penal code,[13] and relying on this section proceeded to examine the extradition request of Senator Augusto Pinochet to Spain. The universal jurisdiction was necessary, because under British law, Spain may request extradition only if the events at the core of the request are a crime both in Britain and in Spain. The events at the center of the extradition request were committed in Chile by Chileans against Chileans, so under traditional notions of sovereignty, they were not a crime *in Britain.* The double criminality was established upon the British statute that criminalizes the alleged offences (because they amount to torture and similar grave crimes) in Britain, even if committed by non-Britons against non-Britons and not on British soil.

We are thus presented with the difficulties associated with universal jurisdiction in the starkest terms: the British polity, through its judiciary, passing judgment on the former head of state of the Chilean polity in response to a request by the Spanish polity (itself exercising universal jurisdiction over the offenses). What can we make of this development as far as our understanding of the relationship between nations? Can we defend the development of universal jurisdiction? I will identify

---

11   For analysis of grounds for jurisdiction, see Diane Orentlicher, "Whose Justice? Reconciling Universal Jurisdiction with Democratic Principles," *92 GEO. L. J 1057* (2004); Luc Reydams, *Universal Jurisdiction: International and Municipal Legal Perspectives* (Oxford: Oxford University Press 2003, reprinted 2005).

12   Convention Against Torture, and Other Cruel, Inhuman or Degrading Treatment or Punishment, Adopted 10 Dec. 1984, G.A. Res. 39/46, U.N. GAOR, 39th Sess., Supp. No. 51, U.N. Doc. A/39/51 (1985) (entered into force 26 June 1987), United Nations Treaty Series, 1987, Vol 1465 p 113, reprinted in (1984) 23 *I.L.M.* 1027.

13   Section 134(1): Criminal Justice Act, 1988, ch. 33, reprinted in *12 Halsbury's Statutes Of England And Wales* 1079 (4th ed. 1997).

four major concerns raised by the notion of universal jurisdiction, and address each of them briefly.

The first and obvious concern stems from the threat to national sovereignty. Universal jurisdiction pierces the shield of sovereignty by subjecting citizens of one nation to the jurisdiction of other nations and thus threatens to undermine the monopoly of legal power each nation enjoys over its citizens and its territory – a central component of sovereignty. Note that by definition universal jurisdiction is exercised by a nation that bears no other ties to the act or the actors other than its membership in the community of nations. If any nation may pass judgment on citizens of any other nation without specific jurisdictional ties to the act the citizens have allegedly committed, sovereignty, it would seem, is significantly challenged.

But sovereignty, of course, should not be treated as providing talismanic immunity. The reason we care about sovereignty in modern times cannot be because we care about the metaphysical extension of the King's flesh or spirit over his subjects, his territory or his particular interests. Both a liberal and a republican understanding of sovereignty would reject this early (and hopefully obsolete) approach. We care about sovereignty because it represents, or embodies, the right of a given people to self-determination. One nation should not adjudicate the subjects of another nation (barring any other jurisdictional ties) because the exercise of jurisdiction is a component of the exercise of self-rule, and as such an expression of collective self-determination.

Upon a closer examination, however, there could be cases in which self-determination itself requires that sovereignty would NOT be respected. If sovereignty is used in a manner contrary to the idea of self-determination, it cannot shield those in power from international intervention. For example, if the Iraqi army bombed a segment of Iraqi citizenry with chemical weapons, Iraq's claim for respect of its sovereignty against a humanitarian intervention could not rely on self-determination. The self-determination of the segment hit by these weapons was equally at stake, and the exercise of unrestrained and indiscriminate power towards this segment cannot be reconciled with the self determination of the Iraqi people as a whole. The same, it would appear, applies to the republics of Libya, Syria, Yemen or any other regime that turns its guns against its own citizens. A polity with republican aspirations cannot turn to republicanism to fend off "external" interventions and at the same time undermine the notion of "the republic" and its built-in solidarity by acts against the fabric that constitutes "the republic."

A similar line of argument could rest on liberal human rights: if a state, created in order to respect and advance the rights of its citizens, uses its power to systemically infringe these rights, it can no longer demand the respect of other liberal states in the name of the right of self-determination. The right of self-determination is itself a component of a broader system of rights. We care about self-determination because it expresses the autonomy and dignity of a certain people. If we care about autonomy and dignity, serious offences committed by those acting *prima facie* as state officials against the autonomy and dignity of others cannot receive absolute immunity from an international community that is organized around the concepts of autonomy and dignity. To the extent that such offences contain an international element—for instance, if they were deliberately committed against members of an ethnic minority or on a large scale—the international community, acting as an agent of a world-order organized around the commitment to the protection of human rights, would be remiss if it would refrain from reacting to the violation of human rights on account of the right of self-determination of the violating nation.

War crimes, for example, can be the subject matter of international law, and claims about self-determination would usually not serve as a good defense against the prosecution of perpetrators of such crimes. More specifically, the defense of subordination—"I was ordered to do so by my superior"—which arguably emanates from self-determination: my polity nominated my superior to exercise official power, and therefore it is no business of the international community to question my loyalty to my sovereign—is usually not considered prevailing.[14] If certain acts are

---

14   For example, the Belgian Act Concerning the Punishment of Grave Breaches of International Humanitarian Law, 1993 (as amended in 1999) (Belgium), 38 I.L.M (1999), 918, specifically states in article 5 (2): "The fact that the defendant acted on the order of his/her government or a superior shall not absolve him/her from responsibility where, in the prevailing circumstances, the order could clearly result in the commission of a crime of genocide or of a crime against humanity, as defined in the present Act, or a grave breach of the Geneva Conventions of 12 August 1949 and their Additional protocol I of 8 June 1977." Subsection (3) states that "[t]he immunity attributed to the official capacity of a person, does not prevent the application of the present Act." This section was later (in 2003) amended to include a proviso at the end: "except under those limits established under international law." See 42 I.L.M 749 (May 2003).

viewed as acts against the international order itself, it would follow that organs of the international order, including national judiciaries, should be available to adjudicate allegations of commission of such crimes.

The focus, then, should be not on universal jurisdiction as such, but on identifying the particular crimes the commitment of which calls upon other nations and the international community to intervene by allowing other nations to pierce the veil of sovereignty and exercise jurisdiction on behalf of humanity itself. This aspect will be further addressed below, in the context of the liberal-republican debate.

The second concern that universal jurisdiction raises is of a second order: due process. The republic owes each of its members the protection of due process before it exercises its sovereign power via the criminal process. Each republic would expect other republics to show similar commitment to due process when adjudicating foreign nationals, not only because this would be prudent, but also because republicanism is sensitive to the notion of reciprocity. As Hobbes argued, the sovereign and the subject are bound by reciprocal relations mediated by laws.[15] The same should hold among sovereign nations as they enter into treaties (or establish customs) for the purpose of self-governance on the international sphere. Reciprocity among republics would therefore establish, via conventions or customs, transnational principles of due process. Similarly, from a liberal point of view, one's liberty may be revoked only pursuant to a fair process. From a liberal perspective, this is a human right containing a universal kernel, and is therefore independent of nationality.[16] Universal jurisdiction, it seems, challenges the commitment to due process. If a remote jurisdiction is vested with adjudicatory powers, evidence before it might not be comprehensive. Moreover, defendants might be at a disadvantage, having to incur high costs when mounting an effective defense. Furthermore, there is a risk of politicization. Judges, as any citizen of a

---

15 Thomas Hobbes, *Leviathan*, ed. Richard Tuck (Cambridge: Cambridge University Press, 1997), chapter 21, 147.

16 It should be noted, however, that the liberal and the republican notions of due process may differ. While both would be committed to some core principles of fairness—a minimum each state must accord to all under its legal authority—a republican approach may allow the state to provide a different standard for citizens and non-citizens beyond that minimum. For example, the extent of state funding for legal representation may be related to citizenship when the offenses are not severe offenses and the accused are of some financial means. It would be much more difficult to justify a differential treatment based on purely liberal principles.

remote jurisdiction, may be subject to a positive or negative one-sided portrayal in the media of actors or events in other countries, and thus may harbor negative or positive political sentiments towards the cause represented at trial. Beyond media representations, there might also be cultural preferences that may influence impartiality. For example, In Northern Ireland, Catholics tend to identify with the Palestinian cause whereas Protestants are more likely to identify with Israel. Israelis are more likely to identify with the Dutch than with the Germans (despite the fact that German politics are more pro-Israeli than Dutch politics). Such cultural biases may impair the right to a fair trial. To the extent that law is a political process, political interests of the country where the trial is held may tilt the proceedings.

It is conceded that indeed there could be cases that raise these concerns. But it is not clear that these are good reasons to reject universal jurisdiction *per se*. Forum non-convenience considerations are certainly a weighty concern. They necessitate that the primary jurisdiction would be vested with states that bear closer links to the event. These states, because of their greater proximity, are usually more accessible to the various players in the legal process, and thus conducting the trial in a state with the closest ties to the event is a good idea. But these considerations do not carry the day if there is no other available forum to adjudicate serious crimes. So, if states with closer connections to the events are either unable or unwilling to adjudicate, accepting the forum non-convenience argument would mean that some crimes would not be adjudicated at all. Assuming that the international order stands to suffer as a result—torture or even genocide might go unpunished—this second-order concern requires that extra care would be given to the due process, not that the jurisdiction be barred *in toto*.

The same reasoning applies regarding possible inequalities between the prosecution and the defense: we should ensure that due process is maintained, not disallow the process altogether. Incidentally, it should be noted that experience teaches us that at least on some occasions, the states of the accused tend to support him or her, changing the balance of power and resources.

In any event, at the end of the day, transparency—and expected reciprocity—could be the most effective remedy for such due process concerns. Given the heightened attention likely to be drawn to any and all procedural aspects of the exercise of universal jurisdiction, there is little reason to assume that due process violations would mire the adjudication as a systemic matter.

As for the danger of politicization—that danger indeed exists. It is unclear, however, if it would be heightened when courts exercise universal jurisdiction compared to the exercise of jurisdiction based upon direct ties to a case. Israeli soldiers in Israel might enjoy preferential treatment by the Israeli legal system (courts included). Can we not claim that external tribunals are actually better situated? Contrary to the argument presented earlier, it may be the case that neutrality and impartiality—key components of due process—actually point away from courts exercising jurisdiction on the bases of the territoriality or the personal attributes of the parties, such as their citizenship. Foreign jurisdictions may prove to be less emotionally involved with the issue, and thus professional judges in foreign jurisdiction may in fact be better situated to adjudicate highly-charged cases. This is the rationale of requiring a change of venue in federal states,[17] or removing cases to another location.[18]And this was the rationale of "importing" foreign judges to sit on national courts in troubled places[19] or on special tribunals.[20]

Nevertheless, universal jurisdiction should be kept as a last resort only, but for reasons other than the concerns previously raised.

---

17 The Sixth Amendment calls for such change of venue when there are concerns for impartiality. Patton v. Yount, 467 U.S. 1025, 1035 (1984); United States v. McVeigh, 918 F. Supp. 1467, 1474 (W.D. Okla. 1996).

18 In the Lockerbie case, two Libyan individuals were accused of planting a bomb on a Pan-Am flight, killing 270 people (all on board and some on the ground). Since Libya claimed the accused are likely not to receive a fair trial in the US or the UK, the trial eventually took place in the Netherlands with Scottish judges (according to Scottish rules of procedure), pursuant to a special treaty signed by the United Kingdom and the Netherland, and as a result of an agreement reached by Libya, the United Kingdom, the United States and the United Nations. See reports by Michael Sharf of the American Society of International Law, available at: http://www.asil.org/insigh44.cfm and http://www.asil.org/insigh61.cfm.

19 Under The General Framework Agreement for Peace in Bosnia and Herzegovina (The Dayton Accords, reached at Wright-Patterson Air Force Base in November 1995, and formally signed in Paris on December 14, 1995), of the 12 judges of the Bosinian constitutional court three will be internationally renowned jurists who cannot be citizens of Bosnia & Herzegovina or of any of its neighboring countries. Available at: http://www.state.gov/www/regions/eur/bosnia/bosagree.html.

20 The special tribunals for Rwanda (ICTR) and the former Yugoslavia (ICTY) were premised on the notion that an international forum is better situated to achieve justice as an impartial venue. The ICTY was established pursuant to UN Security Council 8 November 1994. (S/RES/827 (1993) 25 May 1993). The ICTR was established pursuant to a UN Security Council resolution and at the request of Rwanda (S/RES/955 (1994)).

Republicans and liberals alike would prefer that judges be subject to the rules that they themselves pronounce upon deciding cases. Republicans would prefer that judges be subject, in real life (not only in theory) to the actual implications of their rulings as a form of self-governance of the polity. Liberals would prefer this option because for liberals, judges—a necessary component of a rights-based system—are needed precisely because reasonable people may disagree regarding the proper balance between rights; and judicial discretion must be informed by the possible consequences a particular decision may bring about. If a foreign court exercises judgment in a certain way—for example, if it strikes a certain balance between national security and a particular human right—it would be disturbing if the judges themselves were not subjected to living under the interpretive standard they announced. By "living," I mean having to bear the responsibilities associated with the balance struck. Judges of a system related to the case only by virtue of universal jurisdiction may be too remote to seriously internalize the implication of the balance they need to strike. In other words, universal jurisdiction raises accountability concerns associated with splitting the deciding body from the consequences of its decision.[21] Of course, this need not necessarily be the case, since a particular judiciary trying a given case may in fact be subject to the real-life consequences of its decision, if the state of which the judiciary is a part is facing conditions similar to those prevalent in the states where the crimes where allegedly committed. But since the exercise of universal jurisdiction may equally take place in a context so removed as to raise the concerns mentioned above, the option should be the last resort only.

However, if no viable alternative exists, and if the crimes are indeed grave violations of the fundamental principles of the international order, the risk associated with a decision by a distant court, removed from traditional jurisdictional links, is the lesser evil.

The third concern that the application of universal jurisdiction raises is also related to due process: victims might shop for a forum favorable to them, and file a complaint there. This may raise concerns of equal protection of the laws, and may also lead to disarray. Moreover, today,

---

21   Compare: Amnon Reichman, "Judicial Non-Dependence: Operational Closure, Cognitive Openness, and the Underlying Rationale of the Provincial Judges Reference—The Israeli Perspective," in Lorne Sossin and Adam Dodek (eds.) *Judicial Independence in Context* (Irwin Law, Canada, 2010), chapter 14.

not all courts follow the basic tenets of due process; universal jurisdiction therefore may in theory empower courts in systems that are not fully committed to democratic principles (liberal or republican) that must govern the judicial process for it to be considered "fair."

Forum shopping is indeed a concern. It should be addressed by setting prior conditions which must be met for indictments based on universal jurisdictions to proceed: universal jurisdiction should be exercised only by non-dependent courts fully committed (in law and in practice) to shared principles of due process; and only after systems with more obvious ties to the event have been exhausted, namely found unable or unwilling to provide a bona fide forum. The first condition is obvious: universal jurisdiction would not be legitimate if it is applied by courts which do not or cannot guarantee due process. Admittedly, the application of this condition may prove difficult, in small part because on rare occasions it could be difficult to determine whether a system is indeed committed to principles of due process, but more poignantly, it would be difficult, politically, to establish a two-tiered system of courts worthy of our trust and courts which are not. Nevertheless, as a matter of theory, all courts should adhere to fundamental principles of fairness in order to be considered courts of law, and in practice we already operate under the assumption that verdicts and reasoning generated by democracies are taken more seriously, at least by democracies themselves. As for the second condition—a failure of systems with closer jurisdictional ties—the practical implications are clear. For example, in the Sharon case the plaintiffs should have at least demonstrated that in Israel it would not have been possible to proceed against Sharon and the army generals, or to expect a fair juridical outcome. It could very well be the case that the plaintiffs could have demonstrated that Israeli generals enjoyed a de facto immunity in Israel from such claims. But this argument had to be demonstrated and established at trial; it could not have been assumed or argued without further evidence. It stands to reason that the plaintiffs would have had to point at the very least to attempts made to pursue justice in Israel, before going elsewhere. That they did not do.

But what if indeed a system failure has occurred, and no system with traditional links to the crime is willing and able to adjudicate? Is there no concern that different laws in different countries will give rise to forum shopping? A closer examination reveals an interesting development.

There is a preliminary indication that national judiciaries in Western democracies—the United States excluded[22]—are mindful of decisions rendered by other national courts.[23] Judges, it appears, read the reasoning of other national courts, and examine whether the reasoning is indeed convincing, in search for common substantial standard regarding the interpretation of international norms. Such convergence could inform the judicial approach to national legal arrangements that seek to incorporate international norms into domestic systems, especially in matters pertaining to the foundations of the international legal order. This trend is worthy of notice, and it reflects the possible move toward some form of globalization.[24] If this trend will indeed mature into a full-blown system of substantive law, then the concern of forum shopping is greatly reduced.

Related to this is the concern of disarray. In a nutshell, the concern is that universal jurisdiction opens the door to multiple proceedings taking place with respect to the same events. These proceeding can happen concurrently, but also sequentially, raising issues of conflicting factual findings as well as conflicting rulings of law (or in legal terminology, *res judicata*). This concern, of course, is not unique to the exercise of universal jurisdiction. In any civil claim that involves a multinational dimension, such concerns may arise. Usually, the rules of private international law mitigate its bite. There is no reason why a similar system of conflict rules

---

22   There is strong judicial sentiment in the United States' federal system against comparative constitutional law, at least among some justices. The argument is that comparative law is done in a non-systemic manner (i.e., by way of "cherry picking") and in any event abrogates from the sovereignty of the United States, who fought the British crown to free itself from rules developed elsewhere. This argument has been vehemently contested as failing to capture the commitment among democratic nations to democratic principles jointly developed, as well as the advantages associated with learning from the experience of others. See, Norman Dorsen, "The Relevance of Foreign Legal Materials In U.S. Constitutional Cases: A Conversation Between Justice Antonin Scalia And Justice Stephen," *3 Int'l J. Const. L.* 519 (2005); Printz v. U.S. 521 US 898 (1997); See also Vicki C. Jackson, "Ambivalent Resistance and Comparative Constitutionalism: Opening up Conversation on Proportionality," *1 U. Pa. J. Const. L.* 583 (1999). Dick Howard "A Traveler From An Antique Land: The Modern Renaissance Of Comparative Constitutionalism A.E.," *50 Virginia J. Intl L.* 3 (2009); David Fontana "The Rise And Fall of Comparative Constitutional Law In The Postwar Era," *36 Yale J. Intl. L.* 1 (2011).

23   Ann Marie Slaughter, "Court to Court," *92 Am. J. Int'l L.* 708 (1998); Eyal Benvenisti and George Downs, "National Courts, Domestic Democracy, and the Evolution of International Law," *20 Eur. J. Int'l L.* 59, 59 (2009).

24   Amnon Reichman, "When We Sit to Judge We Are Being Judged: The Israeli G.S.S. Case, Ex Parte Pinochet and Domestic/Global Deliberation," *9 Cardozo J. of Int'l and Comp. L.* 41, 41 (2001); Amnon Reichman, "Universal Jurisdiction in National Courts—Undermining Sovereignty or a New World Order?," *17 I.D.F. L. Rev.* 49 (2004) (Heb.).

will not be developed in the context of universal jurisdiction. Related to this point is of course the doctrine of double jeopardy, which protects a defendant against being tried twice for the same offense (provided the first trial was indeed a real trial, not a charade designed merely to shield the defendant from future prosecution). Furthermore, in order to minimize possible abuse, a pre-condition for universal jurisdiction in national courts should be *in personam* jurisdiction, namely physical presence of the accused in the territory over which the domestic court has jurisdiction. Sharon should not be tried in Belgium if he is not present there at all. If necessary, an extradition request may be submitted prior to the commencement of the actual proceedings.

Two other factors should be taken into account in discussing the concern of legal disarray. First, nation states would often be reluctant, rather than eager, to exercise universal jurisdiction, because such legal fanfare is not only costly to litigate but is also likely to attract diplomatic complications. The Pinochet and Sharon cases are examples on point: the state establishment in Belgium and Britain preferred that the matter would be put to rest, and would have acted to discontinue the suits, if they only could. Judges themselves appear cautious in granting applications to exercise such jurisdiction.[25] Assuming states would develop tools to grant the state prosecution some control over the proceedings, the concern that states would invite such suits and thus that many proceedings would take place simultaneously is exaggerated.[26]

Second, we cannot underestimate the power of reciprocity. The way states act in claims against foreigners in their courts is going to reflect directly on how their citizens are treated in foreign courts. After all, states are the ultimate repeat players. Subjecting foreigners to universal jurisdiction in a domestic court entails the exposure of citizens to similar jurisdiction in other nations. Once the role of reciprocity is recognized, it appears that states would tend to respect proceedings already commenced elsewhere (provided, of course, these are bona fide

---

25 Michael Kirby, "Universal Jurisdiction and Judicial Reluctance: A New 'Fourteen Points'," in *Universal Jurisdiction: National Courts And The Prosecution Of Serious Crimes Under International Law*, Stephen J. Macedo, ed. (Philiadelphia: University of Pennsylvania Press, 2003).

26 Compare: Diane Orentlicher, "Striking a Balance: Mixed Law Tribunals and Conflicts of Jurisdiction," in *Justice for Crimes against Humanity: International Law after Pinochet*, Philippe Sands and Mark Lattimer, eds. (Hart Press, 2003) ch. 8.

proceedings) precisely because they would not want to subject their own citizens to multiple legal proceedings in the future.[27]

The last concern that I will address here pertains to the principle of Equal Protection of the Laws. The fear is that domestic courts would be used in a selective manner, so as to pick and choose among offenders, according to a certain political agenda. Liberals would find this concern disturbing, since the principle of equality demands that the rights of all be respected, not just the rights of those favored by some. From a republican perspective, courts of another polity may be harnessed only in the name of republican values; such values hold for every member of the polity (read: the globalized polity), and if they were violated it would be difficult to turn to universal jurisdiction against some but not against others. Another way of putting it would be that in exercising universal jurisdiction states allow their judiciaries to act as agents of humanity itself. It would follow that, as a matter of law, universal jurisdiction should be applied subject to the principle of non-discrimination. The practical implication of such a rule would call upon states to ensure that their judiciaries are enlisted only if serious efforts were made to bring all the relevant offenders to justice, not censure only offenders of a certain stripe. It should be the rare exception that proceedings are commenced only against one party to a dispute, and there should be weighty reasons given why the proceeding should not be halted until all relevant parties are before the court.

This is the most persuasive argument against the trial of Sharon

———————

27 A related concern must be recognized: as a matter of politics, not all states share equal footing in the international arena. Even if we limit the applicability of the argument presented here to democracies, or at least to those states with independent judiciaries and the commitment to due process and the rule of law, some carry more political weight (on account of their military and economic power but also on account of their reputation and esteem). This raises the concern of a two-tier or even a three-tier system: some states may be just too powerful, and thus other states may be reluctant (or feel intimidated) to exercise jurisdiction when officials of the powerful states are involved. Of course when it comes to the powerful states, they would submit that their officials are more likely to be targeted for law suits as a political tool attack them. Conversely, there could be states too "little" to be considered as respected guardians of the world order. If proceedings would be commenced in these states they may not generate sufficient legitimacy and in any event there may be a risk that the rest of the international community will wave aside the judgments. The discrepancies in power might lead to double or triple standards. While some may suggest that "what is allowed to Jupiter is not allowed to the bull" (*Quod licet Iovi, non licet bovi*), the argument presented here assumes that over time and with respect to the truly serious offenses (i.e., the *jus cogens*) the distinction between Jupiter and the bull may become irrelevant: states may wish to belong to the club of respected nations that apply the rule of law, and may eventually suffer if they do not. For if the gods lose the respect of the bulls, over whom would they reign?

in Belgium. Clearly, Sharon was not the only, and not even the main, villain, even assuming *arguando*, that he was responsible for the death of Palestinian civilians. The massacre was committed by orders of local commander of the Christian militia as a reaction to the killing, allegedly by Syria, of the Christian leader, President Bashir Jumayel. Both the Christian leader and the Syrian operatives were not indicted in Belgium.

4. Universal Jurisdiction, the Liberal-Republican Debate and the Natural Law-Positivism Divide

Is the development of universal jurisdiction an indication of the ascendancy of the liberal ideal of individual human rights? Or is universal jurisdiction actually an expression of a novel form of republicanism? In order to answer this question we have to take a closer look at the structure of the offenses that may give rise to universal jurisdiction, and also at particular interpretations of liberalism and republicanism in our times.

In the present context, let us define liberalism as a political theory of governance that places central value on each individual and his or her self-realization. Under this approach, the state (and the international order) is established in order to protect human rights, and these rights are an expression of the autonomy of all humans qua humans. Liberalism claims that humans are rights-holders by virtue of their "humanness," and not necessarily as an expression of an actual choice made by a particular institution. At best, as John Rawls taught us, rights are an expression of an assumed consent, best reached behind a veil of ignorance.[28] Some would call these rights "natural," in the sense that all rational people would agree that these rights should be (equally) protected. Since the liberal ideal places the individual at the center, the liberal state at its best is a pliable structure that may assume content individuals ascribe to it, provided such content does not run against the core liberal ideals of human rights and self-realization. In fact, liberalism, properly conceived, may do away with the concept of a state

---

28   The veil of ignorance is a construct designed to ensure procedural fairness. John Rawls, *Theory of Justice* (Cambridge, Harvard University Press, Revised Edition 1999), 104.

(or, in the words of John Lennon, "country")[29] altogether, provided an effective international structure is established for the administration of justice and the fulfillment of individual preferences.

Republicanism can be seen today as a system of governance that acknowledges human rights, especially of the civil type, within a given polity. Under republicanism, the fundamental right is the right to self-determination by a polity and its members. The polity, organized as a republic, owes a duty to all citizens of the republic to protect their fundamental rights, because these rights are instruments of a just collective self-determination. Furthermore, the duty to protect rights is fenced by the duty to ensure that such protection does not seriously harm the polity (embodied in the republic) and its members. Republicanism places emphasis on choice: the republic expresses the aggregated will of its members and in so doing reaffirms the belonging of all members into a collective. But choice, and the freedom to choose it presupposes, are components in a greater structure. Republicanism also has a "natural" or "reason-based" dimension. It is difficult to understand modern day republicanism without the concept of "good governance," namely governance that takes seriously the well-being of the collective (and its various components). Compared to the often "thin" (or, pliable) liberal state, the principle of good governance is a rather "thick" (or sturdy) idea. Moreover, as liberalism cannot allow an individual to waive his or her autonomy (and thus cannot tolerate the "freedom" to become a slave) so republicanism cannot allow a republic to "choose away" the basic republican duty to the well-being of the republic and its citizens. So while "the will of the people" is central, it is not unlimited. Furthermore, a republic may embody other values, representing the ethos of the polity beyond membership in a community of moral agents. Conceptually, therefore, a republic may have sections of the constitution pertaining to the character of the state beyond the reach of an amendment by the people, just the way a liberal constitution can place sections pertaining to core human rights beyond the reach of any majority.

At first glance, it would seem that universal jurisdiction is consistent with the liberal ideal. By granting other states or the international

---

29   The full verse calls on us to "[i]magine there's no countries. It isn't hard to do. Nothing to kill or die for; and no religion too. Imagine all the people living life in peace" (John Lennon, Imagine, 1971).

community the power to pierce the veil of sovereignty, the polity is set aside for the protection of universal human rights, which respect the individual as such. But note that this description holds only if universal jurisdiction is exercised for the protection of grave violation of human rights, and is an expression of reason, rather than of the choice of polities themselves to accept universal jurisdiction by other nations. While in some cases the two approaches may converge, there could be cases in which they would not.

It is beyond the ambit of this chapter to examine in depth the various grand crimes currently recognized as warranting universal jurisdiction,[30] but an important distinction should be recognized between acts that were criminalized in order to protect against the violation of human rights, and acts there were criminalized to maintain a republican world order. The latter may include the protection of human rights, but this is just one component of the commitment of the family of nations as sovereign nations, or perhaps even an expression of an emerging supra-sovereign global polity. The torture offense, it would seem, is designed to protect a human right. Genocide, on the other hand, is not "just" about mass-murder (or the right to life); it is about the intentional acts towards the eradication of a nation from the family of nations. Clearly, liberals would also insist on a the criminalization of genocide (and on universal jurisdiction for that crime), because any individual under a veil of ignorance would not accept a state of affairs under which she or he may be subject to such treatment, and if the nation(s)

---

30   For an examination of the uses of universal jurisdiction see for example the research submitted to the Executive Council of the African Union: "Report of The Commission on The Use of The Principle of Universal Jurisdiction By Some Non-African States As Recommended By The Conference of Ministers of Justice/Attorneys General," EX.CL/411(XIII) (24-28 June, 2008). The matter was also analyzed by scholars from various jurisdictions: Philippe Sands and Mark Lattimer, eds., *Justice For Crimes Against Humanity: International Law After Pinochet* (Hart Press, 2003); Stephen J. Macedo, ed., *Universal Jurisdiction: National Courts And The Prosecution Of Serious Crimes Under International Law* (Philadelphia: University of Pennsylvania Press, 2003). See also "The Princeton Principles on Universal Jurisdiction," available at: lapa.princeton. edu/hosteddocs/unive_jur.pdf.; M. Cherif Bassiouni, "Universal Jurisdiction for International Crimes: Historical Perspectives and Contemporary Practice," *42 Va. J. Int'l L.* 81 (2001). As the International Criminal Court (ICC) is taking its first steps, the matter will be further developed. It is sad to note that the list of crimes granting jurisdiction to the Court cannot be fully defended solely on the degree to which such crimes offend the international order. For example, settlement in an occupied territory is such a crime, whereas terrorism is not specifically enumerated in the Rome Statute (the convention that established that court, available at: http://untreaty.un.org/cod/icc/index.html).

associated by closer jurisdictional ties do not adjudicate, courts around the globe cannot remain inert. However, liberals would not necessarily treat genocide differently than other gross human rights violations; republicans must.

Another possible distinction may pertain to the republican and the liberal approaches to the legalistic of universal jurisdiction: liberals are more likely to accept universal jurisdiction even if there is no signed convention on point (provided the crimes directly relate to human rights). Republicans, as a general matter, would usually insist on an actual expression of the choice of the polity to criminalize a certain act, and similarly to invest jurisdiction in national courts (save the rare exceptions where the acts are *per se* against the republican world order, as is the case with genocide).

More generally, crimes deserving universal jurisdiction (as all legal norms) can rest on one of two sources (or on both). They can be crimes because the various republics (and other states) comprising the international community, through a certain convention, decided that certain acts are crimes. Call this source "will-based". Consequently, nations may choose to grant universal jurisdiction to other nations, and thus actually express their sovereignty (provided they do not agree, in a convention, to fully abrogate sovereignty; that would be un-republican). Alternatively, acts may be considered crimes because the conceptual foundation upon which the international order rests requires that these would be crimes. Call this source "reason-based." It is usually the case that the latter offenses relate to human rights, although, as mentioned, there could be instances where the acts directly offend aspects of the world order associated more with republicanism (as in the case of piracy, which started as an offense conferring universal jurisdiction prior to a convention on point, and which is taken as an offence closely related to republicanism because piracy challenges the republics as sovereign nations by undermining their power to protect their subjects in the high seas and thus threatens the world order according to which each republic must ensure the safety of its members).

Recall that the Nuremberg trials were not based on a violation of a written convention, nor were they premised on acts contrary to an established custom.[31] It was difficult to prove a custom prohibiting

---

31   Indeed, some have expressed concern that the proceedings in the Nuremberg Tribunals were

genocide, because for that one would have to show that cases of genocide had been prosecuted before, but they had not. Part of the reason is that genocides, as we understand the term today, were rare in modern times. But nonetheless, as mentioned earlier, even republicans, who would generally require some form of an actual expression of the will of the people before an international crime is established, would recognize crimes against humanity. The notion of crimes against humanity, then, need not necessarily be read as "crimes against universal human rights," and therefore as crimes seen as warranting trans-national adjudication only by liberalism. They can also be taken as crimes whose indictment reflects the emergence of a globalized polity, which shares a duty towards it sub-components—nations and peoples—and towards its individual members as well.

The distinction between will-based and reason-based crimes carries legal implications: if a certain act is criminalized by a certain treaty, it follows that the issue of universal jurisdiction should be regulated by treaty as well. But if the crimes are reason-based, it is not necessary to point to a will-based instrument, such as a convention, to ground universal jurisdiction. Thus, Israel did not have to rely on a specific convention when it put Eichmann to trial. If Eichmann committed crimes against humanity, then humanity, including the Israeli court, may react.[32]

In that context, another historical irony of sorts is revealed. Recall that in the Pinochet case some members of the British House of Lords relied on the Eichmann case, and thus on what I call a reason-based argument, in finding that Senator Pinochet was not protected by the immunity granted to heads of state. In so doing, their Lordships reflected a long

---

based on ex-post facto laws. See discussion in Michael Biddiss, "Victors' Justice: The Nuremberg Tribunal," 45 History Today, Issue 5, May 1995; Danilo Zolo, Victor's Justice: From Nuremberg to Baghdad (Verso: 2009). For an historical analysis of the transition from the Nuremberg Tribunal to the establishment of the International Criminal Court in the Hague, see chapters 1 and 2 (by Richard Overy and Andrew Clapham) in the anthology edited by Philippe Sands, From Nuremberg to The Hague: The Future of International Criminal Justice (Cambridge: Cambridge University Press, 2003).

32 The Israeli Court, as some have noted, could be seen with closer jurisdictional ties, because Israel, the national home of the Jewish people, can be seen as asserting jurisdiction on behalf of the Jewish people for harm done to it even prior to the creation of the state. See Loera Bilsky, "The Eichmann Trial and the Legacy of Jurisdiction," in Politics in Dark Times. Encounters with Hannah Arendt, Seyla Benhabib ed. (Cambridge: Cambridge University Press 2010); Leora Bilsky, "Back to the Territory: Hannah Arendt and The Eichmann Trial," in Hannah Arendt, A Half-Century of Polemics, I. Zertal & M. Zuckermann eds. (Hakibbutz Hameuchad, 2004), 107 (Hebrew).

common-law tradition of reason-based arguments. After all, the common law itself could be seen as a regime which ultimately rests on reason, rather than on will expressed via the ordinary "republican" channels of government. This is not surprising, given the non-republican structure of the British Commonwealth. However, the first Pinochet decision was vacated, on the ground that one of the Law Lords did not disclose that his wife worked for amnesty international, an organization associated with the quest to extradite Pinochet. When the House of Lords addressed the issue again (in a case called "Pinochet III")[33], it relied not on reason-based principles in order to determine that Senator Pinochet's alleged acts could not possibly be considered acts of a head of state and therefore cannot enjoy immunity. Rather, the court turned to the convention against torture, and interpreted Chile's signature of that convention as an implied waiver of the aforementioned immunity[34] (itself a creation of the Vienna Convention).[35] In other words, the House of Lords, the traditional bastion of the reason-based common law, turned to a will-based argument by searching for the expressed (or at least implied) will of the Chilean republic. The ultimate guardian of the reason-based common law appears to have found will-based republicanism more attractive in this case. It might be noteworthy that such a reading dramatically shrunk the scope of offenses for which Senator Pinochet could be charged, since Chile had signed the convention against Torture towards the very end of the period during which the atrocities in Chile took place.[36]

5. Conclusion

The case against Ariel Sharon in Belgium was ultimately dropped in the

---

33   R. v. Bow Street Metropolitan Stipendiary Magistrate and Others, Ex parte Pinochet Urgate (No. 3), [1999] 2 All E.R 97(H.L) (March 24, 1999).

34   See the opinion of Lord Browne-Wilkinson, *id.*, which enjoyed the majority of their lordships.

35   Vienna Convention on Diplomatic Relations, Art. 39(2), 196, available at http://treaties.un.org/doc/Treaties/1964/06/19640624%2002-10%20AM/Ch_III_3p.pdf.

36   Interestingly, in further proceedings in the lower court it was argued that the government may consider events prior to September 29, 1988, when Chile signed the convention, because some of the offenses, such as conspiracy to commit torture, were continuing offences. In other words, the persons who had "disappeared" during the reign of Pinochet prior to the signature were still "disappeared" when the government was called upon to decide the extradition request. Pinochet Ugarte, R (on the application of) v. Secretary of State For Home Department [1999] EWHC Admin 505 (27th May, 1999).

summer of 2003. In April of 2003 (pursuant to pressure by the United States to remove the NATO headquarters from Brussels),[37] Belgium amended the law to allow the exercise of universal jurisdiction only with the approval of the Federal prosecutor, the conclusion, *inter alia,* that a system with closer jurisdictional ties (and with an independent judiciary) is unable or unwilling to litigate the grave crimes that give rise to universal jurisdiction.[38] In so doing, Belgium advances our thinking on this important matter, including our thinking on the proper relation between nations as they seek to protect human rights among sovereign states. Pinochet, as we all remember, was not extradited to Spain. But the British judiciary, in dealing with the case, indicated that it viewed its role as a component of an emerging global judiciary; first, it appears, as an agent of universal human rights, and then, as the shift to the will-based Convention reveals, as an agent of an emerging republican world-order.[39] National judges, therefore, are agents not only of their respective states, but of the international system as well.[40]

---

37 The United States disapproved of the Belgian act because it opened the door to indict U.S. soldiers and commanders, for example, on crimes they allegedly committed in Iraq. For an account see Irit Kohn, "The Suit against Sharon in Belgium: A Case Analysis," in Manfred Gerstenfeld, *European-Israeli Relations: Between Confusion and Change?* (Jerusalem Center for Public Affairs) 2007.

38 The amended section states that the legal system must determine whether "in the concrete circumstances of the matter, it results that, in the interest of administration of justice and in respect of Belgium's international obligations, this matter should be brought either before international tribunals, or before a tribunal in the place where the acts were committed, or before the tribunals of a State in which the offender is a national or where he may be found, and as long as this tribunal is competent, independent, impartial and fair." The statute then deals with a situation in which the tribunal with closer ties fails to act. See *42 I.L.M.* 749 (May 2003). For a brief analysis see Stefaan Smis and Kim Van der Borght, "Belgian Law concerning The Punishment of Grave Breaches of International Humanitarian Law: A Contested Law with Uncontested Objectives" *ASIL* July 2003. Available at: http://www.asil.org/insigh112.cfm#_edn6.

39 Toward the conclusion of the case a decision had to be made whether to disclose the results of the medical examination Senator Pinochet underwent to the four states (including Spain) that sought extradition. Under the extradition agreements, such disclosure was required. But the British government undertook to keep the details classified, and under British law such a governmental promise is binding. So which of the two norms should be given precedent? The Court decided to prefer the disclosure, in no small part because of its conception of the judicial role in the case, as an agent not only of the British system of the transnational legal system committed to checks and balances and democratic principles of governance. Had the materials remained sealed, no other democracy would have been able to rest assured that, indeed, Pinochet's health was the deciding factor that informed the British government's decision, and not a political calculation incompatible with the commitment to ensure the protection against torture and other inhumane treatments. *R. v. Secretary of State for Home Department ex parte The Kingdom of Belgium,* Q.B. Divl. Ct., CO/236/2000 (February 15, 2000), per Lord Simon Brown.

40 Yuval Shany, "Dédoublement fonctionnel and the Mixed Loyalties of National and International Judges," Filippo Fontanelli et al. (eds.), in *Shaping Rule of Law Through Dialogue: International and*

At the end of the day, this essay argues that we are better off with universal jurisdiction than without it, provided the concerns raised are met. Whether universal jurisdiction is a component of liberalism or of republicanism, our understanding of the relationship between human rights and sovereignty in the 21st Century have sufficiently evolved for us to understand that some human rights require the protection of humanity as such, and thus the various nations that comprise the family of nations must be able to rely on each other in order to ensure that sovereignty is not used against the sovereign, namely the people. While universal jurisdiction should be exercised only as a last resort, and only very rarely (if at all) it nonetheless should not be abolished. It may provide an important link in the emerging global chain of mutual responsibility in matters of human rights. The potential embedded in the emerging global judiciary to do its part in fighting serious crimes against humanity—and terrorism is one such crime[41]—cannot be ignored.

The design under which domestic courts are the residual site of international law is better than relying on the International Criminal Court (ICC). It is better because domestic courts are not placed in a hierarchical order: no one court is above any other court. Rather, all national courts are co-equal. This peer-to-peer design forces judges from the different jurisdictions to take their responsibilities as part of the emerging global judiciary seriously, and provide convincing reasons— liberal and republican reasons—as to why they decided a certain case

---

Supranational Experiences (2009), 34, 41.

41   The crimes committed in Sabra and Shatila, as well as crimes committed in 9/11 in the United States or in 7/7 in London, or crimes such as those committed during the wave of suicide attacks against Israel in March 2002, are clearly violations of human rights. To the extent that universal jurisdiction is a component of a transnational regime for the protection of human rights, courts of the various states should be open to adjudicate such crimes, provided no state with stronger jurisdictional ties is willing or able to serve as a forum for ascertaining justice. Upon a closer look, these acts can also be justified as crimes against fundamental republican principles, and therefore warranting universal jurisdiction under that approach as well. These terror attacks threaten republicanism precisely because they undermine genuine self-determination. The killing is directed to sow fear and thus undermine the meaningful exercise of self-governance in the attacked polities. At the same time, the killing cannot be justified as a last resort of an oppressed people denied self-determination. Even if we assume such oppression, clearly there are other, less harmful means to advance the claim against "the oppressive West" or against the occupation by Israel, and in any event, the right of the United States, Britain and Israel to exist must be respected. International terror, therefore, is a prime candidate for a crime that warrants universal jurisdiction. If Israel rejects the very idea of universal jurisdiction, it also rejects universal jurisdiction against terrorists; this position is regrettable.

in a certain manner. In giving judgment they also stand to be judged by their equals,[42] and by the rest of the professional legal community. As the ICC begins deliberating its first cases, it should not be forgotten that international law ultimately resides in states, and not in international organizations.

42   As President Barak noted in HCJ 769/02 Public Comm. against Torture in Israel v. Gov't of Israel (Nevo, 14 December 2006)—which dealt with the legality of the application of force by general-security-service investigators—when the court sits to judge it is also being judged. For analysis see Amnon Reichman, "When We Sit to Judge," *supra* note 24; Eyal Benvenisti, "Reclaiming Democracy: The Strategic Uses of Foreign and International Law by National Courts," *102 Am. J. Int'l L.* 241 (2008).

Republican and Liberal Values
in Coping With the Memory of World War II:
The Swiss Holocaust Assets in a Transnational Perspective

THOMAS MAISSEN

The restitution of Holocaust-related assets was a major issue in the 1990s. Rather surprisingly, at least for the Swiss themselves, Switzerland became the most prominent target in the respective debates. To compare the reactions in the involved countries—besides Switzerland, especially the United States, Israel and the members of the EU—is not only necessary in order to explain the relevant conflicts of the outgoing twentieth century but also conflicts among befriended democratic states. It can also help us understand diverging approaches and inhibitions among some important actors of globalization in the years to come. Such differences can be explained, at least partially, with the role that republican and liberal traditions play in these countries and their national memories. The assumption is that political languages of the pre-nation-state era can help us understand which specific lessons different nation-states drew from World War II and the Holocaust. Since the end of the Cold War, these lessons have affected and go on to affect their position to globalization and a possible new world order.

To explain this argument, the Swiss case will first be discussed both with (1) a characterization of the relevant problem areas stemming from World War II and (2) a summary of the debates in the 1990s, followed by (3) a description of how the payment of reparations has evolved to date and a discussion of the respective problems. The different national patterns of reaction and their foundation in collective memory are analyzed (4) and then confronted (5) using "republicanism" and "liberalism" as ideal typical political languages.[1]

---

1   I have described the whole issue at length in *Verweigerte Erinnerung. Nachrichtenlose Vermögen und die Schweizer Weltkriegsdebatte 1989-2004* (Zürich: NZZ, 2005) and will not refer to that book for details of the account. I will quote the relevant literature, however, where I discuss interpretations. It is limited, if some scholarly standard is applied, as most publications in Switzerland, Israel and the US were quite partisan. The relevant contributions in English are: John

1. The Legacy of the Nazi Era

Dormant accounts, Nazi gold, loot, and the policy towards refugees are different problem areas that all raise questions about the Swiss role during the National Socialist rule in Germany. Switzerland, where two thirds of the population speak German, was immediately affected by Hitler's seizure of power. The Nazi ideology did not appeal to the Swiss who had only one Nazi in their national parliament, and for just one term (1935-9). Unlike Austria, the neutral Swiss were not traumatized by World War I: even though the country was hit by the lasting depression, unemployment remained relatively low (about 5 percent) compared to other countries and especially Germany; Nazi centralism contradicted Swiss federalism with its large autonomy for cantons and communes; dictatorship and Führerprinzip were incompatible with the Swiss democratic parliamentarian system that was the only one on the continent, besides the Swedish, to last throughout the Nazi era; racist references to "blood and soil" made no sense in a country where four different languages (German, French, Italian, Romansh) were not only spoken but also official languages; national identity depended on a shared historical past, not on a social Darwinistic "master race." Such deeply rooted differences manifested in a clear opposition of the Swiss and their public sphere, including almost all newspapers, against Nazism. In the spiritual defense (Geistige Landesverteidigung), organized by the minister of the interior, this position became an official policy.

Switzerland, however, was far from autarkic. The economy of the small but already wealthy country depended on exports, and Germany was a major trade partner. Compared to the present, the Swiss banking-system was still largely national, but the convertible Swiss franc and the accessible banks already attracted an international clientele. Anti-Semi-

---

Authers, Richard Wolffe, *The Victim's Fortune: Inside the Epic Battle over the Debts of the Holocaust* (New York: HarperCollins, 2002); Michael J. Bazyler, *Holocaust Justice: The Battle for Restitution in America's Court* (New York, London: NYU Press, 2003); *Holocaust Restitution: Perspectives on the Litigation and Its Legacy* (New York, London: NYU Press, 2006), ed. Michael J. Bazyler and Roger P. Alford; Regula Ludi, "Why Switzerland? Remarks on a Neutral's Role in the Nazi Program of Robbery and Allied Postwar Restitution Policy," in *Robbery and Restitution: the Conflict over Jewish Property in Europe*, ed. Martin Dean, Constantin Goschler and Philipp Ther (New York, Oxford: Berghahn, 2007), 182–210; Leonard Orland, *A Final Accounting: Holocaust Survivors and Swiss Banks* (Durham: Carolina Academic Press, 2010). Literature on restitution issues in general has become vast; for broad perspectives see e.g. Elazar Barkan, *The Guilt of Nations: Restitution and Negotiating Historical Injustices* (New York: Norton, 2000); *Restitution and Memory: Material Restoration in Europe*, ed. Dan Diner, Gotthart Wunberg (Oxford: Berghahn Books, 2007).

tism, not least among civil servants, was widespread in a country where barely one half percent of the population was Jewish. Anti-Semitism often accompanied the anti-Communism that had become an integrative glue after the failed general strike in 1918. While Nazism remained limited to splinter parties, many exponents of the bourgeois elite, and also members of government and army, admired Mussolini and his Fascist equals in Spain, Portugal or Austria. The Fascist model of a corporative state had influential sympathizers. Authoritarian thoughts and practices were manifest also in the federal government.

After the fall of France, from July 1940 onwards, Switzerland was surrounded by the Axis powers but for a short borderline with Vichy France, which became occupied as well in November 1942. Hence the Swiss had to cope with German hegemony during the war and did so quite well. While general mobilization in 1939-1940 was directed against the Third Reich and a considerable number of Swiss troops remained at the borders throughout the war, Swiss economy produced largely for the surrounding Axis. Strategic material, including anti-aircraft-weapons, was not a small part of these exports. Against the duties of a neutral state, the federal government subsidized this production through considerable credits—with the double aim to maintain jobs and to propitiate the Germans who easily could block Swiss imports and exports. Invulnerable transit for trains passing through the neutral Alps favored the Axis as well—and so did many decisions, from censorship to blackout, the government adopted to appease the Reich.

Most of these facts were not unknown at that time. A well-known joke described the Swiss ambivalence this way: six days a week, we work for the Germans and then spend the *seventh* day saying prayers for the Allied victory.[2] The issues that seemed to appear from nowhere in the 1990s had their origin in this uncomfortable situation in the years 1939-45 which the Swiss, however, had managed to turn into too many comparative advantages. There were essentially four:

Nazi gold refers to the gold that the German Reichsbank sold the Swiss National Bank and—to a lesser extent—the commercial banks between 1940 and 1945. The Germans received Swiss francs in exchange for which they needed to purchase raw materials in other non-belligerent countries, such as Portugal. Of the German gold, worth about 1.9 billion

---

2   Quoted as a "standard joke" in Max Frisch, *Dienstbüchlein* (Frankfurt a. M.: Suhrkamp, 1974), 102.

francs (U.S. $444 million at the exchange rate of 1945), which was purchased by Swiss institutions, a considerable portion had been looted, mostly from the Belgian and Dutch central banks. Confiscated property of individuals was in the booty, too, and a small part of this gold (worth CHF. 0.58 million) even came from concentration camps. Nobody in Switzerland seems to have known about its dreadful origin, while the Swiss National Bank's leading representatives must have known about the monetary gold's looting at latest in 1942. The allied were not sure about that, however, when they summoned the Swiss to Washington in the spring of 1946 to account for controversial financial transactions in favor of the Reich. By signing the "Washington Agreement," Switzerland agreed to pay CHF. 250 million in gold to those national banks which had suffered losses. Claims of private individuals were not taken into consideration.

Loot was a rather vague issue, as it was and is very difficult to determine which private assets German institutions or individuals stole during the War and then deposited in other countries. It is clear, however, that some Nazis had bank safes in Switzerland, and stolen jewelry and works of art were sold by Swiss fences.

Refugee-policy was already debated to some extent during the War, and later in an official, though quite critical report in 1956, which provoked further research, reports and movies. During the War, Switzerland hosted about 28,000 Jewish refugees. At the same time, about 25,000 refugees, mostly Jews, were denied the entry into Switzerland. The number is debated, but those who were sent back to the territory controlled by the Germans faced death in the concentration camps.

Dormant accounts or *heirless assets* describe a problem that only developed after the war. By its end, accounts of unknown value belonging to Nazi victims, especially to Jews, had accumulated in Switzerland. The banks resisted several initiatives to search for the original owners. Their interpretation of the Swiss bank secrecy law implied that a bank could give information only to people authorized by the account holder and that the bank never had to get into contact with its foreign clients. When the law was stipulated in 1934, this was considered a protective measure for foreigners who had to fear draconian punishment, especially in Nazi Germany, for having violated their own country's law prohibiting transactions in foreign currencies or tax evasion. After the War, however, such a policy worked to the disadvantage of survivors who searched for assets that had belonged to their murdered relatives but could not produce a death certificate or authorization. For obvious reasons, this was often impossible for survivors who in addition knew little about the accounts and could not even identify the right bank. There was no institutional help in such cases, and banks often proved to be far from helpful, denying the possible heirs the specific treatment they needed and deserved in respect for the historical circumstances. Although the banks did not appropriate their clients' money but left it dormant, it could be reduced to nil through fees throughout the years. There are also documented cases of criminal bank clerks who plundered accounts whose owners never claimed their assets. Only in 1962, a Swiss Federal Decree ordered that all accounts of Jewish origin and dormant since 1945 were to be declared as such. The procedure was implemented carelessly: until 1974, the banks declared only the sum of roughly 10 million Swiss francs, of which only between 1.5 and 4 million francs were paid to relatives of Nazi victims, part of the remainder to humanitarian associations.

2. The Controversies of the 1990s

In the 1970s, the matter of the heirless assets seemed definitely settled to the few who knew anything about it; and so were in the 1990s the domestic debates about the Swiss wartime past that the new left had initiated after 1968. But soon after the celebrations for the fiftieth anniversary of the War's end in 1995, Switzerland's history became a major international issue for the first time ever. Several newspapers printed articles with titles such as "Secret Legacies" (*Wall Street Journal*, June 22, 1995) or "Give Us Our Money Back!" (*Jerusalem Report*, June 29, 1995). Members of the Swiss parliament reacted suggesting legislation on the matter, and the Swiss Bankers' Association, so reluctant earlier, finally established a central information service for dormant accounts to assist claimants in their search. The Bankers' Association wanted to deal with the matter on a strictly national level, with just the community of Swiss Jews as its partner. But the World Jewish Congress (WJC) and the Jewish Agency (JA) had agreed to investigate the case. In September 1995, their representatives Edgar Bronfman, Israel Singer and Avraham Burg met with some exponents of the Swiss Bankers Association and insisted to be part of further investigations. "Trust, but verify," was his motto, Bronfman declared. But outside verification would have meant a breach into Swiss bank secrecy. Therefore the bankers only proposed an information service working under their own control. When the WJC realized that this was the Swiss approach, it mobilized political backing. U.S. Senator Alfonse D'Amato held several hearings before the Senate Banking Committee that he chaired, the first one in April of 1996. Ten days later the Swiss agreed to sign a "memorandum of understanding" that established a Commission chaired by Paul Volcker, the former chairman of the US Federal Reserve. The Volcker Commission mandated the leading international auditing companies to check whether and how many heirless assets stemming from World War II still were dormant in Switzerland. The auditors got unrestricted access to relevant information on accounts opened in Swiss banks before, during and immediately after the War.

The dynamics did not stop there, however. In fall 1996, British and later American original sources were quoted in the press in order to show the discrepancy between the looted gold acquired by the Swiss National Bank and the sum actually paid in the Washington agreement in 1946. While the heirless assets had been an issue of private companies, the banks, the National Bank was a public institution, and its wartime politics, often justified with the convertibility of the neutral nation's currency, had been part of the overall strategy to keep the country out of the conflict. Although reluctantly, Swiss politics now came into the game. The federal parliament tried to counter growing international criticism by adopting a decree providing for a historical and legal investigation into the matter. The expert commission was chaired by the Swiss historian Jean-François Bergier; the holocaust survivors Saul Friedländer and Władysław Bartoszewski were among its 9 members, and the research would last 5 years, leading to about 30 sub-studies and an encompassing final report in early 2002.[3]

As all the relevant issues, including loot and also refugee policies, were intensely covered by international media, the WJC lost its monopoly in criticizing the Swiss, and with it control of the case. The WJC aimed at an institutional solution, essentially with the Jewish organiza-

---

3   For further information see http://www.uek.ch/en/index.htm, containing also the *Final Report of the Independent Commission of Experts Switzerland—Second World War* (2002), hereafter Bergier Report.

tions themselves. In this perspective, the Swiss case was hijacked when American lawyers opened a new front in October 1996 and launched plaintiff class actions for the restitution to groups of discriminated individuals; and not to institutions. Ed Fagan, an outsider with more media savvy than legal expertise, preceded the heavyweights Mel Weiss and Mike Hausfeld in filing lawsuits against Credit Suisse and UBS for having withheld access to information from potential heirs.

Three scandals in Switzerland marked the decisive escalation in January 1997. The outgoing president of the Swiss government, Jean-Pascal Delamuraz, had to apologize after he had characterized Jewish pressure as "ransom and blackmailing" to undermine the Swiss banking place. This crisis was barely settled when Christoph Meili, the employee of a security company, noticed that documents which, in part, concerned transactions with Germany in the 1930s (but not Jewish accounts) were to be destroyed at UBS. Although this violated the mentioned federal decree for historical and legal investigation, UBS fired Meili for acting against bank secrecy. As if this were not enough, the Swiss Ambassador to the United States, Carlo Jagmetti, resigned in late January after one of his internal reports was leaked to the press wherein he warned about being at war with adversaries that could not be trusted.

The three major Swiss banks, the National bank and some companies of the export industry reacted to the escalation by establishing a humanitarian "Special Fund for Holocaust Victims" that eventually distributed about $200 million; the Israeli politicians Josef Burg and Avraham Hirschson belonged to the executive board. Soon after, in March 1997, the President of the Confederation launched the idea of a 7-billion-franc "Swiss Foundation for Solidarity" with the objective to provide relief for people in need. The Foundation met with fierce political opposition among conservatives who vilified it as surrender to blackmail; after a negative referendum, the Foundation eventually was not established.

While conservative rejection gained strength in the Swiss public sphere, new opponents came forward in the United States, in addition to D'Amato's hearings and the class actions. The representatives, treasuries and comptrollers of several U.S. states gradually joined in the growing movement for boycotts. The Clinton administration opposed such interventions into what it considered its prerogative in foreign relations. But the federal government had its own way to push the Swiss towards compromise. Under Secretary of Commerce Stuart Eizenstat was in charge of the issue and published a report that described the post-war negotiations on German assets and looted gold. In his foreword, Eizenstat criticized the Swiss for having been the principal bankers for the Nazis, thereby prolonging World War II: "In the unique circumstances of World War II, neutrality collided with morality: too often being neutral provided a pretext for avoiding moral considerations."[4] The Swiss were shocked that a member of the government of a friendly nation would so harshly criticize neutrality that had formed the core element of Swiss foreign policy for centuries.

The increasing boycott movement threatened the Swiss banks which were very vulnerable because they were expanding heavily on the American market after acquiring U.S. investment banks, such as First Boston, bought by Credit Suisse in 1990, or Dillon Read, bought by the future UBS in 1997. So a long negotiation process started between the banks, the plaintiff lawyers and the WJC, with Stuart Eizenstat mediating. When, in the summer of 1998, a real boycott of transactions with Swiss banks seemed imminent, Swiss politicians envisaged more or less radical countermeasures; even the boycott of American and Jewish products was proposed by a small rightwing party. On August 12, 1998, however, a global settlement was reached: Credit Suisse and UBS assented to pay $1.25 billion for an extra-judicial agreement prepared by Judge Edward Korman in Brooklyn. This sum covered possible heirless assets that would be discovered through the auditing organized by the Volcker Commission, but compensated also for possible claims against the Swiss Confederation, the National Bank, other banks and other Swiss branches, except the insurance companies which were part of another class action.[5] The boycott movement immediately stopped. While representatives of the Swiss business world welcomed the agreement, many other Swiss complained that blackmailing had proved successful.

---

4   Stuart E. Eizenstat, foreword to William Z. Slany, *U.S. and Allied Efforts To Recover and Restore Gold and Other Assets Stolen or Hidden by Germany During World War II* (Department of State, Washington, 1997), v; http://www.ess.uwe.ac.uk/documents/asetindx.htm.

5   For these litigations see http://www.icheic.org/, containing also the 2007 final report; see also Orland, *Final Accounting*, 95-98.

3. Problematic Compensation, 1998-2010

The global settlement was a political end to the international debate, but it was not one to the judicial issue itself. Judge Korman held a fairness hearing in late 1999, finalized the Settlement Agreement of July 26, 2000 and adopted an institution to implement the Agreement, the Claims Resolution Tribunal II (CRT II) in Zurich and New York. Thus he succeeded in combining his task with the extraordinary audits that the Volcker Commission had organized in roughly 60 Swiss banks. For a remuneration of about $500 million, some 650 international auditors checked 4.1 million accounts of all kinds (hence mostly domestic and unproblematic) for which some documentation still could be traced. The number of 4.1 million was surprisingly high given a record retention of only ten years, but it was opposed to an estimated 6.8 million accounts that may have existed in the Nazi era. Information was missing for an estimated 2.7 million accounts. Out of the 4.1 million examined accounts, the Volcker Commission, in its final report dated December 6, 1999, considered 54,000 as "probably" or "possibly" belonging to Holocaust victims. Among them, there were only few obvious cases. Thus, 417 accounts had been paid out to Nazi institutions after the original owner had ordered to do so, probably under pressure; still, the orders that they had sent to the banks were legally corrected, and fulfilling it may have saved lives of Jews who were captured and blackmailed by Nazi henchmen. The Volcker Commission stated that there were some proven cases of cheating but no systematic looting or destruction of documents by the banks. The category of the "possible" accounts referred mostly to people in countries that were or came under Nazi control between 1933 and 1945 and were "closed unknown to whom," which means that there was just no proof left about who eventually got the asset. The Volcker Commission's approach to auditing was a decisive reversal of the onus of proof: until then, the Swiss banks had considered an account to be Holocaust related only if there was positive evidence that the former owner had perished in the Shoah. Now every account whose final destiny was unclear became a possible victim's account.[6]

For Judge Korman, who had to allocate the settlement money, the work had just begun in the summer of 1998. About 580,000 claimants

---

6   ICEP (Independent Committee of Eminent Persons), *Report on Dormant Accounts of Victims of Nazi Persecution in Swiss Banks* (Bern: Stämpfli, 1999).

filled out his "Initial Questionnaires" to explain their claim. This data was checked to decide whether the claimants fit one of the following classes, each of which got a share of the settlement money awarded according to the provisions of Korman's Settlement Agreement and the Distribution Plan presented by special masters Judah Gribetz and Shari Reig in September 2000.[7]

1. Deposited Assets (bank accounts and other assets deposited in Swiss financial institutions): $800 million. For Judge Korman, the property rights of account holders and the banks' neglecting their duties as a fiduciary were the substance of the litigation. He reserved two thirds of the settlement in order to offer legitimate heirs individual compensations corresponding to the account's original value. The findings of the Volcker Commission provided the basis for the attribution. In contrast, the members of the four other classes received lump sums. Such a procedure is typical for class actions. It was limited to individuals who had suffered personally from Nazi crimes where a relation to Switzerland was possible. They received a legal title that—unlike the claims to assets—could not be bequeathed.

2. Slave Labor Class I (individuals who may have performed slave labor for German and other companies which transacted their profits through Swiss entities). A total of $200 million was put aside, from which $1000 per capita was paid out together with the money from the German settlement on slave labor that was concluded independently in the summer of 2000 and consisted of 10 billion Deutsche marks.

3. Slave Labor Class II (individuals who may have performed slave labor for affiliates of Swiss companies): the few documented cases got $1000 as well.

4. Looted Assets (individuals whose assets were looted and transacted through Switzerland or Swiss entities during the Nazi era). As it was completely impossible to identify members of this class, $100

---

7   Judah Gribetz, Shari Reig, *Plan of Allocation and Distribution of Settlement Proceeds* (New York: 2000), http://www.nyed.uscourts.gov/pub/rulings/cv/1996/96cv4849-erk-smplan.pdf; for their considerations see also their "Epilogue," in Orland, *Final Accounting*, 135-151, where the plan is reprinted to a large extent (293-364), and their article "The Swiss Bank Holocaust Settlement," in *Reparations for Victims of Genocide, War Crimes and Crimes against Humanity: Systems in Place and Systems in Making*, ed. Carla Ferstman, Mariana Goetz, Alan Stephens (Leiden and Boston: Martinus Nijhoff, 2009), 115-142.

million, subsequently increased to $205 million, were designated as a cy-près remedy for humanitarian assistance programs.

5. Refugees: $2500 was granted to individuals denied entry into or expelled from Switzerland; $500 if they were admitted into Switzerland, but abused or mistreated.

These later sums seem ridiculous, as the members of the refugee class had arguably suffered most and most directly from Swiss malpractice. But as mentioned, Korman and Gribetz considered only the assets as actionable in a class action. By earmarking $800 million for the Deposited Assets' class, Korman followed the estimations of Volcker's final report but built himself a trap. It proved absolutely impossible to find enough legitimate heirs for such a considerable total sum. Swiss bankers maintained that the interpretation of the "probable or possible" victim's account had not been serious and largely overestimated their number. The bankers' opponents in the class action, and eventually also Judge Korman, countered that in the decades since the war, the banks had destroyed the evidence that would have been necessary to find the legitimate heirs and that, after having achieved their goal—impunity—in the global settlement, the banks no longer contributed to providing further data that could facilitate its distribution. As a matter of fact, the Swiss banks very consciously left the distribution process to the Judge and the CRT II. They had paid a large sum for the external auditors who had already checked their files for Holocaust related cases, and they wanted to avoid further breaches into bank secrecy; but they wanted to avoid the blame from victim groups that remained unsatisfied in the distribution process.

Under these circumstances, with little additional information from the Swiss banks, the criteria of proof for heirs of deposited assets were increasingly reduced. Simultaneously, the distributors increased both the average values of accounts in 1945—which served as starting point for cy-près calculations—and the interest-rates since the War, which was labeled "adjustment of deposited assets class presumptive values." In other classes as well, the payments were "adjusted," which means increased, because there were less entitled persons than anticipated. With such measures, the Settlement Fund Distribution Statistics from March 31, 2012 show that $716.2 million has been approved for distribution to some 18,000 members of the Deposited Assets Class; $205 million for distribution to over 230,000 members of the Looted Assets Class; over $287.2 million for distribution to over 197,000 members of Slave Labor Class I; $826,500 for distribution to 570 members of Slave Labor Class II; over $11.5 million for distribution to over 4,150 members of the Refugee Class, for a total of over $1.228 billion distributed to over 450,000 claimants. The distribution had been concluded in all classes for some years already except for Deposited assets: in the summer of 2007, only $452.5 million had been distributed in that class ($967.2 million in total). This means that the distribution within the lump-sum classes could be done relatively easily, while the deposited assets took much more time and could not and cannot be resolved by identifying eligible persons, unless the criteria for selection are widened.[8]

If one looks at the list of certified awards as last updated on March 31, 2012, fourteen years after the settlement and ten years after the Settlement Agreement, one will also see that not all the approved cases are really assigned cases yet. In the Deposited Assets class, there is a big gap to the numbers just given: for 2,916 certified awards, $497.4 million has been paid out so far.[9] The distribution proceeds at a slow and arguably decelerating pace. This is not surprising if one considers that the well-documented cases were settled first. The CRT II spends its time checking the probability that present-day claimants are related to persons who lived in the 1930s in European countries and of whom the Swiss lists sometimes just mention the last name. Korman and the CRT are confronted with the Sisyphean labor of establishing legally solid solutions where the lack of documentation makes this impossible.

Criticism was unavoidable in such a situation where interest groups could also hope that there would be considerable unclaimed residual funds. Their allocation was contested for some time (as were the lawyer's fees). While Jewish institutions proposed to organize research or education programs, Judge Korman earmarked these funds for humanitarian aid, such as food relief and health care, to the neediest survivors. In spite of this, the essential beneficiaries of the restitution process were not the many old, needy survivors but, regardless of their wealth, the relatively few and happy who could assert a kinship to individuals

---

8   The relevant information of the court in Brooklyn are to be found here: http://www. swissbankclaims.com/ (accessed August 8, 2012).

9   http://www.crt-ii.org/_awards/index.phtm (accessed August 8, 2012); this homepage contains the relevant information of the *Claims Resolution Tribunal II*, including the individual awards.

named on the banks' lists. This was unavoidable as far as the class actions had been about property rights. In the Deposited Assets class, claims were rewarded not as a moral recompense for misbehavior of the banks or the Swiss in general but as a liability of the banks as fiduciaries towards individuals. But such well documented claims (in a legal sense) were far from attaining the earmarked sum.

The explanation for this fact depends on how one interprets the lacking documents of a period 70 years ago. The Swiss banks maintained that there never had been many well documented cases. As the plaintiff lawyers, Judge Korman took another stand. Document destruction, even though legal after ten years according to Swiss law, became for him the "most contentious subject": if a party destroyed relevant evidence, the law assumed that this would have been harmful to the destroyer.[10] Thus the onus of proof was reversed so that a former account in a Swiss bank became a possible victim's account if the contrary was not positively evident. Therefore, the Swiss banking system of the Nazi era (and thereafter) had to be criminalized as a whole and transformed into a conspiracy built up to rob European Jews and then to cover the tracks. Such a plot cannot be excluded, but it is quite improbable and not supported by existing documentation and the research of the Bergier and the Volcker Commissions although they did not spare the banks from criticism for misbehavior, criminal acts and stonewalling against clients. As mentioned above, there are several other aspects of historical and moral guilt that Swiss agents can be blamed for, and this would be enough for recompensing Holocaust survivors on a humanitarian basis. But Korman and the CRT felt that they had to develop a historical argument against the Swiss banks and Switzerland in order to legitimize payments for deposited assets to claimants with a feeble documentation. In spite of this, the blanket assumptions of many CRT-awards are not convincing.[11] There are good reasons to distinguish between the

---

10   Edward R. Korman, "Rewriting the Holocaust History of the Swiss Banks. A Growing Scandal," in: *Holocaust Restitution. Perspectives on the Litigation and Its Legacy* (New York, London: NYU Press, 2006), ed. Michael J. Bazyler and Roger P. Alford, 115-134, 127-129.

11   See http://www.crt-ii.org/_awards/index.phtm. Maissen, *Verweigerte Erinnerung*, 578-581, discusses some awards. The problem is also manifest where Orland, *Final Accounting*, 51-55, quotes several claimants at the 1999 fairness hearing to suggest Swiss responsibility. They say a lot about their sufferings during the Holocaust, but little about Switzerland; out of 9 quoted declarations, only 4 mention Switzerland at all but only vaguely in the following way: "Germans were coming in every single day to collect the treasures. I'm sure, that I don't know but I'm sure

historian's and the judge's task and why the latter should not be held responsible for establishing historical truth in order to adjudicate individual cases.[12]

4. National Memories and Political Sensitivities

Neither discussing the problems of the distribution process nor alluding to a certain self-righteousness of some American protagonists fighting for the good cause is to be misunderstood as apologetic. The Swiss banks deserved the punishment of the global settlement because they had not resolved the problem of victims' assets when they should have done so, immediately after the War. On the contrary, the banks stonewalled possible claimants and purposely obstructed political initiatives to face the problem in the 1950s.[13] Nevertheless, one might wonder in hindsight, after a distribution process that has lasted for well over a decade and still is unfinished, whether Judge Korman chose and maybe, for legal reasons, had to choose a wrong way for a fair solution instead of going for rough justice. Ironically, it would be a similarly wrong way as those the Swiss banks and the Swiss government had tried. Neither an unprecedented auditing mandate nor a commission of scholarly experts nor a Claims Resolution Tribunal could resolve the problems at stake by precision in the legal sense of clear property rights or in the scientific sense of historic evidence. Too many documents are missing, if they ever existed; and it is arbitrary to make the missing evidence into a case in favor of or against the banks.

Instead of hypothesizing about the years of the War and immediately after, it may be more rewarding to understand the conflict about the Swiss bank case as a phenomenon of the 1990s. After all, against the expectations of some proponents and in spite of their success, the Ho-

---

that some of the money was deposited within the Swiss banks or someplace else..."

12   Edward R. Korman, "Rewriting the Holocaust History of the Swiss Banks. A Growing Scandal," 117, states that "the accountants were not seeking historical truth," obviously claiming this for himself. For the problematic judicialization of historical deeds see both in general and with reference to the Swiss case Stefan Schürer, *Die Verfassung im Zeichen historischer Gerechtigkeit: Schweizer Vergangenheitsbewältigung zwischen Wiedergutmachung und Politik mit der Geschichte* (Zürich: Chronos, 2009).

13   For clear evidence on this matter, see Bergier Report, 445-6, following Barbara Bonhage, Hanspeter Lussy, and Marc Perrenoud, *Nachrichtenlose Vermögen bei Schweizer Banken: Depots, Konten und Safes von Opfern des nationalsozialistischen Regimes und Restitutionsprobleme in der Nachkriegszeit* (Veröffentlichungen der UEK, vol. 15) (Zürich: Chronos, 2001), 474; also 242-9, 337-8, 260-1.

locaust litigations have not lead to extended human rights jurisdiction; class actions have not received a similar momentum in the case of South Africa, for example. One can draw three conclusions:

1. The litigations and what belonged to them had their time: the Clinton administration and the pre-9/11 search for a new world order.
2. They were limited to one highly emotional historical crime, the Holocaust, which was politically relevant not only on the level of a particular nation but for international relations as a whole.
3. After all, the issues at hand were not litigable. The Swiss banks case was the only one to eventually be resolved in court and not through an international—which means political—agreement, a solution that federal trial judges usually preferred. The reason is that the Swiss solution that government strongly opposed participating in what it considered to be a private-law litigation and abandoned the banks in their search for a solution although it turned out, as a global settlement, to include the government. But even this legal settlement, mediated and executed by a judge, was not preceded by court ruling. Legally, the banks probably would have won the case for lack of enough clear evidence; but fighting Holocaust survivors in court would have been a PR disaster, and a disclosure obligation would have caused an unsupportable dilemma between following an American judge and obeying Swiss bank secrecy that prohibits exactly such actions.

At its core, the conflict was neither about historical truth nor about individual rights. It was about collective memory: the collective memory of Jews in Israel and in the Diaspora, of the Americans, of the Swiss, and of the Europeans. Characterizing these collectivities and some changes that their identity underwent is unavoidably a rough but hopefully helpful enterprise.

To start with the Jewish world, it had lost its European roots. The World Jewish Congress had been founded in 1936 in Geneva, where it kept its headquarters for decades. Nahum Goldmann lived there as well and eventually became a Swiss citizen. Chaim Weizmann studied and taught in Switzerland, and Joseph Burg spent his annual holidays in Zurich reading the *Neue Zürcher Zeitung*. His son Avraham Burg had lost that adherence to old Europe when he became one of the protagonists of the Swiss bank case. In a fictive dialogue with Theodor Herzl at the centennial Zionist Congress, Burg Jr. declared: "Europe betrayed us. And six million brothers and sisters of ours, children and elderly people. ... And we shall never have enough tears to cry for the loss of the Jewish people. But we learnt our lesson."[14] The lesson was the Israeli "never again," discussed by Diana Pinto in the next chapter of this volume. When the Swiss ambassador Jagmetti gave the mentioned appraisal that Switzerland had to fight a war against an unreliable adversary, Avraham Burg responded: "A new Jew has arisen, and he does no longer lose a war."[15]

For this new generation of Jews, equally self-confident in the United States and in Israel, the Shoah was no longer a concealed trauma but a legacy towards the past and a tie for a future that united Israel and the Diaspora, all Jews albeit their secular, religious or national differences. It is significant that in the 1990s, the restitution process was brought forward not by the Israeli government but by Jewish organizations mainly of the Diaspora; however, when Israel's interest grew, it shifted, in 1999, from a fiscal matter handled by the minister of Finance to an identitarian issue under the minister of Diaspora affairs.[16] While earlier, one had focused on general damage done to the Jewish people represented by Israel, it now was about individual restitution according to property rights. This shift originated in the fall of the Berlin Wall, insofar as the German principle "restitution before compensation" was not only established in the former GDR but also in Eastern Europe; and not only for property socialized during Communism but also for property once arianized during Nazism. As a result, Jewish organizations and individuals searching through archives rediscovered not only legal titles but also many kinds of historical documents of a past that had been destroyed forever. Hitler, however, would ultimately not triumph, according to Emil Fackenheim's famous dictum, if the murdered were duly remembered.

When memory, stolen property and genocide thus came together as issues of the 1990s, this meant also that the Holocaust was no longer seen as an exclusively German crime. The lost apartments, synagogues,

---

14 Avraham Burg, *Speech at the Centennial Zionist Congress*, Basel August 31, 1997, http://www.jajz-ed.org.il/actual/burgb.html (accessed March 12, 2003).
15 *Neue Luzerner Zeitung*, January 28, 1997.
16 For Israel's position see Arie Zuckerman, "The Holocaust Restitution Enterprise. An Israeli Perspective," in *Holocaust Restitution. Perspectives on the Litigation and Its Legacy* (New York, London: NYU Press, 2006), ed. Michael J. Bazyler and Roger P. Alford, 321-330.

paintings, assets had ended up in the hands of all kind of Europeans who had profited from the killing of their former neighbors. One can quote Israel Singer, secretary general of the WJC from 1981 to 2007: "In fact, the organized theft of Jewish property was an intentional and major byproduct of murder during the war. There were no 'good guys' but for a few exceptions in Bulgaria and Denmark where Jews were saved in an organized effort." This is again a kind of reversed onus probandi: Europeans were guilty for letting the Shoah happen, unless they proved the contrary. They were not used to that particular accounting. When remembering the War, until 1989 every European nation had cherished its heroes and a variant of a résistance narrative. Now, heroes no longer had to comply with national pride but with universal values: defending not their country but human rights, namely the innocent and helpless victims. Most Europeans had betrayed them, to repeat Avraham Burg's quote. Even the many who had fought the Nazis had seldom done so to help the Jewish minority.

Israel Singer's opposition of good guys and bad guys does not only reflect the Jewish experience but also the American rhetoric where Manichean confrontations go back to the religious language of the Pilgrim Fathers. Manicheism could also become part of the self-conscious identities that religious and ethnic minorities developed as a consequence of the civil rights movement, often referring to their own experience as victims of discrimination. Within this general phenomenon, the Holocaust did not remain a particularistic Jewish point of reference but was increasingly interpreted in a universalistic sense from the 1970s onwards.[17] Steven Spielberg's movie *Schindler's List* is particularly illustrative because its hero is a German and even a member of the NSDAP. The message is not only universalistic but individualistic: if human dignity is at stake, every single one of us is asked to make the right choices, regardless of his origin; and even a German Nazi can do the right thing. In the same year of 1993, when *Schindler's List* was released, the U.S. Holocaust Memorial Museum was inaugurated. Located among the central monuments of Washington D.C., it recalled a historical event in which Americans actually had not been involved, neither as heroes nor as vic-

---

17 For this topic in general, see: Peter Novick, *The Holocaust in American Life* (New York: Mariner 2000); Daniel Levy, Natan Sznaider, *Erinnerung im globalen Zeitalter: Der Holocaust (Edition Zweite Moderne)* (Frankfurt a. Main: Suhrkamp, 2001).

tims. The Shoah no longer belonged only to the Jewish memory, it had become the Holocaust: a universalized, a globalized point of reference. When inaugurating the new museum in 1993, Nobel prize laureate Elie Wiesel prompted that President Clinton should intervene in Bosnia. The lesson of Auschwitz eventually legitimized the allied intervention in Kosovo: Clinton himself declared in March 1999 that the Holocaust could have been avoided, if someone had intervened early enough.[18]

One must not forget that the Clinton presidency was marked by pre-9/11 optimism: maybe not an end of history but a new world order seemed ahead. An overarching coalition had defeated Saddam after the invasion of Kuwait. From South Africa to Italy, the rotten regimes of the Cold War had collapsed. Oslo and Madrid spread hope into a lasting peace process in the Near East. The United States as the only hegemonic power was coining these processes with their typical mixture of self-interest and idealism. One of their major instruments was economic boycott. Between 1993 and 1996 alone, the United States used sanctions in 61 cases against 35 countries—more often than during the whole Cold War, when boycotts would have driven the opponent into the Soviet camp. Clinton's administration did not only boycott them, but forced other countries to do so as well. In 1996, the Helms-Burton Act obliged companies that were doing business in the United States not to invest in Cuba. The Under Secretary of Commerce who had to teach this lesson to the unwilling Canadians and Europeans was Stuart Eizenstat, soon after to become the decisive figure of the government in the Swiss bank's affair. Another mentioned protagonist, Senator Alfonse D'Amato, put through the D'Amato-Kennedy Act that forbade investments in Iran and Libya in the same year of 1996.

Jurisdictional imperialism was another tool in establishing a new world order or, depending on the perspective, imposing American rules to a globalised world. The Alien Tort Claims Act (28 U.S.C § 1350), dated from 1789, allowed non US-citizens to file a suit with a federal court against violation of international law. The act was barely used until 1980 when, in Filartiga vs. Pena-Irala, an American court claimed to be the forum conveniens for a "hostis humani generis," an enemy of mankind. In the 1992 Torture Victim Protection Act, the Congress adopted the same principle as a federal law.

---

18   Levy/Sznaider, *Erinnerung*, 2001, 173-205.

Class actions, a legal instrument hardly known in Europe, became a weapon for ethnic groups that went to American courts to fight for recompense after having suffered historical injustice. European companies, which in a time of globalization developed a growing interest in the American market, had to realize that there were sometimes good reasons for them to become the target of class actions, too. As for the Swiss banks, they had prospered in a neutral country not least due to the two World Wars. After the end of the Cold War, the relative importance of the financial center decreased in the new and fast growing global markets of the 1990s. The big Swiss commercial banks reacted by buying investment banks in the English-speaking world: Credit Suisse acquired First Boston in 1990, the future UBS bought S. G. Warburg in 1995 and Dillon Read in 1997. In 1989, Credit Suisse gained only 18% of its benefit abroad, while in 1997 it was already over 50%. As a consequence and under soft pressure from the United States, the Swiss had to adopt American rules against insider dealing or money laundering as well as legislation on product liability or on corporate governance. Globalized markets necessitated global rules, and the Americans were ready to impose their standards if they offered access to their lucrative market.

What turned out to be much more difficult for the Swiss bankers was the requirement of the 1990s: renouncing the national myth of their fathers. As every national history, the Swiss cultivated a narrative of exceptionalism, the "Sonderfall," a unique case of peaceful democratic continuity amidst incessantly war-waging states in the rest of Europe. Since the sixteenth century, there had been neither war nor occupation, with the exception of the Napoleonic era; internal and external boundaries have barely changed. Compared to European history in the nineteenth and twentieth centuries, Swiss history looked like an unquestionable success story bringing together a people with four different languages and with two large confessions in internal harmony, protected from the outside due to armed neutrality. World War II became the climax of this historical narrative: regardless of internal differences, the Swiss had mobilized and were ready to defend their independence against Nazi Germany that, however, never attacked.

After the war, many Swiss interpreted the survival of their independence as a merit of their own military readiness: if Hitler had not attacked Switzerland, it was not for economic reasons, but because he did not dare fight the brave Swiss army in the Alps. The generation that served in the army during those years of siege not only cultivated such narratives but constituted also the Swiss elites until 1990. For them, World War II was the formative experience of their youth as well as the climax of the Swiss success story. For all other Europeans on the continent, Sweden apart, and for most of the world, the wartime included humiliation, moments of defeat, guilt and collaboration. Only the Swiss could cherish their kind of résistance myth that embraced the whole nation: they did not have to pass the true test about who would make concessions to the occupying Nazis and who would not. In the fall of 1989, alone in the world, Switzerland celebrated the memory of the outbreak of the war with national festivities, officially to honor the generation which then had guarded the borderlines—unofficially, to fight against a popular referendum that intended to abolish the army that met with a surprising approval of one third of the voters in the optimistic November of 1989, after the fall of the Berlin Wall. In May 1995, the same federal government that had organized the 1989 celebration originally did not plan at all to commemorate the fiftieth anniversary of the War's end and eventually did so only after intervention of some parliamentarians.

One of those federal councilors was Jean Pascal Delamuraz, mentioned above for complaining about ransom of the Swiss. In the same interview, Delamuraz added the rhetorical question whether one should believe that Auschwitz was located in Switzerland. With his colleagues in government, he shared the conviction that the Swiss had no reason to feel ashamed. If somebody dared to accuse them of misdeeds, he or she must be an extortionist. When one dealt with problematic topics, especially the undeniable repulse of Jewish refugees, this was not interpreted as proper misbehavior that might root, for example, in Swiss traditions of anti-Semitism. Swiss refugee policy was considered to have been merely a reaction, even though an awkward one, to the evil incarnated exclusively in Germany. Nazi racism was just one aspect of many within an ideology that was despised because it threatened Switzerland's existence and not because it was exterminatory to the Jews. The Swiss interpretation of the War never focused on the Holocaust. It was integrated into the tradition of armed neutrality among neighboring great powers that fought another fatal war among each other as they had already done for centuries.

The self-image of a nation that had successfully passed another historical test was diametrically opposed to the Jewish perception of the War as a joint venture of the European goyim to rob and exterminate the Jews. Those who did not actively oppose such a genocidal program favored it—this was the essence of Singer's appraisal of the "good guys" and of the Eizenstat report's introduction. Elie Wiesel formulated it categorically: "When human dignity is at stake, neutrality is a sin, not a virtue; ... neutrality, which used to be, at one time, a high ideal or ideal of nations is wrong. Reject it! You must side with the victim, even if you both lose."[19] More concretely, Israel Singer declared: "Swiss 'neutrality' in the face of evil was a crime."[20] Therefore the WJC demanded an official Swiss apology for which it even suggested a concrete document to the banks in the summer of 1998:

> We, like yourself, are concerned with both moral and material restitution. Our discussions and negotiations of the past months, also aimed to resolve the issue of recognition of moral obligations for any wrong doing by the Big Swiss Banking institutions and their former managements. For these actions we have publicly apologized in our determination to undo past wrongs and to respond with proper deeds.[21]

The Swiss bankers were prepared to pay some additional millions rather than to sign such a text. Out of economic pragmatism and with the American market in mind, they agreed to pay roughly $2.5 billion for all kinds of investigations plus the global settlement. What they could not do was sign a letter of excuse for the misdeeds of their grandfathers and fathers, whom they had seen as national heroes. And much less so could the Swiss politicians who, as everywhere, worried about re-election. There was no official participation of the state in the global settlement; and the mentioned "Swiss Foundation for Solidarity" failed. A majority of the Swiss people opposed most fiercely what it considered humiliating the honor of their ancestors who had been ready to fight the Nazis.

---

19 David Johnston and Elie Wiesel, "The Raoul Wallenberg Forum on Human Rights," in *Nuremberg Forty Years Later: The Struggle Against Injustice In Our Time* (Irwin Cotler, ed. Montreal: Mcgill Queens University Press, 1995), 20.
20 Israel Singer, "Auschwitz is Europe's challenge," *Financial Times* (January 26, 2005).
21 Israel Singer, Draft of a letter on behalf of Rainer Gut (Credit Suisse), July 14, 1998.

The way the Americans dealt with national apologies was completely different.[22] President Clinton declared at a gala dinner of the WJC in 2000:

> In forcing the world to face up to an ugly past, we help shape a more honorable future. I am honored to have been part of this endeavor, and I have tried to learn its lesson. Within our country, I have been to Native American reservations and acknowledged that the treaties we signed were neither fair nor honorably kept in many cases. I went to Africa ... and acknowledged the responsibility of the United States in buying people into slavery. This is a hard business, struggling to find our core of humanity.[23]

This is not the place to discuss whether public apologies are always profound and sincere; they obviously can be thoughtless and cheap. But they symbolize that two former antagonists share values; and they demonstrate to the greater public a commitment to joint responsibilities.[24] That is what people need if they want to make business in a globalised world with partners whom they do not know yet. It creates trust.

That is one reason why the Americans tried to teach the Swiss to face the past the way they thought it should be done. The Holocaust became the universal metaphor for the "never agains" of liberal democracies respecting human rights and capitalist economies respecting property rights. They all made their public apologies: the French president Jacques Chirac in 1995, the Ukrainians as well as the Lithuanians, Hungary, the Netherlands and Britain, the Scandinavians and, in 2000, the Pope himself. Israel Singer commented on this movement:

> Those "I am sorry's" are worth more than all the money

---

22 For public apologies as part of a restitution process see Barkan, *Guilt of Nations*, 2000.
23 Remarks by the President during Bronfman Gala, September 11, 2000, http://clinton6.nara. gov/2000/09/2000-09-11-remarks-by-the-president-at-bronfman-gala.html (accessed February 24, 2011).
24 For these issues see Elazar Barkan and Alexander Karn, ed. *Taking Wrongs Seriously: Apologies and Reconciliation* (Stanford: Stanford University Press, 2006).

that is being given back because they're educational. And those are what we are seeking. It's not just throwing money on the table. It's not this effort that we're participating in with regard to heirless property that merely restitutes, but it also makes whole the people whose lives were destroyed, who were butchered, and whose children were left without parents and without homesteads.[25]

Singer's high moral ground has proven shaky since. But similar thoughts contributed to a vast process, the building of new and supranational collective memory of Europe. At the end of January 2000, a huge international Holocaust conference in Stockholm recalled the liberation of Auschwitz. The German minister Michael Naumann finished his speech declaring: "In the remembrance of the Holocaust we must find the right answer for politics and society of future history." The second article of the conference's final declaration postulated a collective memory of "the selfless sacrifices of those who defied the Nazis, and sometimes gave their own lives to protect or rescue the Holocausts victims." With obvious reference to ex-Yugoslavia, Article 3 declared that the international community shared a solemn responsibility to fight evils like genocide, ethnic cleansing, racism, anti-Semitism and xenophobia.[26]

It was exactly the same Holocaust conference in Stockholm where the EU-representatives decided to boycott Austria if Jörg Haider's FPÖ would join the governmental coalition—a right-wing party that had its very specific ideas about the wartime. Austria's government program reacted to the strong isolation and declared in its preamble: "The uniqueness and singularity of crimes of the Holocaust are an exhortation to permanent alertness against all forms of dictatorship and totalitarianism."[27] Of all politicians, Haider was arguably the first, al-

---

25   House of Representatives, Committee on International Relations, Hearing on Heirless Property Issues of the Holocaust, August 8, 1998 (51–646 CC), http://commdocs.house.gov/committees/intlrel/hfa51646.000/hfa51646_0.HTM (accessed February 3, 2011).

26   For the texts see http://www.dccam.org/Projects/Affinity/SIF/DATA/2000/page877.html (accessed February 24, 2011); for the interpretation also Levy, Sznaider, *Erinnerung*, 2001, 210-216.

27   "Declaration of Responsibility for Austria. Future at the center of Europe," quoted in *Central Europe Review*, 2, 5 (February 7, 2000); http://www.ce-review.org/00/5/austrianews5.html (accessed February 14, 2011).

though under pressure, to make the Holocaust a point of reference for a government program. Thus the Austrians proved, formally, that they belonged to a new, supra-national Europe that had learnt its lessons. What these European countries should have in common, was not an external enemy (such as Turkey, Russia or the United States), the way it had been constitutive for nation building since the nineteenth century. Nor could it be national history the way generations had learnt it to become good and committed citizens of their country. Almost the only historical experience the Europeans had in common was their shared internal guilt after persecuting the Jews all over the continent; in World War II but also many times before. This common experience should lead to a high consciousness and responsibility when dealing with minorities within a European union where all nations became minorities.

With this background, the fellow Europeans—although skeptical about US economic and legal imperialism—did not understand nor support Switzerland during the heirless assets' crisis. The Swiss did not follow the EU-logic of a shared responsibility for a continent traumatized in wars and genocides; and they will not do so for some time. The Swiss know that Auschwitz did not take place in Switzerland; and they believe it never could. They think that the nation state and its neutrality are and remain the best way to cope with a world of states that remain in the state of nature. And they think that one can separate the economic integration of the world's fourth biggest net-investor (in absolute numbers) from a supra-national political participation in establishing the political rules and responsibilities for these economic exchanges.

5. Republican Traditions Challenged By Liberal Universalism

Switzerland's reticence against supra-national cooperation differs from the program of the EU but not necessarily from the United States and Israeli policy. Both states stay away from the International Criminal Court (while Switzerland has signed the treaty). Israel's isolation in the U.N. is mitigated only by the barely conditional support of the veto power of the United States. As for Switzerland, it joined the U.N. only in 2002, after a referendum had passed narrowly. One reason behind these positions is the self-image of a chosen people, albeit of a different kind: in the case of Israel, it originates in Jahveh's covenant with the Jews; in the U.S., it refers to the Protestant dissent building a city set upon a hill and later became part of a civic religion that has transcended the single denominations; in bi-confessional Switzerland, where Protestants and Catholics have fought several rancorous civil wars from the sixteenth to the nineteenth century, it is a secularized conviction that History itself (rather than the Almighty) has decided to spare a virtuous people its rigor if only it remains united.

In the twentieth century, the universal mission for democracy became a driving force in American foreign politics. But the state of Israel also feels a particular responsibility for its potential citizens living all over the world, in the Diaspora. In contrast, the Swiss remain focused on the commonwealth of a tiny nation in its territory and face the rest of the world with neutrality. In a republican sense, they favor positive or political liberty as the privilege of a restricted community of citizens governing itself in direct democracy, with a weak judiciary—elsewhere, the backbone of negative or civil liberty in the liberal tradition granting equal rights to a vast body of inhabitants. Unlike its counterparts in the United States, Israel and many European countries, the Federal Supreme Court of Switzerland cannot declare federal laws unconstitutional, and even if it believes them to be so, it has to apply them. In a direct democracy, the sovereign nation has the last say about the law. Especially the conservative nationalists stick to a democratic absolutism according to the slogan: "The will of the people is always right." Therefore the political process driven by voting citizens is deemed to be much more important than the forensic process based on rights of legal persons. It is barely imaginable that two cantons would oppose each other in court on an issue like the ownership of Ellis Island that the US Supreme Court had to resolve in favor of New Jersey vs. New York. The process that led to the constitution of the new Swiss canton Jura in 1978 was a series of referenda on all levels, communal, regional, cantonal and national. The identity of Jura is rooted in the French language and the Catholic faith, two traditional elements of Switzerland. A sense of exclusiveness inhibits additional plurality in an already multi-faceted country. The emancipation of the Jews was achieved only late, in 1866, under pressure from foreign powers, among them the United States and especially France; and just recently, in 2009, a national referendum that interdicts the building of minarets won by a majority of 57.5%.

In the republican tradition, social conformity of full citizens with their particular privileges and duties and subordination of non-citizens are seen as prerequisites for a stable state within a precise territory. The citizen, in this interpretation, is of Christian imprint and male (which explains the late introduction of women's suffrage in 1971); he is the bread-earning head of the household and a soldier in the militia army, another reason for the inflated memory of the soldiers in service during the War. With his pairs, and without claiming to be an ethnos given by nature, this citizen forms a demos of privileged rulers. Contrasting with such a republican conception of the political realm, the economic sphere, in a liberal tradition, is very little regulated by the state, as became clear in the Holocaust assets' crisis; for example, there does not exist an escheat law that would define what happens with heirless assets.

Not all of these mentioned particularities of Switzerland are unknown to the nations that were its opponents in the 1990s. However, it is the case for the limited role that liberal universal values grounded in the title of human rights and a Supreme Court guaranteeing overriding legal principles receive in Switzerland's republican politics. In the last three decades, the fate of Europe's Jews, the slaughter and robbery of a transnational minority, has become paradigmatic for the need to protect human rights and property rights beyond national territories. The lessons may differ, but the Holocaust has become a major legitimizing experience for the mentioned collectivities. Although fortunately spared by the War, the Swiss will have to learn the lesson that the combatant nations already, painfully, did.

Europe and Israel Today:
Can Their Incompatible "Never Again(s)" Be Reconciled?

DIANA PINTO

In the post-war order, the decline contemplated by early modern philos-ophers with respect to classical times became a reality, with Europe no longer at the center of the Western world. World War II and the Holo-caust recomposed the horizon, both in the immediate post-war period and a second time in the 1990's under the double impact of the fall of the Berlin Wall and the revival of public discourse on the Holocaust (and World War II) through their extensive commemorations. In both cases, the careful sedimentation of political thought going back to the previous centuries—when the difference among full fledged monarchies, consti-tutional monarchies and republics counted—was abandoned. Pedigrees in political philosophy after the war mattered less than the democratic lessons that had to be learned in order to avoid the horrors of totalitar-ian dictatorship. The result was the blending of political thought into a democratic purée. New more immediate references to a post-war 'never again' with respect to the Nazi (and later Soviet) totalitarian horror increasingly took center stage especially after 1989. And to add to the purée, the Hebraists of early modern political thought with their Biblical references now gave way to real life "Hebrews" in the both old and new land of Israel. As a consequence, the democratic thought that emerged concretely from World War II and the Holocaust developed in two poles: a European (in this context the American reflections remained Euro-pean since they were mainly the intellectual product of émigrés) and an Israeli, both the legitimate heirs to the political reflections which emerged from the Nazi horror.

In the following paper, I spell out the theoretical differences that sep-arate the European and the Israeli and Jewish "never again(s)." I do this as an intellectual historian with a European Jewish identity, who has witnessed firsthand the growing divide between the European "never again(s)" and the Israeli/Jewish "never again (to us)."

The scenarios are well known. Europeans (and some Israelis as well) will criticize Israel for its behaviour toward the Palestinians and for what they deem to be the necessarily second class nature of any Israeli citizen who is not Jewish, for Israel's illegal settlements in the occupied territories, for its failure to uphold human rights in these contested lands, for its cavalier military crossing of international borders, especially after the first Lebanon war in 1982, and for its non-protection of civilians during its military attacks, particularly in Gaza in 2009.

Most Israelis and Jews will retort that Europeans do not understand what it means to live in a State whose immediate neighbours from its onset sought its destruction, nor Israel's objective conditions in its daily war against terrorism. The result has been that the Jewish world rebuffs these European criticisms as ongoing proof of hidden and (not so hidden) anti-Zionist and anti-Semitic attitudes. The historical irony is that the United Nations, born out of a post-war order specifically designed with the 'never again' in mind, should have become one of the most mistrusted institutions in Israel. The Jewish State accuses the U.N., and especially its Human Rights Commission, of constantly criticizing it with a quasi-irrational and hypocritical passion, while other countries (mainly in what used to be called the "Third World") with far worse human rights records and even ethnic cleansing on their conscience elicit far less attention and passion. These verbal jousts have produced two Manichean readings of the Jewish State: either as a country on the way to becoming almost a "rogue state" within the occupied territories or as the eternal victim, "the Jew among nations" of a lopsided international system. There is of course some truth on both counts.

I do not enter here into the welter of Middle East politics. These diametrically opposing readings of Israel are the symptom, not the cause of the two "never again(s)." These "never again(s)" have their deep origins in two equally legitimate but incompatible readings of the lessons stemming from World War II and the Holocaust. They embody the same kind of structural incompatibility to be found in the classic philosophical reflection over the master/slave relationship or in the currently academically more fashionable evocation of colonial/post-colonial links between formerly intertwined actors. It is my belief that these two "never again(s)" stand as equally clear, heartfelt and focused mirror images which pit a non-Jewish European reading of new normative laws and policies for Jewish life (and that of other minority groups) to prosper within the continent, and an Israeli reading of what is necessary for the

Jewish people to be safe within their own country. In order to understand this divergence we have to step back into postwar history to see how the two "never again(s)" came about.

The Origins of Europe's Post-War Values

The war had not yet ended when Winston Churchill began reflecting on a new European institution that would incarnate and above all guarantee the founding principles for the continent's new post-war identity. The institution that was born out of these reflections was the Council of Europe, created in Strasbourg in 1949, with its most important institution, because it is binding, the European Court of Human Rights. Its tenets underpinned Europe's values as now practiced by the European Union and its member states. The values in question, which have since then become a European mantra, were: human rights, the rule of law, and pluralist democracy. One must bear in mind that this mantra was a main precipitate of the liberal democratic world-views of the victorious powers based on British and French political philosophy. The British contributed their belief in individualism and the rule of law. The French brought their belief in clearly stated universal rights, their upholding of secularism (laïcité), as well as their political aversion to any ethnic definition of the State. To this they added their fervent post-war belief in the need for historical reconciliation between former enemies.

The result was a set of common values which made no distinctions between republics and monarchies, the political left and right, in order to emphasize universal human rights as the only way to prevent future dictatorships along Fascist or Nazi lines. This set of values did not incorporate the German philosophical tradition assumed at the time (when books such as William McGover's *From Luther to Hitler, The History of Fascist-Nazi Political Philosophy*, 1941, were in vogue) to have underpinned the Nazi outcome, but it allowed West Germany, rebuilt along the lines of Western democratic principles, to become early on a member of the Council of Europe. More important for our concerns, the Council did not have among its post-war members those ethnic nation states that had been created at Versailles out of the ruins of the Austro-Hungarian and Russian empires. Under Soviet hegemony, and hardly embodying the democratic principles of the Council, they were not allowed by their Soviet suzerain to apply for membership.

The Council of Europe instead developed immediate links with the State of Israel, which had been founded one year earlier. If one enters the Council's corridors in Strasbourg, one can see more than one photo dating back to the 1950's of the Council's general assemblies with David Ben Gurion sitting amicably in the front row, wearing no tie, and accepted in Israel's name in the family reunion as a European cousin living 'down the road.' The Council even created a new category of "guest status" within the Parliamentary Assembly, to accommodate a parliamentary delegation from Israel (others from the U.S. and Canada would follow suit later), which could not be a full fledged member since it was outside the geographic limits of Europe. Ironically, Ben Gurion and Israel were thus the only representatives of the East European ethnic state tradition to be found in Strasbourg's corridors, until after the fall of the Berlin Wall, when the end of Communism opened the road for eventual admission (once certain conditions were met) of the other half of Europe into the Council. After 1989, the Council defined the criteria with which former Communist countries had to comply in order to be accepted within the organization, the vital first step for future entry into the EU. The fundamental principles behind the founding "never again(s)" were thus spelled out more clearly, forty years after they had been enunciated, and turned into the current normative framework for European politics.

Europe's "Never Again(s)"

The European "never again" credo is based on the following points:

1. *Never again to war as a political means*: peace in post-1945 Europe was deemed to be effective and final, and became so in Western Europe, even if it was a frozen Cold War peace. Only after 1989 did war return to the continent, but for Western Europeans, the Yugoslav wars took place precisely because none of the countries involved had shared the values of the Council and had not been Council members. Even among more peaceful East European countries, 1989, not 1945, was considered to be the effective end of World War II with the return of their national sovereignties.

2. *Never again to ethnic or religious definitions of belonging to a State*: all citizens had to be absolutely equal in the eyes of the State, even

in those countries with established churches. Any ethnic-based political elections with special ethnic seats in Parliament or specific constitutional provisos for ethnic minorities were banned. Furthermore, the Council provided for maximum rights even for foreign residents.

3. *The absolute primacy of individual human rights over any national or collective rights*: collective religious or cultural rights exist only as incarnations of individual human rights and have no legal transcendence of their own. This implies not only a full protection of minorities (qua groups of individuals) but also of the minoritarian majority in any enclave of a larger minority, leading to a "Matrioshka effect" of pluralist claims and identities, in what is perceived as an ever expanding secular space.

4. *Never again to any ethnic or religious cleansing*: population movements to achieve desired 'balances' for ethnically consolidated majorities were to be banned.

5. *Never again to any Volkgesetz*: i.e. any legal tradition based on ethnic rights that turned those not belonging to the given ethnicity into pariahs with fewer rights, or none at all. The emblematic case of this danger was Nazi Germany.

6. *Full Citizenship as the lynchpin of the entire system*: open to anyone regardless of race or religious affiliation, provided they adhere to fundamental principles, and major rights provided to non-citizens, even mere sojourners, under the human rights conventions which are capped by the European Court of Human Rights.

7. *Never again to hermetic national boundaries*: Europe's goal is to advocate an ever-stronger common space with ever more porous, if not fully open, borders.

8. *Never again to hereditary enmity*: reconciliation became a historic ideal and the Franco-German case its model. In the wake of 1989, others followed, such as the German-Czech, the German-Polish, the Polish-Ukrainian reconciliation. Behind the concept lay the belief that countries could bury their conflicting pasts with honest discussions and calm bilateral historical scholarship.

These values, the backbone of post-war Europe, consciously defined an entirely new political project. Drawing on a revised form of legal civic humanism without any implicit national, much less nationalist, traditions, cultural or religious traits, the European "never again(s)" in-carnated a purified form of secular bourgeois liberalism based on social justice without any Communist input. However, it contained its own dose of historical irony. Its values and contents spelled out a European political and social setting which would have constituted a paradise for Europe's pre-Holocaust Jewry—but which in the wake of the Shoah, no longer seemed pertinent or in keeping with the new needs of a Jewish world as incarnated in the State of Israel.

The Origins of Israel's Post-War Values

If one turns to the Israeli context, the first remarkable difference in the origins of the post-war State is to be found in its pre-war pedigree. Zionism, the official ideology of the State of Israel, was not just based on a renewed reading of the Jewish identity based on the return to the original Biblical lands. It drew its more contemporary essence from strong nineteenth century nationalist, religious, Socialist (and later Communist), corporativist and agrarian currents. Theodore Herzl may have been an assimilated western-style Viennese journalist, reflecting the political complexity of the still standing Austro-Hungarian Empire. His followers, however, came mostly from the vast reservoir of east European Jewry who, within that empire or inside the Russian Empire had experienced the stirrings of nationalist identities defined almost exclusively in ethnic terms. Israel's pioneers were thus imbued with a strong ethnic Jewish identity, bolstered by Socialist-agrarian values close to the teachings of Count Tolstoy, (who also influenced the Kib-butz movement), to which were later added Socialist and Communist working class and collectivist ideals. With such a background, it was logical that the origins of the future Jewish State would be grounded in an ethnic-nationalist vision of the Jewish "people," rather than in a liberal bourgeois concept of power. This vision, it should be emphasized, was initially (during the first half of the twentieth century) not shared by most assimilated Western European Jews, except as a necessary solu-tion for their suffering brethren in less privileged lands.

The Shoah helped to obliterate these differences. For history seemed to have proven the founding generations right in their wish to have their own separate ethnic state. The capitulation to fascism and to Nazi occupation of most of the states of Western Europe led most of their own Jews to the Final Solution and could not palpably validate the pre-war Western European democratic example of Jewish integration. The United Kingdom, by resisting occupation, remained open to Jews, but its tutelary mandate over Palestine and the closing of its borders to Jew-ish immigration after the Holocaust tarnished its own domestic record in the eyes of the future elites of the not yet born Jewish State.

The Jewish "never again (to us)" was thus the direct result of the Jewish horror during the Holocaust, when the Jews both as a people and as individuals went unprotected by any State (albeit in most cases occupied), and experienced directly their condition as non-citizens after having become second-class citizens. Their survival thus depended on the moral courage of individuals or resistance groups within society. No non-occupied State intervened on their behalf. No international agency protected them. No movement "beyond borders" could shelter them. It was thus inevitable that the need for a strong and independent State for the Jews would make itself felt as the logical outcome of having been selected for extermination and abandoned by all of Europe's old estab-lished institutions. This is the historical background that set the tone for Israel's understanding of "never again (to us)."

The Israeli/Jewish "Never Again (to Us)"

The stances which compose the "never again (to us)" are based on differ-ent pedigrees, emphases, and hopes, which were the mirror images of the Europe's own "never again(s)."

1. *Never again will we let anyone else determine our collective fate*: on this count, the lessons of the Shoah are more important than any well meaning "never again to war." Furthermore, for Israel, war was co-determinant with its birth, and has become a defining fixture of its national identity. There has been no ultimate post-war peace.

2. *There is an existential need by the Jews and for the Jews for the State of Israel to protect their collective rights*: this is a classical definition of any nation, but in the Israeli case, the line between a nation and a religion is far more blurred than anywhere else in Europe. This clear-cut monolithic stance is the mirror image response (albeit a belated one) to the unsolvable and protean "Jewish Question," which domi-nated most of Europe's history after Emancipation.

3. *Israel is the State of an ethnic and religious people*: the Jews. Rights and freedoms are guaranteed for non-Jewish residents within the State, but the State, and above all its historical pedigree and narrative, cannot be fully "theirs." There is no equivalent to the old French teaching of *Nos ancêtres les Gaulois* which was extended to all students irrespective of their origins. The Israeli national narrative is watertight.

4. *Equality of all citizens up to a point*: the primacy of the Jewish character of the State is primordial; in political and also in social and economic terms. As a result, Israel has no formal secular space, as proven by the absence of civil marriage, and no neutral collective space. It is precisely this space which Jews across Europe have always invoked as the best protection for their own rights, throughout history and especially in post-1989 Eastern Europe.

5. *No Supranationality*: Israel will not delegate the hard won sovereignty of the Jewish people, nor will it indulge in any borderless rhetoric—despite its own unclear borders. On this count it resembles the other offshoot of Europe, the United States.

6. *Collective Jewish rights take precedence over individual human rights*: these collective rights are political, not just cultural, linguistic and based on individual human rights as in Europe. They emanate from the State. As a consequence, the rights of non-Jewish minorities can only be structurally limited. Non-Jewish and non-Israeli guest workers fall into an undefined hybrid zone, with no clear path to citizenship.

7. *Citizenship of non-Jews*: when citizenship is granted to Israeli, Arabs or Christians, it does not confer the same rights and privileges or duties. The line between religious and ethnic belonging remains hopelessly blurred on this count, the exact opposite of European principles.

8. *Reconciliation is not a virtue*: Israel's national narrative is one of "liberation from," so that it cannot brook easily any dispassionate "understanding of" past and present tensions and wars with the Arabs, when some of the latter have in the past preached, or still preach, the destruction of Israel. Reconciliation would imply a double recognition, the Holocaust for the Palestinians and the Nakba for the Israelis and the Jews. This is not easy even within academic circles, and above all not symmetrical (from the Arab point of view), since

the Arabs were not responsible for the Holocaust; and just as asymmetrical for the Jews given the difference between expropriation and extermination. Most Europeans fail to understand the complexity of this asymmetry, and most Israelis fail to understand the need for such an open acknowledgment that Palestine was never "a land without a people for a people without a land."

Again, I do not wish to enter here into political judgements. What I seek to stress are the divergent philosophies that underpin the principles behind Israel's legitimacy and the legitimacy of European States in the aftermath of World War II and the Holocaust. In practice, Israel and its Supreme Court have maintained extremely high standards of the rule of law (surely linked to Israel's German trained pioneer legal experts educated in the world of the Rechtsstaat). As a result, Israel is not the closed "apartheid" state that some of these differences in principles might imply, and that some radical European hotheads accuse it of being. But one cannot deny that Israeli Arabs and Israeli Jews do tend to live in effect, and even in principle, in separate state spheres.

It is important for Israelis to understand that when they are criticized by Europeans, this occurs not out of any sweeping knee-jerk anti-Semitism or rabid anti-Zionism (although both exist, of course), but because most Europeans (with a certain dose of historical insensitivity) tend to judge Israel by their own "never again" standards, rather than by Israel's "never again (to us)" mirror image version. The situation is thus rife with explicit and implicit misunderstandings.

European and Israeli Misunderstandings

At the heart of the misunderstandings lies one key problem. The European "never again(s)" has allowed Europe's own Jews to live fully in a post-war setting where the European States have guaranteed their rights, freedoms, collective presence and visibility in an unprecedented manner. Jews belong in Europe. The former victims and structural "others" of Europe's millennial past are now full-fledged citizens—even when they also hold an Israeli passport. This is an incredible achievement that would have been simply unimaginable in the pre-Shoah past. One need only remember how, in the early nineteenth century, many a British thinker like the liberal historian Thomas Macaulay had reservations about giving Jews the vote in Britain, on the grounds that they owed their ultimate loyalty not to the British monarchy but to an abstract ideal of 'Jerusalem.' And we need not dwell further on the long pedigree of Europe's suspicions of the Jews for having potential "double loyalties." This accusation has been shelved in the museum of forgotten historical items, but it is worth remembering its previous tenacious hold on both Europe's political elites and its masses.

It is also important for Israelis to understand that Europeans tend to think of Israelis as Europeans living in another geographical neighbourhood (certainly tougher) but still as implicit members of the European "never again(s)." This explains the often moral tone of their condemnations of Israel's behaviour. In European eyes, Israelis are not abiding by the "never again" that European created precisely because of the Nazi horror, hence they are not faithful to the lessons of their own past. The result is the following European "never again" reading of Israel's behaviour since 1967.

1. The Jewish nature of the State is problematic whereas a state with a Jewish majority, Hebrew as an official language and Jewish holidays as official holidays would not be.
2. The lack of secular civil spaces makes pluralist belonging in individual democratic terms impossible.
3. The complex status of non-Jewish immigrants and guest workers and the weakness of citizenship as the only founding element of national belonging turn Israel into a potentially "xenophobic" if not "racist" state, including for those who are only in part Jewish and do not fulfil perfectly Jewish categories of Jewishness.
4. The impossibility of adhering fully to the national compact if one is not a Jew ensures that individual human rights are secondary to Jewish collective rights. Hence the full rights given to a brand new Jewish immigrant compared to the partial rights that Arabs possess even when they have lived on the land since time immemorial.

To these arguments, many Europeans have added the more classic political contemporary objections: first, that after 1967, Israel occupied the lands of another people conquered through war, and it has ruled them in a "colonial" manner while implanting its own settlements on these lands;

and second, that Israel has used disproportionate means of war as a way to carry out its own security, particularly in Lebanon and in Gaza.

All of these criticisms are perfectly logical in the context of the European "never again(s)." In such an interpretation, Israeli and Jewish objections that the Europeans are hypocrites and that Israeli is the only democracy in the Middle East, or that Europeans do not pay enough attention to the far more terrible misdeeds of many African or Asian states, fall on totally deaf European ears. Israelis must realize that for most Europeans, they are "white Europeans" misbehaving in an exotic and surely violent neighbourhood, but Europeans nevertheless who should at least in principle abide by the European "never again(s)."

Furthermore, they are the only "white and western" upholders of an ethnic state. Even the most ethnically oriented Eastern European states have been browbeaten by institutional Europe after 1989 into having to abandon such a self-definition, whether it be the Estonians vis-à-vis their ethnic Russian minorities or the Slovaks and Romanians vis-à-vis their ethnic Hungarian citizens, and increasingly all these countries vis-à-vis the Romas. Israelis are now in the highly uncomfortable position, after the end of apartheid in South Africa, and effective Serbian rule over Kosovo, of being the only "white" people to rule over other surrounding indigenous populations, determining their collective lives on a daily basis. As such they constitute a historical anomaly.

Israelis can object with the reason that their "second class citizens," the Arab Israelis, enjoy far stronger rights, guaranteed protections and opportunities than many a European "minority" (without even referring to the plight of the Romas) in the vast EU. But once again, in the tension over "never again(s)," this argument is also beyond the point. For Europeans have been educated, as part of their "never again" lessons, to respect principles as equally important, if not more important, as immediate and quantifiable pragmatic results. And the Israeli principles on these issues are definitely less identity-blind and universal than Europe's.

Hence the implicit belief, seldom expressed publicly, that Israel in the long run, if it persists with its own "never again (to us)," was a "mistake" in that particular geographical context. Since no small European nation (for instance Luxemburg) has offered to cede its place to create a Jewish state, such a reading amounts to saying that the very idea of a Jewish State was a mistake.

Fortunately, few Europeans would go to that extreme. But I am willing to bet that today most would say that the Israeli "never again (to us)" could only be understood as a temporary post-war measure, perhaps even a necessary crutch given the Holocaust, but one which, once the State had been consolidated, had to give way to the more universal "never again." In this view, this conceptual crutch was hijacked by the larger post-1967 Israel with its annexationist impulses. And Israel can only remain true to its European and western character by removing, now that it is such a powerful country, the "to us" from its own "never again." In purely visual terms, David Ben Gurion belonged of course as a cousin in the front row of the Council of Europe. It is by no means evident that Benjamin Netanyahu would fit the bill, not just because the Europeans may not feel any affinity toward his vision of the world, but equally important because he would see no point in joining what his part of Israel considers as a hypocritical and sanctimonious, and above all powerless Europe.

Yet, Israeli objections to the European "never again(s)" cannot be couched in relevant philosophical categories, for one very simple reason. The rights and well being of Europe's Jews draw their legitimacy from the juridical, political and cultural institutions born out of the European "never again(s)." The only way to avoid this paradox is for Israeli officials to minimize this European achievement. They have done so repeatedly by stressing the ongoing anti-Semitic dangers Europe's Jews continue to face, while also stressing that their small numbers, even if they were happy to live in Europe, make them irrelevant to the concerns and priorities of world Jewry. This argument has been a powerful weapon in Israel's understanding of Europe, one which however fails to distinguish between the State sanctioned anti-Semitism of old Europe (which led to the Shoah) and the current anti-Semitism or anti-Zionism which emanates from particular minoritarian groups or extreme fringes within society, and which are actively fought by European States in the name of their "never again(s)." A few commentators, including a significant number of left-wing Jews, have even gone so far as to say that Israel's own actions whether in Lebanon or Gaza or in the occupied territories are in part responsible for, or at least indirectly related to, the surge of this new anti-Israeli or anti-Jewish climate, especially among new youthful generations who do not have the complex post-war past in mind.

Can the Two "Never Again(s)" Be Reconciled?

In strictly philosophical terms, the Israeli and European "never again(s)" cannot be reconciled except by making the Israeli one a temporary subset of the European one. Nor can one resort to civil society as a bridge between the two visions. Israel's civil society is among the most vibrant in the world, but not necessarily in the multicultural, identity-free or identity-blended meaning which now defines vibrant civil societies throughout the Western world, in Europe, North America, and Australia. One can only hope that Israel will get there eventually (and parts of Israeli society are in the vanguard on this front), but that in itself will not overcome the problem of the philosophically incompatible "never again(s)."

In political terms, however, the two "never again(s)" may be paradoxically reconciled at another level: in three possible geopolitical scenarios, one "rosy," the second "black," and ultimately, in a third "non-European" manner. The "rosy" scenario is the simplest but also the most unlikely and the most conceptually difficult for Israel. The "black" scenario is the most troubling for Europe, while it would fit Israel better. The "non-European" scenario is the most likely, and its consequences will be dire above all for Europe, but also in the long run for Israel.

The "Rosy" Scenario

A two-state solution finally emerges from the welter of peace plans and the outcome would be the peaceful cohabitation of Israel and Palestine side by side, perhaps even with a few Jewish minorities in Palestine, perceived as the pendant of Israel's own Arabs. This implies of course that once the Palestinian problem is settled, Israel would have peaceful relations with all of its Arab neighbours, and that terrorism—with its own logic—would slowly dwindle. In this somewhat far-fetched hypothesis, one would be entering a Hungarian-Romanian scenario, which would then call for a European style of reconciliation between the two sides. Israel would then become more European in its "never again(s)" because it would no longer be threatened by neighbours who had denied its right to exist. Europe would enthusiastically embrace and finance such a transformation. The Israeli Supreme Court would reign even more triumphantly over society, and slowly but surely Israel would become a full-fledged pluralist democracy with many Jewish (and non-Jewish) tribes, and above all individuals.

The "Black" Scenario

Terrorism, demands of ever more radicalized Islamic groups, and un-stoppable immigration will lead Europe to shed its "never again(s)" in favour of a far more restrictive closed nation-sponsored "never again (to us)," based on exclusionary definitions of who can be a resident and a citizen. Citizenship will be conditional on newly defined terms of loyalty, not just with respect to principles but also to culture. In brief, Europe might become more of a security conscious fortress, not un-like Israel, with some of its citizens (those choosing to live according to entirely different non-Western precepts) hampered in their rights or even excluded from full participation in the body politic. We have already experienced some of this. Since 9/11, possessing an American or a European passport does not make all citizens equal. Those who were born in Muslim lands as well as those native born but with clear Muslim names are now treated differently by security authorities, especially at airports, in ways that Tel Aviv's Ben Gurion airport pioneered. Israel, in such a pessimistic scenario, will have been at the avant-garde of the new global threats, not unlike the little canary in a mine, just as Jews in pre-war Europe were the avant-garde victims of Nazi and even Stalinist threats. It is worth mentioning that particularly after the Madrid and the London terrorist bombings, Europe's political elites and sectors of public opinion did perceive Israel in a more favourable light, and above all with greater understanding for its security dilemmas. But once again, such a more favourable reading had no impact on the "never again(s)," and this capital of sympathy was partially eroded with the scope of the Gaza offensive.

The "Non-European" Alternative

Europe's "never again(s)" and its underpinning of the international in-stitutions that were created after World War II (among which of course was the U.N.) may well lose international relevance. None of the newly emerging countries that will inevitably play an increasingly powerful role in the twenty-first century have adhered to the "never again(s)": certainly not China and India. Brazil perhaps does in highly abstract untested terms. Japan certainly comes as close to being a homogeneous ethnic state as possible, and one that still does not understand the dynamic of reconciliation. As for Russia, the country routinely tramples on most of the principles it adhered to when gaining admission to the Council of Europe in the mid-1990s. Even the United States, the ultimate incarnation of a vibrant pluralist democracy based on individual rights cannot fit into a European "never again," if only because it does not accept any supranational jurisdiction beyond its own Supreme Court and has no room for, understanding of, or even need for the very concept of reconciliation (with Canada? with Mexico?). Nor has America ever engaged in an official reconciliation process with Vietnam. One can even wonder whether it is not the entire "west" which may be turning itself into a declining and minoritarian "life style" (certainly in demographic but perhaps also in value terms) compared to the rest of the world.

To return to the European context, it is important to stress that America put an end to the war in Bosnia in 1995 with a solution which went counter to all the anti-ethnic principles embodied in the European "never again(s)." The Dayton Accords stipulated a power arrangement in Bosnia along strict ethnic lines. Serbs, Croats and Bosnians all had a share of power in a federalist system with no reference to the values of democratic pluralism (even in the future) or any reference to the rights of individual citizens. As a result of these accords, a prominent Jew who played a key peacemaking role inside Sarajevo during the city's blockade was unable to run for the country's presidency, since he was not an Orthodox Serb, a Catholic Croat, or a Muslim Bosnian. (He won his case belatedly in front of the European courts in the spring of 2011, but only because Bosnia is in the process of applying for membership in European institutions).

Israel's "never again (to us)," furthermore, has broad implications for all those former colonial countries which still bear a grudge against "old Europe," and who often see Europe's "never again(s)" tenets as a more refined semi-colonial way of still meddling in their affairs, thus trespassing on their hard won sovereignty, even when the issues at hand are as severe as genocide, or ethnic cleansing, two categories which they tend to refuse as driven by western value judgments.

In brief, Israel, which increasingly projects its scientific, military and economic clout toward the new Asian powers of this century, would not be alone in such a post-European group. In this reading, the Jewish State would once again be at the avant-garde of a geopolitical and conceptual shift away from Europe and its pious but "toothless" values. But I wonder: in such a shift away from these principles would Israel remain truly faithful to its own origins and history in the process? Even though in mirror image form, Israel and its "never again (to us)" may be ultimately closer to its European hinterland than it itself is willing to admit. Certainly, in the current Kulturkampf over making the Israeli State both Jewish and democratic in the sense of including all of its citizens equally, the more open parts of Israeli society are closer to the European "never again(s)" than to the increasingly Hobbesian "never again to us" which some of the tougher members of the political class, aided by many in the Jewish Diaspora, advocate. On this count, Europeans would do well to stop the Israel-bashing which is so fashionable in many circles and lend their active support to those who fight these battles daily and literally in the field, often in the Palestinian owned olive groves which constitute the frontier of many a settler colony. This is a battle with very high stakes for Europe itself.

It is too early to tell whether the European "never again(s)" will expand to encompass ever-larger parts of the world or whether it will shrink to the size of a weaker and more marginal European continent. But it is safe to say that whatever the outcome, both Europe and Israel will stand to lose if their ways were to fully part, if the noble principles that underpinned the post-war order's "never again(s)" were to fully give way to an increasingly strong and self-centered international "never again (to us)."

Index

Aaron, 45, 96
Abbadies, Jacques, 77
Abel, 45
Abimelech, 45
Abraham, 19, 45, 162n24
Account of Switzerland, An, 73
Adair, Douglass, 88
Adalah, 202, 204
Adam, 45
Addison, Joseph, 66-67, 69
Administration of National and
    Civic Service, The, 177
Adonitzedek, 45
Afghanistan, 134
Afsprung, Johann Michael, 78
Agrarian Justice, 164
Ahaz, 45
Al-Khalil-Hebron, 187
Alexander the Great, 63
Alps, the, 233, 250
America; see: United States
*American States Acting over the
    Part of the Children of Israel
    in the Wilderness, The*, 96
Amos, 162n24
Antigone, 121
anti-Semitism, 232-233, 250,
    253, 258, 265, 268
anti-Zionism, 258, 265, 268
Annales des Provinces Unies, 76
Appenzell, 78
Aquinas, Thomas, 41, 141, 143
Arbel, Dorit, 15
Archaeologiae Atticae Libri Tres,
    49, 52

Arguing about War, 139
aristocracy, 45, 51
Aristotle, 8, 11, 32, 51n5,
    61n33, 162n24
At the Beginning was the Deed,
    152
Athens, 18, 49-63
Athènes ancienne et nouvelle, 52
Augustine, 19, 142
Auschwitz, 248, 250, 253, 254
Austin, J. L., 117
authority, 21-25, 27, 45, 51n5,
    72, 106, 114, 115-116, 123,
    141-143, 158, 214n16
    ecclesiastical, 19, 22, 159

Babeuf, 163, 164n31
Bagnoli, Carla, 149
Bailyn, Bernard, 88
Barak, Aharon, 48
Baron, Hans, 21
Bartoszewski, Władysław, 236
Basnage, Jacques, 76
Basra, 146
Batavia Illustrata, 78
Basel, 37, 75
Basic Law: The Knesset, 48n51,
    200
Belgium, 207-211, 213n14,
    220, 222, 227-228, 234
Ben Gurion, David, 7, 194, 195,
    260, 268, 270
Ben Shalom Commission, 197
Bentham, Jeremy, 129
Bercovitch, Sacvan, 91

CPSIA information can be obtained at www.ICGtesting.com
Printed in the USA
BVOW011331040113

309369BV00007B/12/P

9 781936 235551